The Wild Flavor

MARILYN KLUGER

ILLUSTRATED BY
MARY AZARIAN

A Owl Book
HENRY HOLT AND COMPANY
New York

THE WILD F

Published by Henry Holt and Company, Inc.,
115 West 18th Street, New York, New York 10011.
Published in Canada by Fitzhenry & Whiteside Limited,
195 Allstate Parkway, Markham, Ontario L3R 4T8.

Library of Congress Cataloging-in-Publication Data
Kluger, Marilyn.
The wild flavor / Marilyn Kluger ; illustrated by Mary Azarian.
1st Owl book ed.
p.   cm.
Reprint. Originally published: New York: Coward, McCann &
Geoghegan, 1973.
"An Owl book."
ISBN 0-8050-1330-X (alk. paper)
1.   Cookery (Wild foods)   I.   Title.
TX823.K47   1990   90-4509
641.6—dc20   CIP

Henry Holt books are available at special discounts for bulk purchases for sales promotions, premiums, fund-raising, or educational use. Special editions or book excerpts can also be created to specification. For details contact: Special Sales Director, Henry Holt and Company, Inc., 115 West 18th Street, New York, New York 10011.

First published by Coward, McCann & Geoghegan in 1973.

First Owl Book Edition—1990

Illustration by Mary Azarian
Printed in the United States of America
Recognizing the importance of preserving the written word,
Henry Holt and Company, Inc., by policy, prints all of its
first editions on acid-free paper. ∞

1 3 5 7 9 10 8 6 4 2

The following sections of this book have appeared, in slightly different form, in *Gourmet Magazine*: The Peaceful Pursuit, Gathering Morels, Spring Greens, Blackberrying.

Permission has been granted to quote from the following:

Robert Frost, "Blueberries," from *The Poetry of Robert Frost*, edited by Edward Connery Lathem. Copyright 1930, 1939, © 1969 by Holt, Rinehart and Winston, Inc. Copyright © 1958 by Robert Frost, Copyright © 1967 by Lesley Frost Ballantine. Reprinted by permission of Holt, Rinehart and Winston, Publishers.

Marjorie Kinnan Rawlings, *Cross Creek*, p. 222. Copyright 1942, © 1970 by Norton Baskin. Reprinted by permission of Charles Scribner's Sons.

For Kurt Kluger
and our sons, James and Robert,
my companions afield and in many pursuits

ACKNOWLEDGMENTS

Many friends joined me in my pursuit of the wild flavor and shared their hunting grounds and recipes with me. My thanks to everyone who contributed to the experiences I have written about.

When this book was slowly taking shape over a period of ten years, several people had key roles in moving it forward, sometimes unknowingly. In particular, there were Berton Roueché, who suggested I write a book when I had only one essay on paper; the late John Schaffner, then my literary agent; and Gail Zweigenthal, executive editor of *Gourmet* magazine, where portions of this book were first published.

Finally, sincere thanks go to Jane Jordan Browne and Elizabeth Crossman, who have had the most essential roles—that of agent and editor, respectively—in bringing this edition of *The Wild Flavor* to print.

CONTENTS

9

THE PEACEFUL PURSUIT

At our house, we relish the wild flavor on our table. Everyday meals become exciting, even exotic, when the wine is dandelion and the shortcake is topped with sweet mounds of tiny red strawberries found in daisy-strewn meadows. Nothing adds as much zest to our dinners as the natural delicacies we gather from the fields and woods. And nothing adds so much flavor to our days as the peaceful pursuit of wild foods for our cupboard and table.

From the time the sap rises in spring until the first snow falls, we roam the countryside, baskets in hand, searching out the secret places where nature hides her bounty. The wild harvest is ours for the finding. Day after day we gather the elusive fungi, the savory potherbs, the wildling fruits, the rich nuts, and bring them to our table.

We take no more than our fair portion of the provender we find in meadows and woodlands, for we share the bountiful wild board with our natural brethren—the fox, the deer, the blackbird, the raccoon, the squirrel. It is they who are dependent solely on nature's provision, while we take only a part of our sustenance directly from the land. The native foods we gather from the countryside highlight our meals, supplementing the other good foods on our table that we grow in our garden and buy at the grocery. Their flavors satisfy our taste for the unusual. To us, no imported mushroom is so rare as the morel, no tame fruit so unique as a pawpaw, no foreign vintage more charming than wine brewed of elder blossoms.

Sometimes the wild foods hunt is a family outing, an all-day excursion to the country, spent nutting or mushrooming or berrying, and picnicking—an occasion to remember together in years to come. Or it may be a companionable search shared by two of us, a quick examination of the serviceberry tree on the hillside or a careful search for tender spring greens. Sometimes it is a solitary pursuit, a productive pastime that takes me outdoors, for an hour or a day, away from my usual routine, where I can observe and discover and reflect in sunny summer meadows while gathering foods for our table.

Searching for the wild flavor has become second nature to us, no matter what we are doing. Kurt, my husband, enjoys long walks on the rolling hills of my father's southern Indiana farm. Wherever he goes, he keeps alert for places that promise bounty. Late-ripening persimmons and frost-sweetened wild grapes, found on a brisk November day's hike, make the persimmon pudding for his supper and the tangy dark jelly for his breakfast muffin. Our younger son, Bobby, sets his lines for fish in his uncle's pond, then wades out to collect golden cattail pollen to be stirred into tasty yellow pancakes. Jim, my older son, spies a colony of puffball mushrooms in a grassy field while riding his horse along the country roads near our home; he dismounts and gathers them for dinner. Gathering wild foods is so natural to our way of life that any outdoor activity may lead us to a delicious—and unexpected—discovery for our table.

Hunting for wild foods brings the panorama of nature into sharp focus; whoever sees keenly enough to isolate the succulent morel from its camouflage of brown leaves will certainly find also the lovely shy orchis hidden in the leaf mold. I delight in the coincidental findings of the wild foods hunt: the grass-canopied meadowlark's nest, with four cinnamon-speckled white eggs inside, where I knelt in the wild strawberry field; the pearly everlastings growing on the mountainside among the blueberry bushes; the neat hoard of black walnuts stored away in a treeside cache where I gathered my own winter's supply while a saucy squirrel, high up in the branches, chattered and scolded me for invading his larder. The excitements of these discoveries are never completely separated from the wild flavor itself. Later on, at dinner time, when a flood of sweet juices from the blueberries engulfs our taste buds, all the imagery of the hunt surges back to be savored again, indivisibly, with each morsel of blueberry pie. Even from the dinner table, I can recall a sudden crashing in the brush and visualize proud antlers disappearing in the bush. There is a clatter of plates and forks as the delectable dessert is passed about, but I still hear an echo of the metallic *plink! plink! plink!* of blueberries dropping into Jim's empty pail. I see now the circle of dear, eager faces, intently devouring the blueberry pie, but the vista of mountains, green with conifers and topped with haze, is indelibly fixed in my mind's eye. Soon there is only a pool of thick, purpling juice left in the bottom of the pie tin and a scattering of flaky crumbs on the red-checkered tablecloth; we are replete with the soul-filling wild flavor of blueberry pie and content with the satisfactions of blueberrying.

The intangible satisfactions of gathering wild foods are important to us and inherent to the hunt. But the harvest of wholesome natural foods, ripened by nature, is our foremost aim when we go afield. "The fields and hills are a table constantly spread," Thoreau wrote. But nature, often a mysterious hostess, has spread her concealing green napery over the country feast. The wild foods hunter must search first this hill, then that field, lifting a corner of green here and there, before he uncovers her generous feast.

We have our favorite places to hunt wild foods, places we know intimately after years of careful searching and regular harvesting. Perhaps we know none so well as our own backyard—a sampler of the immense natural harvest that ripens annually in the surrounding meadows and woodlands. Dandelions are welcome in our lawn; not only are their pert yellow blossoms the most charming of all spring-time flowers, but their young leaves are the most piquant greens in our supper salad. Elderberry bushes volunteer in the hedge and we value them—more than privet—for their lacy corymbs of fragrant white blossom, called elderblow, and for the clusters of dark fruits that make our delicious elderberry pies, sparkling jellies, and heady country wines. Pokeweed sprouts prosper near the asparagus row; one vegetable is as acceptable as the other on our table and in our backyard, and the wildling requires nothing of us—no hoeing, no weeding, no fertilizing.

We open the gate and walk a short way down the graveled road in front of our house, through the avenue of towering catalpa trees, to the open country. Along the county road right-of-way, we have gathered, during our sixteen years' residence here, wild pecans, black walnuts, wild plums, Jerusalem artichokes, wild asparagus, blackberries, day lilies, black cherries, elderberries, and various wild greens. One summer I found two enormous clumps of garden-variety kale growing right by the side of the road, sown there by a strange caprice of nature. Last July, Bobby and I discovered several rogue raspberry bushes growing high on the steep road bank, and we harvested from them several pickings of sweet black raspberries for Bobby's breakfast. The surprises we find while walking along our road are remarkably varied.

Unfortunately, from time to time, county road crews undertake to "improve" the roadway. They appear periodically, with buzz saws, weed killers, bush hogs, bulldozers, and road graders to embark upon senseless projects that have no beginning and no end. When the noise and vapors and smoke subside, we are left with deeper ditches, perhaps, but also with road banks denuded of foliage and in prime condition to erode at the next downpour. We who enjoy walking here take little joy in a wider passageway that requires the sacrifice of stately century-old walnut and pecan trees. We mourn the despoiling of our roadside beauties by weed killers—not only the fruitful elderberry hedge and the hardy wild asparagus, but also the rustic black-eyed Susans and the lovely, frothy Queen-Anne's lace that gave our road its country charm.

But there are places where we hunt wild foods that change little in the name of progress through the years, or even revert to more primitive conditions that guarantee good hunting. My father's southern Indiana farm, with its rolling terrain and overgrown fencerows, with its wooded thickets and old orchards, with its treasured berry patches and persimmon trees and wild grape vines, is such a place. Here, in earlier days, my mother and I searched its far corners for wild fruits and nuts and greens while my father and brothers hunted its acres with game bag and creel. I like to go back now with my own children. Few things we do let us transpose our childhood experiences like roaming over the homeplace together. When we retrace the old route to the long-enduring plum thicket where I picked red plums for Mother's shimmering crimson jellies, we walk along the same worn path that I followed then, bare feet plop-plopping. The red plums we pick at the old thicket are borne by descendants of the very trees I climbed then; their sourness assaulting my mouth assures me of it. But we find more than the pleasant nostalgic remnants of my own childhood when we hunt over these acres together, my sons and I. They, too, have their own special places to revisit each season when they return to their grandfather's farm, their own discoveries to make for themselves, their own rewards to garner. I suspect that the intangible, unending riches of Grandpa's untidy fencerows and brushy thickets are our most important harvest.

There is another place where we hunt wild foods that is becoming as familiar to us as my family's Indiana homeplace. That is our rocky, mountain farmstead in northern Vermont where we vacation in a century-old red-clapboard farmhouse overlooking its own magnificent waterfall and the village below. We plan our vacation trips to coincide with the ripening seasons of the wildlings we gather there on our forty acres of woodland and mountaintop meadow. We plant no crops, although our land is listed on the tax rolls as farmland, but we reap marvelous crops from our acreage—crops we have not sown. The boulder-strewn meadow at the top of the mountain is said to have been a hayfield and pasture in earlier days, but it is now a wild berry field. The path up the mountain is carpeted with strawberry vines and the meadow abounds with dewberries, blackberries, and red raspberries. The woods and waterfall are bordered by chokecherries and elderberries. Wild apples grow at random along fencerows and bordering the woods. The woods are deep and moist, filled with ferns and inhabited at times by mushrooms, including the delicious apricot-scented chanterelles and the ephemeral morels and shaggymanes. On the steep slope in front of our house is a profuse growth of common milkweed, wild potherb *par excellence*, from which we take the esculent shoots, leaves, broccolilike flower buds, and silvery green pods for our table; later, when the field of milkweed is in bloom, we reap a second harvest of beauty and sweet fragrance. And on a neighboring mountainside, we gather the prize of Vermont's wild berries:

> Blueberries as big as the end of your thumb,
> Real sky-blue, and heavy, and ready to drum
> in the cavernous pail of the first one to come!
> . . . It's a nice way to live,
> Just taking what Nature is willing to give,
> not forcing her hand with harrow and plow.*

*From "*Blueberries*" by Robert Frost.

There are other places where we take what nature is willing to give: our neighbor's twenty-acre woods near our home in Newburgh, Indiana, where we find morels and pawpaws and wildflowers; my brother's acreage in southern Indiana, originally my grandfather's hill-country farm, and the surrounding environs—these are our hunting grounds where the wild harvest is ours for the finding, there for the taking, our right by invitation or ownership.

We do not violate nature's hospitality by gathering wild foods on posted property or trespassing on a farmer's land. What joy is there in stolen apples? We take the wild abundances only in the country places where we have rightful entry. We would not plunder the secret patch of a fellow wild-foods hunter or damage a future crop by ignorant, greedy foraging. Our conservation ethic, like Marjorie Kinnan Rawlings', begins with the blossom, and before—

> I did not break the may-haw bough,
> Nor pull the flowering plum,
> For ripe fruit follows April's plow
> And falls when locusts drum . . .

and embodies a sense of sharing with our fellows—

> . . . And windy summer nights I know
> New-weaned raccoons will come.
>
> I left the fox the pawpaw bud
> To ripen near his lair . . .

but also the freedom to take from the plenty what we need for ourselves—

> . . . But brambleberries strewed the wood,
> And they had bloom to spare.
> I picked a thorny spray and stood
> And tucked it in my hair.

I discovered that I had a taste for wild flavors in my childhood. It was not an acquired taste; it was simply there, naturally, to be gratified with the sweet wild berries, the sour apples and tart plums, the rich nuts and juicy dark grapes that were also simply *there*, inviting me, in the meadows and woods where I roamed as a child. I understand the lines of John Greenleaf Whittier:

O,—fruit loved of boyhood!—the old days recalling,
When wood-grapes were purpling and brown nuts were falling!

My reminiscences of the fruits loved in childhood are not bittersweet because my taste for the wild flavor was never tamed, never obscured by more sophisticated tastes. In our woods, dusky wood-grapes are still purpling and brown nuts are still falling. Every excursion to gather them revives my appetite for them and sustains the little bit of wildness—and child-ness—that remains in my spirit and exists, I believe, in all of us.

PART I

Springtime Pursuits

SASSAFRAS TEA

Anyone who lives with the seasons reckons a year by its visible phenomena, not by arbitrary dates on a calendar. The natural year begins for me whenever swift arrows of geese point northward; when sleepy chipmunks pop out of their dens; when mottled green spathes of skunk cabbage push through the soil; when ice crashes out of the waterfall; when there are gentle stirrings inside old sugar maples; when the thawing earth turns into a quagmire of mud; when pale spring beauties appear in the woods; and—most surely—when spring peepers trill from the creek.

These are the living symbols of the land announcing a new yearly cycle for plants and animals that is more meaningful in my notation of time than dates set down in an almanac. The natural year begins with the coming of spring. But spring is a movable feast; by the time the vernal equinox arrives, I have already torn off the calendar of winter and turned to a new season. At each sign of life's resurgence, I feel within myself a revitalization that comes of the new season.

One of spring's harbingers in my grandmother's kitchen was the pot of sassafras tea that simmered on the back of the stove during Lent. Grandpa said drinking it "thinned the blood." Since the alternatives to sipping the dread liquid were choking down sulphur and molasses or having our blood seep sluggishly through our veins, we children drank our grandmother's springtime elixir without complaint. But it was years before I relished the flavor of sassafras tea with a fondness to match that of my grandparents'.

The pungent odor of the sassafras roots was easier for a child to enjoy. When my grandfather prepared the roots and bark for the teapot, the whole house smelled of sassafras. In February, before the sap started, Grandpa dug the roots of red sassafras (*Sassafras albidum*) from the small trees that grew on the road bank near the house. He carried the muddy roots to the barn well, in a gunny sack slung over his shoulder, where he washed them in a tub filled with water. Then he brought the roots into the kitchen to scrape away the dark, thin outer bark, to prepare them for the brewing.

This was a task requiring the use of Grandpa's most fascinating and untouchable possession—a multiple-bladed, sharp-honed pocketknife that he always kept safely buttoned in the bib pocket of his overalls. The soft hiss of the blade being honed into readiness always brought his many grandchildren, on the run, to the bench behind the kitchen table, where we would line up like owlets on a limb to watch him use the awesome knife—whether he was peeling an apple in one long red curl, whittling for pleasure, or splitting sassafras roots into short, precise pieces for the springtime brew.

Some people brew only the bark of the roots for sassafras tea, but the whole root, cut into inch-wide pieces, also makes the fragrant, rosy-colored tea. Sassafras roots may be boiled again and again, as long as there is enough strength in them to color and flavor the spicy tea.

Sassafras roots may be gathered anytime in the spring, or all year long. But the best time to dig them up is in the spring when the roots are dormant, just before the sap begins to move up in the branches of the tree. Sassafras roots and bark that have been prepared for brewing may be dried to use for tea in any season.

Hoosiers have laid claim to sassafras tea as their own regional folk drink. October vagabonds who go to Brown County, Indiana, to see the autumn foliage know that the Nashville House menu always includes sassafras tea, hot or iced (and baked apple butter, fried biscuits, and hickory-smoked country ham!). The same trees that give color and spice to the sassafras tea tint Indiana's hillsides with yellow, orange, salmon-pink, red-orange, and bright vermillion leaves. Tourists at the Covered Bridge Festival in Parke County, Indiana, can sip sassafras tea on the green at Billie Creek Village or buy russet

sassafras jelly and sassafras candy—even sassafras ice cream—at the Cook House. And in Spencer County, Indiana, at the Lincoln Hills Arts and Crafts Fair, sassafras tea is served to all of the guests. If sugar and milk are added to the Hoosier's spring tonic, it is called "saloop."

In areas where the sugar maple grows, sassafras tea is sometimes brewed in a kettle of maple sap that has been boiled down for awhile—a double spring tonic! If the flowing sap of a tree contains vital and mysterious elements powerful enough to bring new life to leafless branches, surely, then, it somehow benefits my poor protoplasm.

Another interesting tea is made of sassafras. A fellow spinner, who uses sassafras roots, as I do, to make natural dye colors of rosy tan and rosy brown for hand-spun yarns, once told me to try the spicily scented greenish-yellow sassafras blossoms for tea.

"Get some this spring," she wrote. "The tea has a better flavor. Most people never look for these delicious blossoms."

I had never noticed sassafras blooming before, but the next April when my sister-in-law, Pat, and I were out hunting morels, we saw the pretty but inconspicuous six-petaled blossoms hanging on short stalks where later the long blue berries would be. We found no morels that day, but when we came back to the farmhouse we made a spicy, pale-yellow tea of the sassafras flowers and tasted, with the delight of new discovery, a flavor we had never before imagined.

But sassafras tea does not belong exclusively to Indiana's natives any more than moonshine belongs to hillbillies. Sassafras grows from Maine to the Gulf of Mexico and throughout the heartland of this country. Wherever the tree is found, teas have been made of its bark and roots since the earliest days when the American Indians taught the explorers to use its brew to cure scurvy. Sassafras was the "smelling stick" of the Onondaga Indians; they and their brothers made great use of all parts of the tree as a curative and for food. The Choctaw Indians taught southern settlers to use *kombo* (gumbo) in cookery. Filé powder, made from the dried, finely ground young leaves of sassafras, is still an essential ingredient in gumbo filé and in Creole recipes.

All rustic children and thirsty outdoorsmen know sassafras and nibble its leaves, spicy twigs, and flowers. But the mucilaginous quality of the leaves that thickens the soups and stews is not the real charm of the tree leaf. Young sassafras leaves are not all shaped alike. Some of them are oval or fan-shaped, like the leaves on older trees, but many

are shaped exactly like mittens. Who could pass by a "mitten tree" when out tramping the countryside without stopping to search the branches for a matching pair of mitts? This is one of childhood's retrievable joys, to be found again and again in fencerows and woodland borders.

And who could let a springtime pass without drinking a cup of sassafras tea? My grandfather's quaint spring tonic has become a part of my own rites of spring. When I drink it, I welcome the new natural year as joyfully as *Hyla crucifer*, the spring peeper, who trills a song of spring from the creek.

GRANDPA'S SASSAFRAS ROOT TEA

Dig the roots of small red sassafras trees early in spring, before the sap starts, if possible. Scrub clean and cut into lengths to fit into a large enamelware kettle. Use a generous handful of the roots—4 or 5 chunks—to a quart of cold water. Bring kettle to boil and simmer, covered, for 10 to 20 minutes until the water is a pretty rosy color. (The color indicates the strength of the tea's flavor: delicate rosy pink is mildly flavored; rich, orange red is strong.) Strain and sweeten to taste with honey or sugar. Add lemon or milk, if wanted, and serve.

Save the roots from the kettle to brew several times more, until the strength is gone.

ICED SASSAFRAS TEA

Make the brew of sassafras a bit stronger than usual. Strain the tea and chill in refrigerator. To serve, pour over cracked ice and add a twist of lemon to each glass. Sweeten to taste.

SASSAFRAS BARK TEA

4 pieces sassafras bark   5 teaspoons sugar
  (4-by-2 inches)   Cream
5 cups boiling water

Place the pieces of the rosy outer bark of sassafras root in enamelware pan or teapot. Pour boiling water over bark, cover container. Let steep in a warm place for 5 minutes, or until it is colored nicely. Strain into cups or into a hot teapot. Add cream and serve with sugar to make "saloop," or sweeten with honey. Serves 5.

Filé Powder

Gather young leaves of the red sassafras tree in the spring. Spread them in a single layer on a cookie sheet, and dry them in a warm oven (150° F) with the door ajar until the leaves are crisp and crumbly. Grind them in a mortar with a pestle until powdery. Put powdered leaves through sieve. Then store in covered jars until used.

Dried crushed thyme and bay leaves may be added to the filé powder, if desired.

Gumbo Filé

1 two- to three-pound chicken, cut into pieces
Salt and black pepper
Cayenne pepper to taste
1 large slice ham
2 tablespoons lard
3 tablespoons flour
1 small onion, chopped fine
1 fresh tomato, cut into small pieces

1½ quarts boiling water
1 bay leaf
3 sprigs thyme or 1 teaspoon powdered thyme
2 dozen oysters and their liquid
2 tablespoons butter
3 sprigs parsley, chopped
1 tablespoon filé powder (recipe above)

Sprinkle chicken with salt, pepper, and cayenne pepper. Cut ham into small pieces, and fry for about 5 minutes in a large heavy pan in the lard and some of the fat removed from the chicken. Remove ham. Add chicken pieces to fat and brown on both sides; do not cook, but remove from fat as soon as pieces are brown.

Add the flour to the hot fat and make a roux, stirring constantly until it is brown. Add onion and cook until golden. Add tomato, and let it cook for a few minutes. Add boiling water gradually, stirring well.

Return ham and chicken to pot, add the bay leaf and thyme (if sprigs are used, tie with white thread so they can be removed later). Add ½ teaspoon pepper and 2 teaspoons salt. Set the pan on a slow fire and cook until the meat is almost tender.

Add the oysters and their liquid, butter, and chopped parsley. Cook for about 15 minutes longer. Add more salt and pepper, if needed.

Remove from heat and slowly add the filé powder, stirring well. (*Do not add filé powder while gumbo is cooking* or it will be stringy and unfit to serve.)

Serve over steamed rice in a large, flat soup bowl. Serves 6.

NOTE: Both filé powder and okra may be used in the gumbo, but not so much filé is needed if okra is added. Turkey, shrimp, or crab meat may be used in place of chicken. The gumbo is concocted of whatever meats, seafood, vegetables, and herbs the cook has on hand.

To use okra in this basic gumbo filé recipe, fry 1 pound of okra, cut into pieces, in the roux with the onion and tomato. Add more water if necessary. Adjust the salt, pepper, and filé powder to taste.

KITTY'S SASSAFRAS JELLY

12½ cups strong sassafras tea
   (page 25)
9 ounces powdered fruit pectin

16 cups sugar
5 drops red food coloring
2 drops yellow food coloring

In a large kettle, combine the sassafras tea and the pectin. Stir and bring to a boil. Add the sugar and bring to a rolling boil, stirring constantly, and boil hard for 5 minutes. Remove from the heat and add the food coloring. Skim and pour into hot, sterilized, half-pint jars and seal. Makes 18 jars of jelly.

SUGARING OFF

As we turned off the main road onto a narrower one leading up the mountain, the huge, soft flakes of a springtime "sugar snow" began to swirl around us. Kurt and I had come to Vermont from Indiana, leaving the boys at home, after a telephone call from our friends proclaimed the first good sap run of the brief, unpredictable season of maple sugaring. Now we were hurrying to Mary and Tom Azarian's home, where we would help them gather and boil the sap from the majestic, ancient maple trees on their farm. We knew that the Azarians would get an early start in the sugarbush, and we did not want to miss a moment of this long-anticipated day. We did not even stop at our own house a few miles away. We had rented it for the winter and planned to stay with our tenants, the Ruddicks.

The road up the mountain was unsurfaced, and the freezing and thawing temperatures of the previous nights and days had turned it into a mile-long mud hole. But this seesawing of temperatures that

renders the roads almost impassable, especially to a rented car without a four-wheel drive or chains, also causes the wonderful, mysterious movement of sap within the winter-dormant sugar maples. When the thermometer does not sink below twenty-four degrees at night nor rise above forty degrees by day, the sap flow begins.

It was rough going, but my husband shifted the automobile into the lowest gear and kept on, determinedly, as if he were a native Vermonter. We slipped and slid along the deep ruts of the road and careened wildly up the hill. By some miracle, we reached level ground without getting stuck.

"We'll make it now." Kurt peered past the swishing windshield wipers that cleared an arc in the layer of wet, clinging snowflakes on the glass. "But we may not make it home tonight."

"It's only a sugar snow," I said wisely, drawing on my reading knowledge. "It makes the sap run better."

"Sugar snow!" Kurt hooted. "In Indiana, this would be a blizzard!"

When we had left Indiana the day before, jonquils and forsythia were blooming. Now, this morning, we seemed to be plunged back into winter. Snowflakes swirled in the air; deep windrows of snow lay on the fields; the mountains were lightened with white; mounds of plowed snow banked the roadsides. But under the coverlet of snow, the roots and branches were stirring with vitality. On the sidehills, great billows of steam rose above sugarhouse cupolas; icicles hung from eaves, and there was a fresh edge to the westerly wind. In Vermont, contrary to appearances, spring had begun. It was *sug'rin' time*.

Sugar maple spring blossoms

No one can say in advance exactly when the sugaring season will begin or when it will end with the budding of the trees. We knew that Tom had cleaned his sap buckets and spiles while the snowy winds of February howled around the snug, winter-weathered farmhouse. Before March 21, he had traversed his mountaintop sugarbush on

snowshoes, boring new tapholes in the maples and inserting sap spiles and, finally, hanging covered buckets on the spiles to catch the first drops of maple sugar.

Now we saw the tall, gaunt maples, hung with covered sap buckets, lining the lane that leads to the Azarians' farm. A maple tree must be forty years old and sixty feet tall before the first bucket can be hung on the sap spout to wait for the coming of warm days and freezing-cold nights that make the sweet sap drip. These craggy, gray-trunked maples along Tom and Mary's lane were surely one hundred and fifty years old.

The Azarians live in a charming old red-roofed farmhouse that is covered with grayish-brown, weather-darkened wood shingles. Their house is close to the road; Mary's *Farmhouse Press* studio is connected

Sugar maple leaf and seed

to the house, and another small building is hitched onto the studio, in snow-country fashion. The barn, too, stands very near the house. As we drove up, we saw Mary and Tom in the wide doorway of the barn, hitching up the team of draft horses to the gathering rig.

Mary and Tom greeted us and we stepped into the barn, out of the shower of snowflakes that clung wetly to our hair and clothes.

"Good thing I brought snowshoes," Kurt remarked.

"Oh, this is sugar snow," Tom said, nodding at the sky, which was obscured by thick, swirling snow. "It won't last ten minutes."

"Maybe," Mary commented dryly.

Our arrival caused a stir among the barn animals. The golden retriever ran happily, barking and making circles in the snow outside the door. A pair of African geese came up and looked us over, then waddled away, hissing and honking. Somewhere up high on the barn's big beams, a banty rooster crowed shrilly. Speckled hens scratched in the straw bedding on the barn floor, at the rooster's bidding. In their stalls, sheep and cows were rustling.

Tom's barn is stout, old, unpainted, festooned with cobwebs, and redolent of the hay of a hundred summers. It is the kind of barn I like being in. I was glad the horses were not quite ready to go.

The matched horses were huge light-chestnut Belgians with flaxen manes and tails, and long blond eyelashes. They were shedding their heavy winter coats, and Tom warned me about getting their long hairs on my clothes. There were bells on their harness, and when they moved there was a merry tinkle in the barn that matched the cheerful mood of the day.

Tom hitched the team to a red-painted jack sled and called, "Let's go!"

Kurt and Mary and I stood on the back and sides of the sled, holding on to the big gathering tank that was mounted on the sled. We were off to the sugarbush in a flurry of jingling bells, past the barn, past the mean ram who was tied to a stake in the snowy pasture, past the flock of white ducks, through the swirling snowflakes.

I think: *Are we really a part of this delightful scene? What we are doing could have happened fifty years ago—or a hundred years ago.* In other sugarbushes, sap now drips through plastic tubes into storage tanks, sleds are pulled by tractors, and oil fires burn under the evaporating pans in the sugarhouses. But Mary and Tom see no reason to abandon the old-fashioned method of collecting and boiling the sap. It is practical for their small family and in keeping with their simple, self-sufficient style of life, that Kurt and I envy.

The golden retriever raced alongside the sled and disappeared into a stand of hemlock trees. The sugarbush is downhill from the barn, facing southwest. Where the sap trail forks, Mary and I got off the sled and walked toward the sugarhouse; Kurt and Tom took the other snow trail to the lower part of the sugarbush to collect the buckets of sap.

Mary and I followed the winding path made by the sled through the hemlock and pine trees. Some of the trees along the trail were hung with old wooden piggins that have survived the years, but most of Tom's covered sap buckets are made of galvanized metal. Stepping out of the sled's tracks, I looked into one of the buckets. The sap was dripping at a good rate and the bucket was almost brimful, with bits of icy slush floating on top of the clear maple sap. When I tasted it, it was as cold and clear and fresh as water from a flowing spring and with barely more flavor. The delightful flavor of maple syrup is not in the sap as it drips from the tree. As the sap is boiled down to make the syrup, the color, flavor, and sweetness develop and concentrate.

The trick of maple sugaring is to be ready when the sap starts. A run may last only two or three days, and the next one will not begin until the winds and the temperature are exactly right again. It takes a cold north or west wind to make the sap flow, while a warm east or south wind stops the sap movement. If a cold snap freezes everything up at night or the temperature does not rise above freezing during the day, no sap runs. When Kurt and I were flying here from Indiana, we knew that we could very easily miss the sap run altogether. Vermonters often say, "If you don't like the weather, wait a minute." But the weather held and the sap was dripping into the buckets with a musical *plink! plink! plink!* on the second day of the sap run.

Mary and I rounded the curve in the sap trail, and there was the "sugar shack." It looked as picturesque as a postcard, with a deep ridge of snow clinging to the edge of its roof, icicles hanging from the eaves, and a light covering of new "sugar snow" on the cupola.

The sugarhouse is nestled against the hillside, surrounded by pines, hemlocks, and stately, bare-limbed, hard rock maple trees. It is built of rough lumber with log supports. It looks quaintly ramshackle, leaning a little here, sagging a little there. A woodshed adjoining the sugarhouse is stacked full of logs to fire the arch, or firebox, under the long, flat evaporating pans inside the sugarhouse where the maple sap is boiled down into syrup. A cupola on the peak of the roof vents the clouds of steam that rise above the open evaporator when the sap is boiling. Outside the sugarhouse is a huge sap storage reservoir that supplies the evaporating pans with sap.

Mary waded through the deep snow at the side of the sap trail to check the amount of sap left in the reservoir after yesterday's boiling.

"There is enough to begin boiling as soon as we get the fire started," she said.

We swung open the heavy door of the sugarhouse and stepped inside, grateful for its shelter. But it is almost as cold in the sugarhouse as it is outside, where the temperature is not much above freezing.

"I'll make some tea as soon as we have a fire," Mary said, looking around for kindling wood. Not finding enough, she took an ax and split some small logs.

Soon the fire flamed in the arch and bubbles began to show in the shallow maple liquid standing in the evaporating pan. The liquid was left there last night when the fire was put out with snow after Mary and Tom had drawn off nine gallons of new maple syrup from the first boiling.

Now Mary opened a valve to let some of the sap from the outside reservoir run into the evaporating compartments. But no sap ran out of the tube. The outside line leading from the reservoir to the evaporator was frozen! There was not enough sap in the pans, and the fire was blazing. If any of the pans burned dry, the evaporator would be ruined.

Mary slammed shut the draft of the furnace and dashed outside with newspapers to thaw out the line with a torch of fire.

I felt helpless, standing by the big pans, watching wisps of steam rising from the sap. First there was a little ripple of boiling, and soon one pan after another broke into a rolling boil. Clouds of steam began to rise toward the roof. Already the sap in the pans seemed shallower and the frothy boiling made a rushing sound, like a bubbling brook. The air began to feel damp and humid as the steam rose.

Soon Mary came back to check the sap line. There was still no sap coming through the tubing.

"It's thawing," she said. "I think we are safe but let's scoop up a bucket of snow, just in case."

The bucket of snow standing by the door was comforting. The fire had quieted down and I began to enjoy the atmosphere of the sugar shack.

There are windows on the west side of the sugarhouse that look out on snowy evergreens and the craggy sugarbush. The sugar snow had indeed stopped, and everything looked refreshed and wintery. There was soft snow on the hemlock branches and a pine grosbeak and a junco at the tree. Down in the sugarbush, I could see Kurt and Tom collecting the sap. The sounds of the jingling harness bells and the shouts of *Giddap!* and *Whoa!* drifted up the hill.

Inside the sugarhouse, a long table covered with red-checked oilcloth was set under the window. On one end of the table, the shiny new syrup cans stood ready. On the other end was the basket that Mary had brought from the house. Our lunch, wrapped in a cloth, was packed in the bottom of the basket, and Mary's art tablet, palette, and brushes were on top. Mary told me that she often brushed watercolors on her woodblock prints down here at the sugar shack when the boiling is underway. Not all of the sug'rin' activity is frantic rushing around.

There were possessions scattered about the sugarhouse that gave me glimpses of other days, similar to this one, when steam billowed above the rooftop cupola. On the sod portion of the sugarhouse floor, where Mary split the wood, lay left-behind toys—teddy bears, trucks, and a plush bunny; the Azarian children had spent some time here, too. On the small shelves built between the wall studs beside the window, next to the peanut butter, matches, and Twinings tea, were a few books— *Civilisation, Animals, Walden, Black Elk Speaks,* and *The Female Eunuch.* Lanterns hanging from the ceiling beams and a kerosene lamp on the shelf showed that the boiling sometimes goes on into the night.

But the most interesting record of past days is penciled on the wall. In 1910, Mr. Brimblecombe noted the first day of sug'rin' on the wall of his sugar shack and, in recent years, the Azarians added dates to the record:

1910	April 28	1921	March 14	1932	April 4
1915	March 21	1922	March 31	1934	March 31
1916	March 31	1923	March 29	1935	March 23
1917	March 27	1924	March 21	1969	April 5
1918	March 21	1930	March 28	1970	March 21
1919	March 21	1931	April 1	1971	April 15
1920	March 25				

When Mary came back into the sugarhouse, red-cheeked and cold, with news that the ice plug in the line had melted, I reminded her, "Don't forget to mark down the first day of this year's sugaring off."

"You do it," Mary suggested. "I'll make tea."

With a pencil, I added the date to the record: *April 4, 1972.* Soon the fire was roaring again and the sap was running steadily out of the tube into the first compartment of the evaporator. Mary dipped some of the boiling maple sap out of one of the compartments and made our tea with it. We drank the tea from chunky white pottery mugs. I discovered that the flavor of the tea made from partly boiled-down sap is odd. The faint taste of sweet maple vies with the delicate flavor of the tea, and I am not sure that I like it a lot, but I do not mind its taste, either. It is pleasantly warming and it seems fitting that sap is drunk in the sugarhouse.

Now that the boiling was under way, Mary took the skimmer, a utensil that looks a bit like a perforated dustpan with a long handle, and skimmed the yellow-tinged foam from the boiling sap. She threw the foam on the dirt floor under the evaporator. When the sap at the back of the huge, rectangular evaporator began to boil, Mary read the temperature on a thermometer suspended in the sap: 208° F. Maple syrup has boiled long enough when it reaches a temperature 7 degrees above the point at which water boils on the same day in the sugarhouse. The maple sap, fresh from the tree, is very close to water, so Mary calculated the temperature according to the temperature at which the fresh sap boils. On this day the maple syrup would be finished boiling at 215° F.

Mary tested the maple syrup another way, too. She dipped a wooden paddle into the syrup in the drawing-off pan at the front of the evaporator where the maple syrup finally ends up after having circulated from back to front through a maze of flanges in the evaporating pan. Mary held the paddle up vertically to let the liquid run off its edge. When the golden syrup "aprons off," it is finished; this happens when the drops of syrup merge, instead of falling off separately, and slide off the rim of the paddle together in a sheet, or apron. Testing maple syrup for doneness is very much like testing jelly, but the syrup, of course, does not jell when it cools.

It takes two hours or more for sap to boil down to syrup, but on the day of our visit the first batch would be drawn off sooner than usual because the sap in the front pans had been partly boiled the night before.

Mary put some brown-shelled eggs in the sap in the back pan to boil for our lunch. When Tom and Kurt came in with the load of sap on the jack sled, we would have a picnic by the bubbling, steaming evaporator.

There is much to be attended to in the boiling of maple sap. Every so often Mary checked the depth of the sap in the pans and adjusted the flow of sap from the reservoir into the evaporator. She skimmed off the yellowish foam and fired the roaring furnace under the steaming evaporator, hardly taking her eyes off the frothing, bubbling, stormy surface of the boiling syrup. A cautious boiler, Mary keeps the sap in the evaporating pans at a good depth because a shallow, concentrated sugar solution that is boiling hard can be dangerous. A pan that burns or boils over can end the sugaring for a season. When one of the pans seemed to be in too much of a hurry, Mary dropped a speck of butter into the pan and the wild boiling subsided instantly. A drop of cream works as well.

"People used to suspend a piece of pork above the pan so that it hung just below the rim," Mary said. "When the sap boiled too high, it touched the piece of pork and melted enough fat to tame it down."

There was a tinkling of harness bells outside, and soon Kurt came through the door, after stomping his boots against the foundation to knock off the snow. He leaned his new snowshoes up against the wall by the door.

"That's hard work!" he commented. "No wonder maple syrup costs so much!"

It takes about forty gallons of maple sap to produce just one gallon of pure maple syrup. All of the sap yielded during an entire season by four trees each hung with one bucket makes only one gallon of maple syrup. A log as big as a man is needed to produce the heat to boil down the forty gallons of sap into one gallon of syrup. And at least two people, struggling uphill and downhill in deep melting snow, must collect the load of sap in a rig holding about fifty gallons to get enough sap to make a single gallon of syrup. Another person must tend the evaporator while the sap boils down into syrup. Yes, maple syrup is a precious commodity and its production is hard work. Still, most syrup makers regard sugaring as fun. It is the first work of the spring season and it marks the end of winter's snowy isolation for many Vermonters. So wrote John Burroughs: "A sap-run is the sweet good-by of winter."

"All this snow and cold can become monotonously dreary," Mary told me. "I always look forward to sugaring because it gets me out of the house; it is something different to do."

Tom finished draining the newly collected sap from the gathering rig into the reservoir outside the sugarhouse, and Mary unpacked our lunch. She cut a fat, round loaf of home-baked bread into thick slices, took down from the shelf a squat glass jar of peanut butter, home-ground from fresh peanuts, and dipped the boiled eggs out of the hot sap. She made coffee for Tom and Kurt, using hot maple sap, and tea for us. When the picnic was spread out on the red-checked oilcloth under the window, we helped ourselves—spreading peanut butter on the bread, peeling the hot eggs, and eating ravenously.

Nothing ever tasted better than the plain peanut butter on thick bread slices, or the salt-sprinkled eggs, hot from the maple sap, or the tea laced with maple syrup. And the lush, maple-scented steam surrounding us was the most spring-like of fragrances.

Suddenly I had an appreciation for the taste of maple sap in my tea.

A little later, when Mary dipped the wooden paddle into the amber syrup in the front pan, the bubbles began to break and plop instead of frothing and the drops of syrup aproned off. Tom said, "Let's draw it off!"

He held a bucket under a spigot at the side of the drawing-off pan, and a stream of amber-colored syrup flowed out. Mary caught a small amount of the syrup in a vial and compared it with the syrups in a grading set that all sugar makers obtain from the Vermont Department of Agriculture. Vermont maple syrup is strictly graded according to color. Fancy Grade is the finest, with a light amber color and a delicate, sweet maple flavor. Grade A is slightly darker, medium amber in color, and it has a sweet maple flavor. Grade B is a dark amber color with a rich caramel taste that is generally used for flavoring and cooking. Another grade, Unclassified, is very dark, and it is used in commercial maple and blended syrups.

"We have Grade A today," Mary said.

While Tom drew off the syrup, Mary took our mugs and held each of them under the spigot to catch cupfuls of the steaming hot syrup. Then she passed the cups around and we sipped the fresh hot maple syrup, straight from the evaporator. I could not believe that I was drinking pure maple syrup! But I sipped it as the others did. It was clear, light, golden-amber, and delicious! I was amazed that I drank the whole cupful.

But what better brews could be drunk at the sugaring off than the sap tea and then the syrup itself? John Burroughs wrote, "When made in small quantities—that is, quickly from the first run of sap and properly treated—it has a wild delicacy of flavor that no other sweet can match. What you smell in freshly cut maple-wood, or taste in the blossom of the tree, is in it. It is then, indeed, the distilled essence of the tree."

Mary strained the rich new maple syrup through a felt filter and poured it into shiny, gallon-sized tins. Each container was filled up to the very rim with hot maple syrup, then a metal inner seal was snapped into the top of the opening. Dribbles of syrup were carefully wiped off before the screw cap was fastened on.

When Kurt and I left in the middle of the afternoon, two more loads of sap had been added to the reservoir and the fragrant golden syrup was boiling at a nice even rate. Mary had drawn off several gallons of the syrup and now, with the afternoon sun streaming through the window of the sugarhouse, she had spread out her paints on the red-checked oilcloth.

"Come back tonight after supper and bring the Ruddicks," Mary said when we left. "We'll have sugar-on-snow for the children."

Kurt and I walked back up the hill to the barn, he skimming along easily on the deep snow with his new snowshoes and I struggling in the snowy tracks made by the sled runners. Even in the sap trail, the snow was much too deep for walking. In the sugarbush, Kurt told me, it still lay five feet deep in places.

It seemed colder now, and the sun's rays were weakening. The lovely blue sky had turned gray and was spitting snow again.

Kurt buttoned his coat over the heavy ski sweater he had worn while collecting sap. "The sap is really going to freeze up tonight," he predicted.

The drive home was even more treacherous than it had been that morning. An inch of sugar snow hid the slick spots from sight. Out in the middle of nowhere, the car skidded on an icy spot and the back wheel slid into a snow-filled ditch. When Kurt tried to drive out of the ditch, the front wheel also slid into the ditch, headlight-deep.

By then it was snowing steadily—the same big, wet, clinging flakes we had delighted in that morning—and dusk was coming on early. Kurt walked off down the road to find the nearest house. But soon he returned in a truck with two helpful Vermonters he had flagged down on the road.

For a time it looked as though we would need a wrecker with a winch to get out of the ditch. The truck wheels spun on the slick road when the men tried to pull us out with a chain hooked onto the bumper. But when they finally put chains on the truck tires, they were able to get enough traction to pull our car out of the ditch.

When we were on our way again, escorted down the slippery, isolated road by the Vermonters in their truck, Kurt vowed not to travel this road again in the rented car we were driving.

"We can't get around on these back roads in this snow and mud without tire chains or a four-wheel drive," he said. "We'll have to miss the sugaring-off party."

But, when we drove up to our farmhouse where we were to stay for the week, we saw that our tenants, the Ruddicks, had acquired a Volkswagen since we last saw them.

So that night, after supper, we set out again for the Azarians' snowbound house atop the slippery mountain, this time in the little blue Volkswagen with Pat Ruddick and her children, Victoria and Max. The temperature had dropped well below freezing but it was still snowing, and now the bushes and trees were white-frosted with wet snow. It was incredibly beautiful and quite dangerous to be out on the roads.

When we reached the Azarians' house—not without sighs of relief—we found that Mary and Tom were not expecting us after all. The lower part of the house was darkened.

"We didn't think you would try it in this snowstorm," Tom said.

"Snowstorm!" Kurt exclaimed. "In Indiana, this is a *robin* snow. No one ever passes up a party because of a little robin snow."

Mary built up the fire in the black iron cookstove in the chilly kitchen. The golden retriever dived under the stove and everyone else gathered around it, warming up. The oldest Azarian boy ran down to the sugarhouse to get the thermometer Mary needed to make the maple sugar. To make soft maple sugar, maple syrup is boiled to 227° F and then beaten until the mixture turns creamy. While she was waiting for her son to return with the thermometer, Mary made a pot of hot tea for us and popped a panful of popcorn for the children. Now the kitchen was warm and cozy and busy again. The sugaring-off party was under way!

Mary poured about two quarts of maple syrup into a deep aluminum kettle. She greased the rim of the tall kettle with butter—a precaution against its boiling over—and hung the long thermometer over the kettle's rim so that the end of it touched the syrup. Then she put the kettle on the front burner of the stove, over the hottest fire, and soon the amber syrup began to boil hard. Mary watched the boiling kettle closely and we all sat near, in the red-painted kitchen chairs, chatting and eating popcorn and keeping in touch with the kettle from which a delicious caramel fragrance wafted. When the thermometer reached 227° F, Mary picked up the hot kettle with pot holders and carried it outside where she set it on a waist-high snow-bank by the porch. Then she packed a large tray with fresh snow and set it on the kitchen table. She brought in the slightly cooled kettle of syrup and called the children to the table. Then she dipped out a cupful of the steaming hot, dark syrup and poured it on the snow, a little at a time, making amber spirals over the surface of the snow. With forks we gathered up the snow-cooled syrup that hardened into a most wonderful candy—"sugar-on-snow." All of us, children and adults, alike, ate the waxy, taffylike maple candy, with new-fallen snow clinging to each mouthful, until it became overpoweringly sweet to our tastes. Then Mary offered us a sour pickle to take away the taste of sweet so that we could start all over again when she poured another cupful of hot syrup on the snow.

When we had all had quite enough of the sugar-on-snow, or "leather aprons" as it is often called, Mary served us steaming cups of fresh coffee and plain raised doughnuts.

Taking turns, we beat the hot syrup that was left over from the sugar-on-snow until it turned a pale tan color and became thick and creamy. Mary poured the soft maple sugar into jars and gave it to us when we were ready to leave. And Tom gave Kurt the traditional wage for helping with sug-rin'—a generous share of the maple syrup we had made that day.

After sugaring-off with the Azarians, Kurt and I both have a new appreciation for the sweet products of the hard rock maple. There are nuances of flavor in the delectable maple syrup that we were not able to perceive and enjoy until we had drunk cold clear sap, fresh from the tree, and hot sweet syrup, straight from the steaming evaporator. There are delicate, volatile qualities in it that we tasted at the tree and in the sugarhouse that we can still detect when we pour the amber syrup from the can onto our steaming pancakes. But the new quality that now exists for us in the maple flavor is the very essence of our most memorable springtime pursuit of the wild flavor—sugaring off in Vermont.

VERMONT BAKED BEANS

2 cups yellow-eye beans
   or other dried beans
½ pound salt pork with rind

and a strip of lean
½ teaspoon powdered mustard
½ to 1 cup maple syrup

The night before, wash and pick over the beans. Soak the beans overnight in cold water. In the morning, drain the beans and boil them in a quart of salted water (about 2 teaspoons salt) until the skins crack when a spoonful of beans is blown upon. It will take about half an hour. Do not overboil. Drain the beans.

Place half of the salt pork, rind down, in the bottom of a bean pot. Cover with the parboiled beans. Add the mustard and ½ cup of the maple syrup. Place the remaining pork, rind up, on top of the beans and add enough boiling water to cover the beans. Cover the bean pot with its lid. Bake in a slow oven (300°F) for 6 hours. Keep the beans moist during the baking by adding a small amount of *boiling water* from time to time. During the last hour, remove the cover to brown the beans and pork and add the remaining maple syrup, if more is wanted. Serves 6.

Maple Glazed Squash

2 small acorn or butternut
   squashes or ½ Hubbard
   squash
4 tablespoons melted butter

½ teaspoon salt
¼ teaspoon cinnamon
⅛ teaspoon freshly ground nutmeg
⅓ cup maple syrup

Cut the squashes into halves; clean out the seeds and stringy fibers. Cut a thin slice off the bottom of each squash so that it will stand upright. Place the squash in a baking pan and add ¼ inch water to the pan. Combine the butter, salt, spices, and maple syrup; spoon into the centers of the squashes. Brush the syrup mixture over the inside of each squash. Bake in a moderate oven (350°F) until very tender, for 45 minutes to 1 hour. Baste with the butter-syrup mixture during the baking period. Serves 4.

Maple Barbecue Spareribs

4 tablespoons tomato puree
½ teaspoon chili powder
Dash Tabasco sauce
1 teaspoon salt
¼ teaspoon freshly ground pepper
1½ tablespoons chopped onion

1 tablespoon Worcestershire sauce
1½ cups maple syrup
2 tablespoons vinegar or
   lemon juice
3 pounds spareribs

Combine all ingredients except the spareribs. Mix well. Place the spareribs in a shallow roasting pan, in a single layer. Pour the maple sauce over the ribs and marinate for several hours. Bake in moderate oven (350° F) for about 1½ hours, or until ribs are tender, basting frequently with sauce during baking and turning ribs occasionally. Serves 4.

Maple Baked Apples

4 unpeeled large tart apples
¼ cup seedless raisins
¼ cup chopped pecans, hickory
    nuts, or walnuts

2 tablespoons lemon juice
¾ cup maple syrup
1 tablespoon butter

Cut the core out of the apples with an apple corer and stuff the centers of the apples with the raisins and nuts. Pour the lemon juice over the apples, then the maple syrup. Top each apple with a portion of the butter. Bake in a covered baking dish in moderately hot oven (375° F) for 40 minutes. Baste during the baking time with the maple syrup. Serve warm or cold, with the syrup. Serves 4.

Maple Rice Pudding

¼ cup uncooked rice
2 cups milk
¼ teaspoon salt
2 tablespoons butter

2 eggs, separated
⅓ cup maple syrup
⅛ teaspoon freshly grated nutmeg
½ cup seedless raisins

Cook the rice, milk, and salt in the top of a double boiler over simmering water for an hour, stirring frequently. Remove from heat and stir in the butter. Slightly beat egg yolks, stir a little of the hot rice mixture into them, then add to rice. Add the maple syrup, nutmeg, and raisins. Cool. Beat egg whites stiff enough to hold their shape, then fold into the rice mixture. Pour into a 1 or 1½ quart-sized greased baking dish, and set in a pan of hot water. Bake for 30 minutes in a slow oven (325° F). Serves 4.

Maple Mousse

2 egg yolks
½ cup maple syrup

½ cup milk, scalded
½ cup heavy cream, whipped stiff

Beat the egg yolks until they are light colored, then beat in the maple syrup. Add the scalded milk very gradually, stirring constantly. Cook in a double boiler over simmering-hot water until the mixture thickens enough to coat a clean metal spoon. Remove from heat at once. Do not overcook. Cool the custard before adding it to the whipped cream. Pour the mixture into a refrigerator tray or into individual paper cups and freeze for 3 hours before serving. Serves 6.

MAPLE CUSTARD

3 cups milk, scalded
3 eggs or 6 egg yolks, beaten
½ cup maple syrup
1 tablespoon maple sugar

¼ teaspoon salt
1 teaspoon vanilla
⅛ teaspoon freshly grated nutmeg

Add the scalded milk very gradually to the beaten eggs. Add remaining ingredients and pour into 8 to 10 custard cups or into a baking dish. Place in a pan of hot water and bake in a slow oven (325° F) until the center of the custard is barely set, about 40 or 45 minutes. Serves 8 or 10.

MAPLE BUTTERNUT PIE

3 tablespoons butter
¾ cup brown sugar, packed
3 eggs
¾ cup maple syrup
1 teaspoon vanilla extract
½ teaspoon salt

1½ cups butternut or walnut meats,
   chopped
⅛ teaspoon freshly grated nutmeg
Pastry for 9-inch single-crust pie
   (see below)

In the bowl of an electric mixer, cream the butter with the brown sugar. Add the eggs and beat well. Then add the maple syrup, vanilla, and salt. Stir in the nutmeats and pour into a pastry-lined pie tin. Grate nutmeg over the top of the pie. Bake in a hot oven (450° F) for 10 minutes; then bake at 325° F for 25 minutes more or until a knife inserted in the center of the pie comes out clean. Cool and serve with vanilla ice cream. Serves 6.

PIE PASTRY

For 9-inch single crust
   1 cup sifted flour
   ½ teaspoon salt
   ⅓ cup shortening*
   3 tablespoons cold milk (about)

For 9-inch double crust
   2 cups sifted flour
   1 teaspoon salt
   ⅔ cup shortening*
   6 tablespoons cold milk (about)

Sift the flour and salt together. Add the shortening, and cut in with a pastry blender until the mixture resembles coarse cornmeal. Sprinkle the cold milk, a tablespoonful at a time, over the mixture while tossing it gently with a fork to distribute the milk evenly throughout. Enough

*Hydrogenated vegetable shortening or pure lard.

milk has been added when a small amount of the mixture pressed between the fingers holds together. Turn the mixture onto a square of waxed paper, gather up the edges and press from the outside with the hands to form a compact ball. For easier handling, the pastry dough may be chilled before rolling.

On a lightly floured board, roll out the pastry dough to at least a ⅛-inch thickness, making a circle about 2 inches larger than the pie pan. Line the pie pan with the pastry and, with a knife, trim off the excess at the rim of the pan.

If the pie shell is to be baked unfilled, prick the dough on the bottom and sides of the pan with a fork. Flute the edges. Bake the shell in a hot oven (450° F) for 12 to 15 minutes or until lightly browned.

For baking filled pies, note the directions in each recipe.

MARY'S MAPLE CRESCENTS AND BREAD

2 cups scalded milk
½ cup butter
2 teaspoons salt
⅓ cup maple sugar or
   ½ cup maple syrup
2 envelopes dry yeast

2 eggs, beaten
12 cups unbleached flour (about)
Butter
1 egg yolk, beaten, for glazing
   crescents (optional)

Combine the milk, butter, salt, and maple sugar or syrup. Cool to lukewarm and add the yeast. Stir until dissolved. Add the beaten eggs and mix well. Add enough flour, stirring in a few cups at a time, to make a stiff dough. Place in a large, greased bowl, cover, and let rise in a warm place until doubled in size. Punch down and let the dough rise a second time. Then turn out on a floured breadboard and knead until the dough is smooth and elastic. Divide in half.

Shape one half into a loaf and place in a 9-by-5-by-3-inch bread pan. Let rise in a warm place until doubled in size.

Out of the remaining half of the dough, roll out two 10-inch circles and spread each with 2 tablespoons of soft butter. Then cut each circle into eight pie-shaped slices. Starting at the wide end, roll each buttered triangle up, and bend each roll into a crescent shape. If glaze is desired, brush beaten egg yolk on the rolls. Place on a greased baking sheet and let rise until doubled in size.

Bake the rolls and the bread in a moderate oven (375° F) for about 20 minutes, until the rolls are browned and the bread sounds hollow when tapped with the finger.

Mary Azarian said, "These should have a faint, almost indefinable, maple taste."

Makes 16 fat crescent rolls and 1 loaf of bread.

Maple Butternut Divinity

Using the recipe for Maple Sea-foam Frosting (page 47), beat the egg-white–syrup mixture until it holds its shape, then quickly fold in 1 cup of chopped butternuts or walnuts. Drop the candy by teaspoonfuls onto a sheet of waxed paper, and let cool.

Makes about 36 pieces of candy.

Mr. Parker's Maple Fudge

Cook 3 cups of maple syrup until the candy thermometer registers 236° F. Set the pan containing the syrup in another pan containing cold water, and cool to 110° F. *Stir* until the syrup thickens and turns dull. Pour into a greased pie pan, and press the candy down, using the bottom of a water tumbler. Let cool, and cut into pieces. The candy will fill one 8-inch pie plate.

Mrs. Tibbets' Maple Butternut Fudge

3 cups maple syrup or maple sugar   ½ cup butternuts shelled and
½ cup cream   chopped
1 tablespoon butter

Combine the maple syrup or maple sugar with the cream in a heavy pan. Cook, stirring often, until a soft ball forms when syrup is dropped into cold water, or to 234° F. Remove pan from heat and add the butter. Set pan into another pan containing cold water; cool to lukewarm. Beat until the candy thickens. Add the butternuts and turn out onto a buttered platter.

If the candy hardens before turning out, add a little milk and put over the fire; stir until it warms up enough to spread.

Makes 3 dozen pieces.

Maple Sea-foam Frosting

2 cups sugar
½ cup water
⅛ teaspoon cream of tartar

⅔ cup maple syrup
2 egg whites, beaten stiff
⅛ teaspoon salt

Combine the sugar, water, cream of tartar, and maple syrup in a saucepan and stir over low heat until sugar dissolves. Boil, covered, for about three minutes, then remove lid and boil without stirring until a soft ball forms when a small amount of syrup is dropped into cold water, or to 240° F on the candy thermometer. Pour the hot syrup in a thin steady stream into the stiffly beaten egg whites, beating constantly with the electric mixer. When all of the syrup has been added, add the salt and continue beating until the frosting is of proper consistency to spread on cake. If frosting hardens before spreading, beat in a few drops of hot water. Makes enough frosting for two 8-inch layers.

NOTE: Do not attempt this recipe on a rainy or humid day.

Raised Doughnuts

1 cup buttermilk
2 tablespoons shortening
2 tablespoons maple syrup
2 teaspoons salt

1 envelope dry yeast
1 egg, slightly beaten
3 cups sifted flour (about)

Scald the buttermilk and combine it with the shortening, maple syrup, and salt. Stir until shortening is melted, then cool to lukewarm. Sprinkle the yeast over the buttermilk mixture and let stand for 10 minutes, until yeast dissolves. Stir, then add the egg and mix well. Beat in sufficient flour to make a soft dough that is firm enough to handle. On a floured board, knead the dough well and roll or pat to ⅓-inch thickness. Cut with a doughnut cutter, cover with a towel and let rise in a warm place for about 1 hour. Fry in deep hot fat (375° F) for about 1 minute on each side until nicely browned. Drain on absorbent paper. Serve at a "sugar-on-snow" party. Makes about 20 doughnuts.

MAPLE BREAD PUDDING

4 cups stale bread pieces
2 eggs, beaten
3 cups milk
⅔ cup maple syrup

⅛ teaspoon nutmeg, freshly grated
¼ teaspoon cinnamon
½ cup raisins
1 tablespoon butter

Use good, substantial bread for this pudding, preferably homemade bread or French bread, with the crusts removed. Break the bread into pieces rather than cubing it.

Beat the eggs and milk together with a rotary beater, add the maple syrup and spices. Add the raisins and bread. Pour the mixture into an 8-by-12-by-2-inch baking dish. Dot with butter, and bake in a moderate oven (375° F) for 1 hour. Serve warm with cream. Serves 6.

GATHERING MORELS

T he arrival of morels is the gastronomic event of the year for the wild foods enthusiast. For a brief two-week period, these succulent miracles of early spring can be found in open woods, old orchards, greening pastures, and thickets. There is no precise date on the calendar when they are due to appear, but the dedicated morel hunter pinpoints the exact moment of their emergence by his own timetable of vernal blossom, by the very feel and scent of the air, and by his own quickening instinct for their discovery.

In greenly veiled woods, there must be ruby globes of bloom on three-leafed stems of trillium. There will be delicate white Dutchman's-breeches and clumps of purple violets nestled against tree stumps and fallen logs. Short green umbrellas of mayapple leaves are unfurling but their waxen white flowers are still locked in buds. There are pale jack-in-the-pulpits in mossy woodland cloisters, and yellow adder's tongue—far lovelier than the image of its name—with orchidlike flowers and sharp, speckled leaves. On the hillside, the

49

glowing pink of blossoming redbud trees lights up the dark thicket beyond the creek. In the old orchard south of the house, apple blossoms are just beginning to show.

Such are the fragrant spring blossoms that tell the eager morel hunter that the brief season of mushrooming is at hand. Without the proper conditions of weather, though, these charming signs of mushroom time signify nothing.

The air must be moist, with a gentle wind running over the warming earth. In the most favorable circumstances, a soft rain falls during the night and the next morning the sun comes out of gray clouds and shines hotly on the damp leaves and spawn-filled earth. Beneath the soil, where old plant debris and dead wood lie decaying, the hidden mycelium of the morel fungus takes food and grows until the proper warmth and moisture reach it, which sometimes takes years.

Then, at that rare moment when the signs of spring and conditions of temperature and moisture are exactly right, the magic of mushrooming occurs. In an incredibly short time, perhaps a few minutes, the mycelium of the underground fungus quickly absorbs the moisture, swells rapidly, thrusts upward to the surface of the earth, and rises as a full-blown morel mushroom. It bursts through the ground with remarkable force, this delicate morsel of edible fungus, pushing away leaves, sticks, clods of dirt, small branches, or any other obstacle.

Once released to the surface of the earth, the morel remains for only a few hours until its spores ripen, scatter, and return to the earth to renew the cycle—or until it is found by a keen-eyed morel hunter in search of the delicacy for his table.

I am one of those keen-eyed, eager, dedicated, and slightly mad mushroom hunters who spend the whole of two delightful weeks every April in pursuit of the delectable morel, until the last mushroom fades away with the coming of the hot, dry weather. Each spring I return first to my secret hunting grounds where I have found morels in other springs. These secluded places are the most rewarding sites for hunting because morels rise in the same spot year after year. Occasionally, when conditions are not right for their growth, the mycelium of the fungus fails to send up its fruit in season, but it lives on beneath the soil for many years feeding on decaying vegetation. When all the conditions for their growth are perfect once more, the mushrooms will spring up where they have been before.

"They can be anywhere," my father has said when we hunted morels together, "but you're more likely to find them around old apple trees and elm trees."

Country people may know nothing of mycorhiza, the name given to the relationship that exists between certain trees and certain fungi, but they accept the affinity of morels with apple trees and elms from long experience.

As my father and I walked across the familiar fields, heading for the old apple orchard, my nose fairly yearned for the scent of mushrooms. The aroma of morels is one that a perceptive morel hunter with a keen nose thinks he can detect on the air itself when he nears the spot where they rise rootless from their mysterious, invisible beginnings.

With reckless optimism, I carried a paper bag that I hoped to fill with morels. Many a seasoned morel hunter believes it bad luck to show confidence by taking any sort of container on a mushroom hunt.

"They'll hide if you take that sack along," Dad warned as I rummaged around in the kitchen that morning.

But the day seemed so right for morels that my greedy appetite would not allow me to heed superstition. Nothing could be worse than finding a good crop of morels and then being forced to leave some behind for lack of a container.

Dad ambled along the greening fencerow, head bent and eyes intent on the ground. He stopped where a fallen elm tree lay rotting and raked aside the leaves with the toe of his heavy shoe.

"This will be a good spot someday, if they ever get started here," Dad said. "Morels favor old elms." But we found none, so we went on to inspect the locust grove which Dad had planted for his fence posts in the days when the farm was fenced for cows.

"I never knew that morels grew in this locust grove until one morning, some years ago, I noticed how old Mooley Cow ran directly to the grove when I turned the herd into pasture after milking time," Dad said. "I was going a-mushrooming right then, myself, so I decided to see what the old gal was after."

Dad chuckled. "It was morels, all right, but Mooley beat me to them that day. All I could see was round stubs of stems where she'd nipped the mushrooms off at the ground. From then on, I never let cows pasture here at mushroom time." Dad chuckled again. "I figured that made old Mooley Cow and me about even. She battered my milk bucket every time I got near her."

Dad looked around the locust grove, getting his bearings and continuing his musings about contrary old Mooley Cow, who had shown him where morels grow, a favor not to be expected from even the most loyal of human friends.

"Right about here," Dad made an arc in the air with his hand, "is where old Mooley's mushrooms should be." He looked hard at the ground in front of him for a moment. "Look," he said, and there, camouflaged against a background of curled, matted, brown leaves (the morel's color) was our first one.

"They're out today!" Dad's exclamation of discovery was as jubilant as I remembered it from other springs when we found the first morels together.

Dad reached down and nipped off the brittle stem close to the ground. He took off his battered felt hat and deposited the first morel in its crown.

Finding buried gold on a treasure hunt could not bring more joy than that felt by mushroom hunters at the discovery of a fine crop of morels. With cries of delight I dropped to my knees on the fragrant leaf mold, and the hunt was on.

I gently pushed aside the leaves and looked for the morel's mate, which always hides nearby. When our eyes grew accustomed to the mushrooms' protective coloring, we saw them all about in a space no larger than the top of a dinner table. They were like a forest of tiny brown Christmas trees, rising at odd angles out of the damp humus. Their delectable, yellowish-brown caps were small conical sponges, intricately webbed with an irregular network of deep pits.

Now we really *saw* them!

Instead of blending into the background, as they had before, they now stood out against the leaves, like figures in bas-relief on a woodland sculpture.

"These are the big yellow ones," Dad commented as we plucked off the brittle stems at the ground.

To the mycologist, the big yellow ones are *Morchella esculenta*, the most delicious of all wild mushrooms. Countrymen call them sponge mushrooms because the light yellowish-brown cap resembles an oval sponge, both in appearance and color. *Morchella esculenta* grow larger than the other varieties of morels that we find on the farm. Their average height is three to four inches, but some years we find whoppers that measure five to six inches or more. A single one of these mammoth morels makes a fantastic meal for one person.

Soon after the flush of *Morchella esculenta*, or overlapping it, the smaller and very delicious *Morchella vulgaris* appears. Its conical cap

Morchella vulgaris

and coloring closely resemble the *Morchella esculenta*, but *Morchella vulgaris* is usually shaped more definitely like a Christmas tree, and the pits in the cap are more tightly compressed. The cap of *Morchella vulgaris* is darker than the cap of *Morchella esculenta*, ranging from dark grayish-brown to bister. The stem of *Morchella vulgaris* is white or perhaps only slightly yellowish, whereas the darker stem of *Morchella esculenta* is definitely yellowish. If, by good fortune, both varieties are found at the same time, they may be served up together, indiscriminately. Their flavor is the same· a morel is a morel.

Sometime earlier, another variety, *Morchella conica*, appears in the woods. These are called "snakeheads" by countrymen. They have big, hollow stalks and small, pointed, deeply ridged caps that are shaped, of course, like heads of snakes. The pits on snakehead caps are arranged more neatly than the pits on caps of other morels, in more or less vertical rows. The ridges surrounding the pits of the snakehead are darker than the rest of the cap, giving it a striped appearance. My father refers to snakeheads as "little black-striped fellows."

The stems of the three varieties of morels that we gather at the farm for our table are squat, hollow, and equal in height to or shorter than the hollow caps of the morels. On all three, the base of the cap is not free from the stem, but curves inward at the bottom and is attached firmly over the top of the stem with no overhanging edge.

Another variety of morel found at the farm has a tiny cone of a head, similar to the snakehead, atop a long white stem. The base of the morel cap is *not* firmly attached to the stem; the edge of the cap is free of it and hangs over slightly. The stem may be twice as long as the cap of the morel. Local country people call this variety of morel by the homely and descriptive name "dog pecker." It is edible, but thin-fleshed. My father shuns it and I, too, have always left it behind. When the dog pecker is plentiful, so are the delectable *Morchella esculenta* and *Morchella vulgaris*, and I have always found plenty of these morels without having to harvest the less desirable kind.

Morchella conica

In southwestern Indiana, where I live on the banks of the Ohio River, the morel is never as abundant as it is in some areas along the eastern border of the state and in its wooded, hilly central section. There, fellow mushroomers report to us, morels are harvested by the basketful. My brother, teaching school in mideastern Indiana one year, said that morels made truants of his pupils; school attendance dropped as drastically in mushroom season as it did during a flu epidemic, with whole families leaving home for a day of hunting.

Still, comparatively few people gather morels. Though they are highly touted by American gourmets and spoken of in the same reverent tones Frenchmen reserve for truffles, only a handful of epicures have so much as tasted the succulent morel. Rarity is one factor, of course. And morels are shunned as food by those who suffer from "mycophobia," the fear of mushrooms.

Mycophobia is born of old die-hard superstitions and folklore. Mushrooms have been considered strange, mysterious, malevolent, unearthly things that spring up in the dark of night. Lightning, witches, elves, fairies, and demons are their company. Compounding these superstitions is the unfortunate fact that several mushrooms are poisonous if eaten. Actually, only one family, the relatively rare Amanita, contains a fatally poisonous member, although several other varieties of wild mushrooms cause illness ranging from mild allergy to indigestion to acute gastric distress.

But no one who has seen a morel, or studied a picture of one, can possibly mistake it for any other mushroom.

Clyde M. Christensen, plant pathologist at the University of Minnesota, includes morels in his famous "foolproof four." The foolproof four—morels, puffballs, sulphur shelf mushrooms, and shag-gymanes—are absolutely safe to eat and easily recognized by definite characteristics that positively distinguish them from other mushrooms. He urges the beginner to study and gather them and to eat them without fear.

One excursion after morels, one day spent afield when woods, orchards, and pastures are in their most beautiful season, one dinner of the most delectable and succulent of wild mushrooms, will transform foolish fears into the greatest enthusiasm.

The discovery of a rich stand of morels in springtime is one of the excitements of the year. Besides the obvious reward of having this delicacy for the dinner table, there are the rewards of the season itself to be savored and enjoyed.

I like the clear spring brooks that bubble and gurgle over clean slick stones and smooth round pebbles. I thrill at glimpsing a small red fawn jumping out of a patch of briars; he is as startled as I. I treasure the nosegays of violets blooming around mossy rocks and at the brook's edge. I chill at the surprise of a quick black snake slipping across my path. I enjoy the stereophonic serenade in the thicket where I am surrounded by the wild trilling of cardinals, thrushes, and orioles. I admire the hieroglyphic markings on the shiny black and bright yellow carapace of the slow box turtle who hisses and withdraws into his shell when I pick him up. I welcome the sudden spring shower, drinking up its freshness through my skin as the plants do, and the sunshine that follows rain, unfolding stored-up petals of contentment. I memorize special places known only by me and the wildlings. Most of all, I cherish the serenity I find in the midst of the excitement of the new season, with everything beautiful about me budding, bursting, sprouting, springing, unfurling—beginning again.

Hunting morels is my spring ritual, linking this spring to others. When I hunted morels with my father this past spring for the first time in twenty years, it was as if there were no empty years between those remembered Aprils and this one. The pleasures of other hunts and other springtimes were as vivid and near as yesterday. It was a good day, with Dad telling tales and recollecting the bounties of other years.

Now his hat held a nice mound of morels, and he took one off the top and held it up for our admiration.

In earlier days, when my father hunted many country things, we knew at the sound of his jubilant, booming voice that it was time to fire up the kitchen range and get out the skillet. He began hollering for us at the top of his voice as soon as he came into the barn lot at the back of the house.

"Oh, Laura!" he'd thunder.

"Oh, Marilyn!" His voice could be heard as far away as the back pasture, although we mightn't be farther away than the kitchen.

"Come see what I found!"

Every word rang with the triumph of the returning hunter. By the time he came stomping up the back steps and slamming in the screen door, we were all rounded up and waiting to see what surprises were in store.

"Look what a fine mess of morels," he'd say, holding out his hat for my mother to see. He always had his hat with him, ready to be filled to the brim with savory wild mushrooms, choicest of all the wild flavors he relished, or with sweet wild strawberries found on Havill Hill, or with frosty, ripe persimmons found while out hunting quail. Sometimes he would line his hat with a fragrant layer of green fern fronds, or with his red bandanna kerchief, to keep it from being stained with the juices from nature's bounty.

The wild treasures my father gathered in his hat were always very special. When he brought back morels, Mother made a great to-do of counting them and spreading them out on the kitchen table for us to admire.

Mother sliced each spongy morel down the middle and quickly rinsed the hollow halves in the cool water that I drew up from the deep well near the kitchen door. Then she soaked them, ever so briefly, in salted water to draw out any tiny gray insects that might have crawled into the honeycombed caps before Dad found them.

Mushrooms, like many wild delicacies, are so fragile and ephemeral that only the lightest shower of water is needed to rinse away flecks of earth clinging to their pale, brittle stems and soft, faded-brown caps.

A cool woodsy scent from the mushrooms filled the kitchen almost at once. It is a spicy aroma, evocative of the leathery, rain-soaked leaves and damp mossy places where morels spring up from the earth, an aroma that can never be separated from the flavor of the morels when they are cooked and served for dinner.

Soon the kitchen crackled with activity as Mother prepared a hearty country meal to accompany the delectable morels. Dad always settled down at the kitchen table, in the midst of the hustle and bustle, and we had to walk around him to get to the dish cupboard and sink. His presence was welcome and companionable, but very distracting. Every few minutes he got up from his chair and made a trip to the stove, where he lifted lids and prodded the frying meat with a fork. All the while he kept up his rambling accounts of one matter or another, and I never knew how Mother ever managed to get all the ingredients into the soda biscuits that she stirred up and rolled out while concentrating on his conversation.

At the last minute, when the places were set at the table, when the thick slices of crusty pan-fried steak were browned, when the creamy mound of mashed potatoes was heaped into a bowl and set in the warming closet, when the fluffy biscuits were as high as the side of the pan and beginning to brown behind the oven door, Mother turned all her attention to the morels.

On the back of the stove, a chunk of pale-yellow churned butter was put to melt in the best iron skillet. When the melted butter bubbled and sizzled, Mother laid the morels in the pan, side by side, and sautéed them gently over the back burner until they were lightly browned. Then, quickly, onto the platter in a ring around the steak and to the table—they were at last served up to our zesty appetites.

The morel's best companion at dinner is beefsteak. The flavor of one enhances the other. Morels should be sautéed lightly in butter and seasoned sparingly with salt and pepper. They may be dredged in flour or not, as desired, before being sautéed. Sometimes I dip them in egg and milk and then roll them in cracker crumbs before I sauté them.

Rich sauces and exotic seasonings for the morel? Never! I let its flavor speak for itself. To drown the morel in wines or hide it in condiments is sacrilege.

When we have only a precious few morels in our harvest, I serve them for supper or breakfast, chopped and butter-browned, stirred into a panful of fluffy scrambled eggs.

These two simple ways of preparing morels are the best, I'm convinced, but morels may be cooked in other ways, too. Large, handsome morels are elegant when split lengthwise and filled with a stuffing made of meat or fowl. The stuffed halves are then put together again and baked. Or, I stir morels, browned, into a cream sauce and serve them over triangles of toast.

In those springs when the harvest is plentiful, we eat our fill and freeze the surplus to be used later (extravagantly!) in sauces and gravies.

Morels have a wild, wonderful flavor that can never be separated completely in my mind from the context of greenly veiled woods and wet dripping leaves, from the fragrance of Mother's kitchen, or from the memories of old Mooley Cow and Dad's battered felt hat.

Sautéed Morels I

Cut morels in half lengthwise, rinse in cold water, and soak for a few minutes in a mixture of 1 quart water and 1 teaspoon salt. Drain the morels thoroughly and dry on paper towels.

In a heavy skillet, sauté the morels in several tablespoons of sizzling butter over low heat for a few minutes or until lightly browned. Do not overcook. Sprinkle the morels with salt and pepper to taste while they are cooking.

Sautéed Morels II

Cut morels in half lengthwise, rinse in cold water, and soak for a few minutes in a mixture of 1 quart water and 1 teaspoon salt. Drain the morels thoroughly and dry on paper towels.

Roll the morel halves in flour and sauté them in a heavy skillet in several tablespoons of sizzling butter over low heat for a few minutes or until lightly browned. Season the morels with salt and pepper to taste while they are cooking.

Sautéed Morels III

Cut one pint morels in half lengthwise, rinse in cold water, and soak for a few minutes in a mixture of 1 quart water and 1 teaspoon salt. Drain the morels well on paper towels.

In a bowl mix together 2 eggs and ¼ cup milk and dip each morel half in the mixture. Roll the morels in fine cracker crumbs and sauté them in a heavy skillet in several tablespoons of sizzling butter over low heat until the crumb crust is crisp and brown. Season the morels with salt and pepper to taste while they are cooking.

Stuffed Morels

8 to 10 large morels	2 tablespoons finely chopped onion
2 cups bread crumbs (from firm white bread)	Juice of ½ lemon
	1 teaspoon salt
½ cup chopped cooked chicken	¼ teaspoon pepper
⅓ cup melted butter	½ cup light cream

Cut the morels in half lengthwise, rinse them in cold water, and soak for a few minutes in a mixture of 1 quart water and 1 teaspoon salt. Drain the morels well and dry on paper towels.

In a bowl combine the bread crumbs, chicken, butter, onion, lemon juice, salt, and pepper. If there are additional morels, chop them finely and mix them with the stuffing. Loosely fill the morel halves with the stuffing, join the halves together, and tie them with string. Put the stuffed morels in a buttered casserole and pour the cream over them. Bake in a hot oven (400° F) for about 25 minutes.

NOTE: The morel halves can also be stuffed and baked open-faced, substituting a mixture of ½ cup chicken broth and 2 tablespoons white wine for the cream. Bake them in a hot oven (400° F) for 18 to 20 minutes.

MOREL BISQUE

Morels, one cup or more
2 tablespoons butter (about)
2 scallions, chopped
2 cups shredded tender greens
    such as dandelions, docks, poke
    leaves, alone or in combination
Fresh parsley, chopped

¼ cup sauterne
½ teaspoon celery salt
Salt and pepper
1 quart hot rich chicken stock
1 cup heavy cream
2 egg yolks

Cut morels in half lengthwise, rinse them in cold water, and soak them for a few minutes in a mixture of 1 quart cold water and 1 teaspoon salt. Drain the morels well, dry on paper towels and cut into small pieces. You will need at least 1 cup.

Sauté the morels gently for several minutes in enough melted butter to cover the bottom of a large saucepan. Stir in the scallions and cook for a few minutes longer. Add the greens and some chopped fresh parsley. Simmer, stirring frequently, for 5 minutes. Add the sauterne, celery salt, and salt and pepper to taste. Add the chicken stock and cook for 15 minutes.

In a bowl, thoroughly mix the heavy cream and egg yolks, stir in a little of the soup, and gradually stir the cream mixture into the hot soup. Heat, stirring constantly, but do not let bisque come to a boil.

Serve in heated soup bowls with a slice of lemon and a sprinkling of paprika. Pass a bowl of crisp croutons. Serves 4 to 6.

MORELS IN CREAM I

Cut four big morels in half lengthwise, rinse them in cold water, and soak them for a few minutes in a mixture of 1 quart water and 1 teaspoon salt. Drain the morels well and dry on paper towels.

Over gentle heat, sauté the morels in enough butter to cover the bottom of a skillet. Cook until most of the pan juices are absorbed. Stir in ½ cup heavy cream and salt and pepper to taste. Serve the morels on slices of bread, preferably home-made, toasted and buttered.

Morels in Cream II

Cut morels in half lengthwise, rinse them in cold water, and soak them for a few minutes in a mixture of 1 quart water and 1 teaspoon salt. Drain the morels well and dry on paper towels.

In a buttered casserole, arrange alternate layers of the morels and buttered bread crumbs. Over each layer pour enough heavy cream to moisten the crumbs and season them with salt and pepper to taste. Bake the morels in a moderate oven (350° F) for 25 to 30 minutes.

Scrambled Eggs with Morels

Rinse four big morels in cold water and soak them for a few minutes in a mixture of 1 quart water and 1 teaspoon salt. Drain them well, dry on paper towels, and chop into small pieces. In a skillet, sauté the mushrooms in several tablespoons of sizzling butter over low heat until they are lightly browned.

In a bowl, beat 8 eggs and stir in ½ cup milk and salt and pepper to taste. Pour the egg mixture over the morels and cook them over low heat, stirring constantly and gently, until the eggs are cooked but still moist. Serve at once. Serves 4.

SPRING GREENS

I was still young enough to be enchanted by fairy tales when Grandmother taught me to "tell greens." In springtime, as soon as wild lettuce, lamb's quarters, dandelion, and black mustard were the right size, the children and women of the farm literally swarmed over the fields to fill the bushel basket with these tender greens. At the picking place, Grandmother gave each child a sample leaf to hold in his hand during the hunt. We scattered out across the fields, shrieking with pleasure at the discovery of every leaf of wild treasure while Grandmother tucked up her long skirts and settled down to gather new life for her larder from a green fence corner.

My grandmother's kitchen was a place of wonderful aromas. It smelled good even when the wood fire was out and nothing was cooking on top of the kitchen range—a mixture of freshly made coffee, baked bread, buttermilk, vanilla, and cinnamon—will-o'-the-wisp fragrances to remind me of every good food that I had ever eaten in her kitchen. But when the greens were in the pot, with a piece of salt pork for flavor, gently being coaxed into tenderness on the back of the range, and a big flat pan of yellow corn-bread batter was swelling to lightness behind the oven door, there was no question what was cooking for dinner. The only question was, How much longer?

Those first greens were like spring tonic to winter-wearied appetites. By the time Grandfather and the others came into the dooryard, we were washed up and waiting on the bench behind the long kitchen table. Greens and "pot-likker" for dinner meant that winter was finally over.

Greens and pot liquor on my table today are just as symbolic of winter's end as they were in those days. When winter dwindles down to the last few dreary days and I cannot bear being housebound for another minute, I dress in some old clothes, pick up a basket and a keen-edged knife, and go out looking for greens.

Going afield to gather the crisp young potherbs for the springtime "mess of greens" is a tonic in itself. Who could not feel lighter, more buoyant, after spending an afternoon in a fragrant, bee-humming meadow collecting spring leaves for dinner, with hundreds of brilliant yellow dandelions bursting like tiny suns underfoot? Part of the feeling of renewal surely comes from the day spent in greening fields with the energies of new lives and cycles surging about. Who would not absorb some of the surrounding excitement and feel more vital? Though I take my spring tonics lightheartedly, I vouch for the sense of rejuvenation that follows expeditions into the countryside to hunt spring greens as well as the feeling of well-being that follows the healthful feast.

When I take my children with me into the greening fields, I give them each a leaf to match and find, as I was given it as a child. They tumble through the meadow, shouting their discoveries to one another: "Woolly britches!" "Dandelions!" "Narrow dock!" "Wild lettuce!" They run back and forth, flinging contributions at the basket. Then one shouts, "Hey! Robin's nest!" and they disappear in greener pastures to make their own discoveries: birds' nests, crayfish holes, tadpoles growing legs, and very special rocks.

My dog, Tippy, goes with me, running ahead to sniff out trails of small animals that belong to the meadow, barking furiously, his tail a plume showing above the weeds, when he finds a lazy snake stretched

Dandelion (*Taraxacum officinale*)

Black mustard (*Brassica nigra*)

Many of the greens pictured here are shown in a size too large for eating, but once identified in mature form, the immature, edible leaves are more easily recognized.

Broad-leafed dock (*Rumex obtusifolius*)

Curly dock (*Rumex crispus*)

Spinach dock (*Rumex patientia*)

Wild lettuce (*Lactuca*)

Pokeweed shoots (*Phytolacca americana*)

Pokeweed blossoms and fruit

Lamb's-quarters (*Chenopodium album*)

Milkweed shoots (*Asclepias*)

Milkweed flower buds

Milkweed pods

Sheep sorrel (*Rumex acetosella*)

Peppergrass

Purple violet

Plantain

Blackberry-briar tops

across the path. Tippy is excellent company afield; no hunt is complete without a companionable dog, even a wild greens hunt. When I have settled down beside the basket in *my* green fence corner, he disappears down by the creek, amusing himself at a groundhog den until he hears my whistle.

Sometimes I share my spring ritual with a friend. Often someone who is eager to learn to "tell greens" suggests a hunt, and it is satisfying to initiate another to the pleasures of the meadow. But my favorite of companions afield is the older person who has picked greens for years, who can introduce me to still another tender, succulent, edible weed, who will enchant me with folk-names for plants that I know by other names. While hunting greens with Maude Knowles, my friend and helper, I learned to know plantain as "sheep's tongue," peppergrass as "white mustard," sheep sorrel as "rabbit's-ear," and asparagus as "sparrowgrass." There were other greens Maude picked for our springtime dish that have fascinating colloquial names: "woolly britches," "spring sprout," "speckled Dick," "cliff lettuce," and "wild cabbage." But to Hazel Marshall, a fellow greens-hunter from another town nearby, "woolly britches" are "fuzzy britches" and "speckled Dick" is "wild beet." And so the hunt for spring greens becomes an exercise in etymology.

There are hundreds of common names for the dozens of edible wild greens that the experienced potherb hunter gathers for the traditional springtime "mess." But the novice can concoct a safe, savory dish of wild greens using only the most familiar plants.

Dandelions (*Taraxacum officinale*) are everywhere in springtime, "star-disked dandelions . . . lying in the grass," disdained and dug out of immaculate lawns by determined gardeners but welcomed by enlightened cooks who dish up such garden nuisances for dinner. At our house, we enjoy these delicious intruders in our lawn and on our table. In the basket of "weeds" dug out of the bluegrass are the first green leaves of the field for the healthful salad wilted with hot sweet-sour dressing and sprinkled with crumbled crisp-fried bacon. My family also likes the unique delicately bitter taste of dandelion greens cooked in the rich broth of a meaty ham bone, and I always include lots of dandelions in my traditional mess of greens.

Dandelions for salads and greens must be picked when they are as tender, fresh, and new as spring itself. Later, after the blossoms appear, the greens are too tough and bitter for salads and potherbs. Then we pick the bright yellow flowers to brew into a pale golden *dent-de-lion* wine, a sprightly beverage that evokes the April scent of dandelion blossoms and the bright image of fields yellow with blooms.

Almost as familiar as the dandelion with its golden-rayed flowers and green, notched leaves is the black mustard plant (*Brassica nigra*). Before the bright yellow four-petaled flowers bloom on the maturing plants, the young leaves are picked for potherbs. Mustard is hot to the taste and it adds a fiery tang to the springtime dish of greens, so one must be careful not to add an overpowering amount to the pot. No single green should predominate but, rather, all of the greens should mingle to create the tangy, inimitable wild flavor of the countryman's most savory feast.

Here by the Ohio River, we have fields of wild mustard in the spring that were sown by nature. When the leaves have grown too old to be gathered for greens, the yellow flowers of mustard tint the meadows a golden color. But more beautiful to the Southerner than the sight of lovely blooming fields is the steaming tureen of mustard greens and turnip greens cooked with ham hock. This is the favored combination for mustard greens below the Mason-Dixon line.

When black mustard and dandelion are ready for greens, the new leaves of the docks (*Rumex*) are also at their best. Several species of docks are gathered for potherbs. The most popular in this area is the common curly dock or narrow dock (*R. crispus*). It is an abundant, sometimes troublesomely rank, plant of roadsides, pastures, gardens, and cultivated fields. The dark green leaves of curly dock are long and narrow, with wavy edges. A few plants furnish enough of the foot-long leaves for the springtime mess of potherbs. It is so plentiful here that few hunters bother to gather broad-leafed or bitter dock (*R. ob-tusifolius*) but its wider, rounded leaves are tender and edible when the plant is very young. Later, the broad-leafed dock becomes bitter and cannot be used for greens. Another dock commonly used for greens is patience dock or spinach dock (*R. Patientia*). It is very similar to curly dock except that the leaves are longer, sometimes two feet long, and the plant is taller. Several species of dock might be found within the same area, to the confusion of the novice, but all of the species are edible.

Wild lettuce (*Lactuca*) has a very subtle flavor that is indistinguishable in the bouquet of greens but I look for it to tone down the stronger flavors of dandelion and mustard. There are two kinds of wild lettuce that I gather. The leaf of one species of wild lettuce (*L. canadensis*) looks very much like a dandelion leaf at first, when it is young and tender enough to eat, but later it grows into a large, rough, prickly leaf. Wild lettuce exudes a milky juice from the leaf when it is broken away from the stem, but this does not make the leaf bitter until later, when it is older. Then the wild lettuce can be parboiled before adding it to the spring pottage to remove the milk and the bitter principle. The flavor of the other variety of wild lettuce that I gather is even milder. Prickly lettuce (*L. scariola*) is very tender when it is young and can be added to the mess of greens or served raw in a salad. Maude called this wild lettuce "smooth lettuce," even though there are tiny, weak prickles on the lower part of the rib of the toothed leaf and on the stem, and she liked to use it to make a dish of wilted lettuce whenever we could find enough of the succulent leaves.

Very early in the spring when I begin to look for greens—about the time I begin to look for morels, too—pokeweed (*Phytolacca americana*) shoots are pushing out of the ground. When the plant is only a few inches tall, the entire sprout with its unfurling leaves is edible and delicious in the dish of mixed greens, or cooked alone as "poke greens."

Poke greens are my favorite of the spring greens. I like their delicious vegetable flavor and the delicate taste of iron in the cooked leaves, and the young stalks are better than asparagus.

"A mess of poke is as good for you as a round of sulphur and molasses," Maude said when we were gathering the thick, succulent shoots on the roadbank one day in April.

Young poke shoots, no taller than six or eight inches, and the new leaves at the branching top of the young plants before the blossoms appear, are wholesome and safe to eat; but the root of pokeweed is poisonous and should not be eaten. The seeds of the purplish-black berries that form in racemes on the plant in autumn are also said to be poisonous, and the purple rinds of the mature plant stalk take on some of the harmful quality of the root. However, those who would shun the young leaves and shoots as food because other parts of the plant are dangerous if consumed should remember that many plants have both an edible and a poisonous portion, such as potatoes and rhubarb.

The citizens of Harlan, Kentucky, honor the lowly pokeweed during an annual "polk sallet" festival. One day in late spring is designated Poke-Eating Day. Everyone feasts on poke greens. The governor of Kentucky, who serves as the Chief Poke Warden, is charged with the duty of protecting the bounty of poke from greedy harvesters who would break the unwritten code of the hills concerning when and how to gather it.

When the stampede of spring has started, there is very little time to gather poke greens at their best. Maude's and my code for picking poke is simply to get out and get it when it is at the right stage. We use poke greens in an amount equal to the dandelions, mustard, and dock, and we freeze the surplus to be used later.

Lamb's-quarters *(Chenopodium album)* are another spring green that we like to gather. When Maude and I go picking for the first time, we do not find as many lamb's-quarters as we find a little later on, but we find a few early plants, especially in the flower beds and in last year's garden patch. Lamb's-quarters have a delicious, mild, spinach flavor that is good in the kettle of greens or cooked alone. Throughout the spring and summer, after the early greens such as dandelion, docks, and wild lettuce have grown too large to eat, new lamb's-quarters continue to spring up anywhere rich soil has been disturbed. It is especially plentiful in cultivated gardens, and the vigilant gardener unwittingly weeds out a wild vegetable that is as delicious as the spinach, kale, chard, or lettuce that he must plant, hoe, water, and weed. The entire young plant of lamb's-quarters can be eaten as greens and later, when the plant grows taller, the tender top portion can be plucked off. The small, grayish-green leaves of lamb's-quarters are oval-shaped with a white, mealy bloom on their undersides. The fresh leaves have a peculiar water-repellent quality, but when they are steamed they quickly lose this resistance and shrink in bulk by at least one half their quantity, like other wild greens.

"Pick plenty," Maude always advises. "Greens cook down to nothing."

If we find some early sprouts of milkweed *(Asclepias)*, Maude and I include them in our April dish of greens. In the weeks of late spring and early summer, we will go out again and again to gather milkweed. We will hunt along the roadsides, in unplowed cornfields, along the garden's margins, for the tender young plants that can be cooked and served in asparaguslike ways, then later for the unopened flower buds of milkweed that look like broccoli-flower buds, and finally, for the tiny, young milkweed pods. Milkweed is a worthwhile food plant, one that is beautiful and fragrant in blossom as well. When a milkweed plant volunteers to grow in my garden or flowerbed, it is as welcome as an eggplant or a marigold.

Sheep sorrel (*Rumex acetosella*) is a relative of garden sorrel, or French sorrel. It is found in the spring in dry fields with poor soil and again in the autumn when such greens as the docks and dandelions bravely send up tender new growths. Sheep sorrel is sometimes called sour grass because the light green, arrowhead-shaped leaves are delicately sour and have a pleasant, refreshing taste. In Indiana, sheep sorrel is often called rabbit's-ears. The tart leaves of this small plant can be used generously in cooked soups and sauces but only small amounts of it should be eaten raw, as in salads. It is one of the greens used sparingly in the springtime mess of greens because of its sourness.

Anyone recognizing these common wild greens—dandelion, black mustard, wild lettuce, pokeweed, lamb's-quarters, milkweed—can gather and prepare a savory springtime dish.

"Mix the common greens, about equal parts," Maude instructed me. "Then, to give the greens a good flavor, find a little elder, some blackberry-briar tops, a few violet leaves, a handful of rabbit's-ear, sheep's tongue, wild beet, and the like—but not too much of any of them, mind you."

When it comes to gathering the uncommon wild greens that give a good flavor to the springtime dish, a long-time greens hunter is the best instructor. Gathering greens and cooking them is an esoteric country skill that is best passed on from one person to another by demonstration.

A number of women have shown me delicious spring greens, beginning with my grandmother, and my kettle's contents increase with wild flavor each time I am fortunate enough to go hunting with one of them. Grandmother first taught me to "tell" the basic greens. Christine Day showed me how to find "speckled Dick," Phillipia Barnett introduced me to "woolly britches," Hazel helped me find "rabbit's-ears," Loretta Ingram gave me "spring sprout," Angie Willett told me about "poke sallet," and Maude taught me to find "white mustard," "wild beet," "smooth lettuce," and many others.

None of these women has ever looked in a botany book but I trust their teachings completely. None of them would ever foolishly experiment with an unknown wild green for food. They learned what they know from other hunters. Each has her trusted repertory. When I asked Maude why she did not pick a certain plant that I knew to be edible and good, she said, "I only pick what my mother showed me to pick."

Excursions into the greening fields and meadows with these

delightful women are, for me, half the pleasure of dining on spring greens. The memory of the day spent kneeling on the stirring earth, surrounded by spring's recurring miracles, with the sun's warmth burning my back as I bend over rosettes of curly dock and dandelion, cannot be separated from the wild flavor of the greens. All the sensory joys of the day are recalled by tantalizing scents that flood the kitchen as the steamy kettle simmers on the stove and the crisp leaves of the meadow wilt and tangle into what can only be called a "mess of greens." When the steaming tureen of potherbs is served up for dinner, the essence of the greens hunt is savored again—even more completely. The delightful spring mixture, swimming in its own pungent green pot liquor, served with buttery slabs of corn bread, black-eyed peas, scallions, slices of fried smoky country ham, and buttermilk, is the most flavorful of the countryman's traditional feasts.

Spring Greens

Gather a basketful of mixed spring greens when they are young and tender, picking at least 2 or 3 gallons of greens. Combine dandelion, narrow dock, pokeweed leaves and shoots, black mustard, wild lettuce, and lamb's-quarters in about equal amounts. Add smaller portions of other edible wild greens such as violet leaves, plantain, blackberry-briar tops, peppergrass, sheep sorrel, and milkweed shoots. Do not add any leaves that are not young and tender and *do not add any leaves you do not positively recognize as edible potherbs*, no matter how attractive in appearance. Wash the greens through several waters as soon as you reach home, until the last water runs clear, and store the cleaned greens in the refrigerator.

In a large soup kettle, 1½-gallon sized, simmer a ham bone with plenty of meat left on it, in 3 quarts of water. Let the ham bone cook until the meat begins to fall away from the bone and the broth is well flavored. Then fill the pot with cleaned greens. When they cook down, add more greens. Cover the kettle and let the greens simmer until they are tender and have cooked down into a savory "mess of greens," about 45 minutes. Season with salt and pepper to taste during the cooking period and add 1 pod of red pepper, if desired.

Serve the spring greens with sliced hard-boiled eggs and vinegar to accompany the traditional menu.

NOTE: Pot liquor dodgers may be cooked with the greens, or fluffy dumplings may be added during the last 15 minutes of cooking. See recipes below.

Pot Liquor Dodgers

2 cups yellow cornmeal,
  stone ground
1 teaspoon salt
½ teaspoon baking powder

2 cups hot pot liquor from
  Spring Greens (recipe above)
1 tablespoon fat, melted

In a bowl, combine the cornmeal, salt, and baking powder. Stir in the pot liquor and the melted fat. Let stand for 15 minutes. Shape into cylindrical biscuits, 2½ inches long and 1 inch wide. Place the dodgers on top of the greens during their last 20 minutes of cooking time, and cover the kettle tightly. Lift dodgers out carefully before removing the greens. Serve with the pot liquor. Makes 12 dodgers.

Cornmeal Dumplings for Greens

1 cup flour
1 cup yellow cornmeal,
  stone ground
2 teaspoons baking powder

1 teaspoon salt
1 egg, beaten
¾ cup milk
1 tablespoon shortening, melted

Sift the dry ingredients together. Combine the egg, milk, and the cooled, melted shortening. Stir into the flour mixture and mix quickly until well blended. Drop by tablespoonfuls on top of the greens 15 minutes before they have finished cooking. Cover the kettle tightly and steam the dumplings without removing the lid for 15 minutes. Serve immediately. Makes 10 to 12 dumplings.

Poke Sallet

3 quarts tender young
  pokeweed leaves

¼ teaspoon baking soda
12 slices bacon

Clean the pokeweed leaves, cover with 1 quart of cold water, and bring to a boil. Cook gently for about 10 minutes. Add the baking soda, stir, and drain thoroughly.

In a large skillet, fry the bacon until crisp. Drain on paper towels. Add the pokeweed to the fat in the skillet and sauté until the liquid has almost evaporated. Crumble the bacon over the "poke sallet" and serve at once with black-eyed peas, scallions, corn bread, and butter-milk. Serves 6.

Hoosier Poke Sprouts

16 to 20 poke sprouts
2 tablespoons butter
2 tablespoons flour
1 cup milk
½ teaspoon salt
Freshly ground pepper to taste

½ cup grated mild Cheddar cheese
12 slices crisp-fried bacon
 (or 4 slices Canadian bacon)
4 squares buttered toast (or 4
 buttered toasted English muffins)
1 tablespoon chopped chives

Gather the poke sprouts in the early spring when they are 6 or 8 inches tall, snapping off the entire stalk with its unfurling leaves above the ground, as you would pick asparagus. Clean the poke sprouts and boil them gently in salted water to cover until the stalks are just tender. Drain the sprouts and keep them warm until served.

While the poke sprouts are cooking, make a white sauce of the butter, flour, milk, salt, and pepper. As the sauce thickens, stir in the Cheddar cheese and continue cooking until the cheese is blended. Have ready and keep warm the slices of bacon, drained well, and the buttered toast. For each serving, top a toasted bread slice with 3 slices of bacon and put 4 or 5 poke sprouts on top. Cover the poke sprouts with cheese sauce and sprinkle with chopped chives. Serves 4.

NOTE: Poke sprouts may be forced indoors during the winter. See page 88.

Yankee Corn Bread

¼ cup soft shortening
1 cup flour
¼ cup sugar
4 teaspoons baking powder

¾ teaspoon salt
1 cup yellow cornmeal
2 eggs
1 cup milk

Divide the shortening between two round 8-inch pie tins and put them in a hot oven (425° F) to allow the shortening to melt, about 5 minutes. Meanwhile, mix the remaining ingredients as follows.

Sift together the flour, sugar, baking powder, and salt. Stir in the cornmeal. Beat the eggs and milk together until mixed well, then add to the dry ingredients. Beat until just smooth. Remove the hot pans from the oven and pour the hot fat into the corn-bread batter. Stir quickly. Pour the batter into the sizzling pans and put in the oven to bake at 425° F for 20 to 25 minutes. Cut into pie-shaped wedges and serve from the tins. Makes 12 wedges.

KENTUCKY DANDELION GREENS

Gather 1 to 1½ gallons of tender dandelion greens and wash well. Simmer a meaty ham bone in 1½ quarts of water until the broth is rich and the meat is tender, about 1 hour. Use the bone of a country-cured or smoked Kentucky ham, if possible. Add the cleaned greens to the kettle, cover and simmer gently until the greens are tender and well-flavored, about 1 hour. Season the greens with salt and pepper, as needed, during the cooking. Serve the greens in a hot tureen with the pot liquor poured over them. Serve with corn bread or cornmeal dumplings, and with a cruet of vinegar. Serves 8.

REDUCING BITTERNESS OF DANDELION GREENS

As the season progresses, dandelion greens become increasingly bitter, but as long as the plant has not blossomed, the greens are edible. If the bitterness is objectionable, reduce its tang somewhat by soaking the cleaned greens overnight in cold water with a teaspoon of salt and the juice of half a lemon. Next morning, drain them and use in the usual way. Or, cover the greens first with *boiling* water and pour this off before cooking them according to the recipe.

DANDELION AND LETTUCE SALAD

1 pint fresh cleaned dandelion greens
4 Bibb lettuces (an amount equal to dandelion greens)
4 scallions
½ green pepper
1 cup halved cherry tomatoes
⅓ pound coarsely shredded

Swiss cheese
Salt
Black pepper
3 tablespoons salad oil
4 tablespoons wine vinegar or herbal vinegar
2 sliced hard-boiled eggs

Cut into small pieces the dandelion greens, Bibb lettuce, scallions, green pepper. Add the cherry tomatoes, and Swiss cheese. Add salt and freshly ground black pepper to taste and toss lightly. Add oil and vinegar. Toss well and garnish with the hard-boiled eggs. Serves 4.

WILTED DANDELION GREENS I

4 cups tender young dandelion
greens
4 slices bacon
3 tablespoons vinegar

2 teaspoons sugar
½ teaspoon salt
¼ teaspoon dry mustard
Pepper to taste

Coarsely shred the dandelion greens. In a skillet, fry the bacon until crisp. Remove bacon, leaving the fat, and drain on paper towels. Crumble the bacon over the dandelion greens. To the bacon fat in the skillet, add the vinegar, sugar, salt, dry mustard, and add pepper to taste. Heat the mixture and pour it over the greens and bacon. Toss the salad until the greens are wilted. Serve at once. Serves 4.

WILTED WILD LETTUCE SALAD

Follow same recipe as above, using the tender young leaves of wild lettuce instead of the dandelion greens.

WILTED DANDELION GREENS II

4 cups tender young dandelion
greens
4 slices bacon
½ cup sugar
½ teaspoon salt

1 tablespoon cornstarch
1 egg, beaten
¼ cup vinegar
1 cup cream

Coarsely shred the dandelion greens. Fry the bacon slowly until crisp, and drain. In a saucepan, combine the sugar, salt, and cornstarch. Mix well. Add the egg and vinegar, mixing well. Crumble the bacon and add with the cream and the bacon fat. Cook to the desired thickness and pour the mixture over the dandelion greens while hot. Toss until the dandelions are wilted. Serve at once. Serves 4.

BATTER-FRIED DANDELION BLOSSOMS

36 dandelion blossoms
1 egg, beaten
1 cup milk

1 cup flour
½ teaspoon salt
⅛ teaspoon pepper

Pick new dandelion blossoms—those on short stems—and rinse well in cool, lightly salted water. Cut off the stem ends as close to the flower heads as possible, without cutting off so much that the petals fall apart, because the stems and greenery are bitter. Roll the dandelion blossoms in paper toweling to blot up the excess moisture, then dip each one in a batter made of the egg, milk, flour, salt and pepper. Drop the batter-coated blossoms into deep hot fat (375° F) and fry until lightly browned. Drain on absorbent paper, sprinkle with more salt, if needed, and serve at once as a hot hors d'oeuvre. Serves 6 to 8.

NOTE: Squash or pumpkin blossoms from the garden may be fried by this recipe, too.

DANDELION CROWN OMELET

1 cup blanched dandelion crowns   3 teaspoons cold water
3 tablespoons butter   ¼ teaspoon salt
6 eggs   Freshly ground pepper

Prepare the dandelion crowns from dandelions that have been blanched outdoors in the springtime or forced in a cellar flat (see page 88). The crown is the portion beginning above the brown roots and ending where the leaves start to turn green. Cut away the root and leaves and wash the crowns.

Sauté the dandelion crowns in 2 tablespoons of the butter for about five minutes. Drain and keep warm.

Break the eggs into a bowl, add 3 teaspoons cold water, salt and pepper, and beat with a wire whisk for 30 seconds. Put 1 tablespoon butter in a French omelet pan and melt over medium heat until the butter sizzles. Tip the pan to coat the sides with the melting butter. Pour in the eggs and cook slowly over low heat until the bottom begins to cook, then arrange the dandelion crowns over the omelet. Lift the edges of the omelet and let the egg mixture run under. Continue cooking over low heat, shaking the pan back and forth over the burner to keep the omelet from sticking, until the omelet is firm except for a barely-soft portion in the center. Fold the omelet and serve at once. Serves 2 or 3.

NOTE: Dandelion crowns can also be served as a stewed buttered vegetable or eaten raw in salads.

BAKED DANDELIONS

2½ cups cooked dandelion greens
3 tablespoons butter
2 tablespoons minced green onion
3 tablespoons flour
2 cups milk
1 teaspoon salt
¼ teaspoon pepper

3 hard-boiled eggs,
   coarsely chopped
¼ teaspoon nutmeg
¾ cup buttered bread crumbs
½ cup grated American cheese
¼ teaspoon paprika

Using an electric blender, puree the cooked dandelion greens. Melt the butter in a skillet and sauté the onion in it. Stir in the flour, add the milk, salt and pepper. Cook and stir until smooth and thickened. Add the dandelion puree, chopped eggs, nutmeg, and additional salt and pepper to taste. Place the mixture in an 8-by-12-by-2-inch buttered baking dish, and top with the buttered bread crumbs, cheese, and paprika. Bake in a moderate oven (375° F) for 20 minutes.

DENT-DE-LION WINE

2 quarts dandelion blossoms
4 quarts water
2 lemons, cut into small pieces

2 oranges, cut into small pieces
3½ pounds sugar
1 cake of yeast

Pick dandelion blossoms early in the morning, taking care not to have a particle of bitter stem attached. Snip off the end of each dandelion blossom to remove the green collar at the base of the blossom. Cover the blossom petals with water and boil for 20 minutes. Pour the hot mixture over the lemons and oranges and allow to cool to lukewarm. Add the yeast cake and let stand for 48 hours. Strain and add the sugar. Stir to dissolve. Pour the liquid into a jug, such as a glass cider jug, and cover with a lid but do not screw the cap down tightly. Or use a cork with a tube inserted through it for a stopper, and put the other end of the tube into a glass of water. Let the wine stand for about six weeks, or until still. Strain and bottle. This pale wine improves with aging. Keep for 6 months before drinking. Makes five 4/5-quart wine bottles.

PINK DANDELION WINE

2 quarts dandelion blossoms
2 quarts boiling water
Juice of 3 lemons
1 10-ounce package frozen red

raspberries
3½ cups sugar
1 cake of yeast

Gather the dandelion blossoms early in the morning while they are still fresh. Prepare the blossoms for the wine as soon as you return to the house, as they soon wilt. Snip off the end of each dandelion blossom to remove any remaining bitter stem particles as well as the little collar of leaves at the base of the blossom. Do not wash the flowers. Put the petals in a one-gallon stoneware crock and pour the boiling water over them. Let stand overnight. In the morning, strain the liquid from the flowers, squeezing all of the juice out of them. Combine the dandelion juice, lemon juice, raspberries, and sugar. Boil gently for 20 minutes. Pour back into the crock, cook to lukewarm, and add the yeast. Cover the crock and let ferment for about 10 days, or until it stops hissing. Using filter paper or a double layer of cheesecloth, strain the liquid into a scalded cider jug and let stand for about 3 days to settle. Then strain again into clean quart wine bottles with screw-on caps, but do not tighten the caps. Let stand until the wine is still before corking or capping the bottles tightly. Age in the cellar until Christmastime. Fills three 4/5-quart wine bottles.

Teetotaler's Dandelion Beverage

1 quart fresh dandelion blossoms	2 cups cold water
2 quarts boiling water	2 oranges, sliced thin
3 cups sugar	2 lemons, sliced thin

Fill a 1-quart measure firmly with fresh dandelion blossoms. Rinse the blossoms and cut off the stem ends close to the flower heads. Cover the blossoms with the boiling water and set the mixture aside to cool. Combine the sugar with the 2 cups of cold water and bring to a boil; this will make 3 cups of syrup. Add the syrup, oranges and lemons, and let the mixture stand for 2 or 3 days. Strain and serve over cracked ice. To keep longer, either bottle the strained liquid and cork tightly, or keep under refrigeration. Makes more than 2 quarts of a healthful, nonintoxicating drink.

Dandelion Wine Pudding with Ladyfingers

6 egg yolks, beaten	¾ cup Dandelion Wine
4 tablespoons sugar	(either recipe above)
1 tablespoon lemon juice	6 egg whites, beaten stiff
Grated rind of an orange	6 tablespoons confectioners' sugar
1 teaspoon cornstarch	1 dozen ladyfingers, split

Combine egg yolks, sugar, lemon juice, and orange rind. Dissolve the cornstarch in part of the wine before adding to egg-yolk mixture. Cook over simmering hot water until thick, stirring constantly. Let cool. Make a meringue by gradually adding confectioners' sugar to the stiffly beaten egg whites while beating. Place split ladyfingers in the bottom and around the sides of an oven-proof serving bowl. Pour in the dandelion custard and top with meringue. Bake in moderate oven (350° F) for about 12 minutes, or until peaks of the meringue are tipped with brown. Serve with a small glass of Dandelion Wine to accent the flavor of the pudding. Serves 6.

LAMB'S-QUARTER WITH LITTLE FELLOWS

1½ gallons lamb's-quarter
Smoked-ham bone
1½ quarts water

1 pound potatoes, peeled and cubed
Little Fellows Dumpling Batter
(recipe below)

Gather a quantity of lamb's-quarter, at least 1½ gallons, in the springtime before the plants are 6 inches tall. Pick the entire plant. If you gather the lamb's-quarter later in the season, when the plants are larger, pinch out and use the tops. Rinse the greens well and drain.

In a large kettle, cook a meaty smoked-ham bone in 1½ quarts of water for about 1 hour. Add the lamb's-quarter to the broth along with the potatoes. Cover and simmer for 10 minutes. Remove the ham bone, cut off the meat, and cut it into ½-inch cubes. Return the meat to the cooking greens. With a teaspoon, drop little fellows dumpling batter on top of the lamb's-quarter mixture and simmer the dumplings, covered, for 15 minutes. Serve the lamb's-quarter and the dumplings from the kettle. Serves 6 to 8.

LITTLE FELLOWS DUMPLING BATTER

½ cup flour
½ teaspoon salt
½ teaspoon baking powder

Pepper
1 egg, beaten
2 tablespoons milk

Into a bowl, sift together the flour, salt, baking powder, and pepper to taste. In another bowl, mix together the egg and milk. Add the flour mixture all at once and blend well with a fork. Makes enough batter for 12 dumplings.

MILKWEED CASSEROLE

2 dozen young milkweed shoots 1 teaspoon salt
4 tablespoons butter ½ teaspoon coarse black pepper
4 tablespoons flour 1 cup bread crumbs
2 cups milk 4 tablespoons melted butter
1 cup Vermont Cheddar cheese, grated

Gather young shoots of the milkweed plant when they're no more than 6 inches tall. Wash well. Fill 3 large pans with enough water to amply cover the milkweed shoots, and put all of the pans on the stove to heat at the same time. As soon as the water boils, drop the milkweed shoots in the first pan and bring the water to a boil again. At once, lift the milkweed shoots out of the first pan with tongs and transfer them to the boiling water in the second pan. Again bring the milkweed shoots to a lively boil. Transfer the milkweed to the last pan of boiling water and repeat the process for the third time. Drain the greens thoroughly. Boiling in three waters removes the bitter principle from the milkweed.

In a saucepan, melt 4 tablespoons of the butter. Stir in the flour and cook slowly, stirring constantly, until the mixture begins to turn golden. Gradually add the milk, stirring well to prevent lumps. Cook over medium heat, stirring constantly, until the mixture thickens. Add the grated cheese, salt, and pepper. Stir the sauce until the cheese is blended.

Arrange the milkweed shoots in the bottom of a 2-quart greased baking dish, and pour the hot sauce over the milkweed. Combine the bread crumbs with the melted butter and sprinkle on top of the sauce. Bake in a moderate oven (350° F) for 20 minutes, or until the sauce is bubbling and the bread crumbs are browned.

MILKWEED "BROCCOLI"

Pick clusters of unopened flower buds of milkweed before they begin to show any of the purple color of the coming bloom. Parboil them quickly in three waters as described in Milkweed Casserole recipe above. Then cook the buds in a small amount of water for 5 minutes. Drain, season with salt, pepper, and lots of butter. Serve at once.

NOTE: Milkweed flower buds turn a beautiful bright green as soon as they are placed in boiling water. The cooked flower buds have a pleasing, mild vegetable flavor: not like broccoli flower buds, which they resemble in appearance, but like milkweed.

MILKWEED SEED PODS

Pick the tiny seed pods of milkweed that begin to form as soon as the flower withers. They must be firm and not one bit spongy when pressed with the finger. Cook them by parboiling them in three waters as described in Milkweed Casserole recipe above. Then boil them a few minutes longer until tender, cooking them about 10 minutes in all. Drain, season with salt, pepper, and butter. Milkweed seed pods are also good served with meat and a sauce of meat gravy.

SORREL SOUP

1 cup sheep sorrel leaves	2 cups chicken stock
5 tablespoons butter	2 egg yolks
1 tablespoon flour	1 cup cream
2 tablespoons parsley, chopped	¼ teaspoon salt
2 rosemary leaves	¼ teaspoon pepper

Cut off the stems, wash the sheep sorrel and dry on absorbent paper. Chop fine. Heat the butter in a pan, then add the sheep sorrel. Cook, stirring over medium-to-low heat, until the sorrel is soft (at least 5 minutes). Stir in the flour, parsley, and rosemary. Combine the chicken stock, egg yolks, and cream, and beat with a fork until the egg yolks are blended. Add to the sorrel, stirring well. Simmer for one minute, but do not boil. Season with salt and pepper. Serve hot with croutons, or chill and serve with a tablespoon of chive-sprinkled sour cream in each portion. Serves 4.

SOUR GRASS BUTTERMILK PIE

5 tablespoons butter	3 tablespoons sheep sorrel
1⅓ cups sugar	leaves, minced
3 eggs	Pastry for 8-inch pie, single
⅔ cup buttermilk	crust (see page 44)

In the small bowl of an electric mixer, cream the butter and add the sugar gradually while beating. Add the eggs, one at a time, beating well after each. Slowly add the buttermilk while beating. Last, add the minced sheep-sorrel leaves. Pour into a pastry-lined pie tin and bake in a moderate oven (350° F) for about 45 minutes, when the filling should be set in the center and the top of the pie browned. Serves 6.

Buttermilk Pie

Use the recipe above, but omit the sheep sorrel and flavor the pie with 2 teaspoons of vanilla extract or 2 tablespoons lemon juice.

Rainbow Trout with Sorrel Butter

½ cup butter
½ cup sheep sorrel leaves,
    chopped fine
1 teaspoon Wagner's lemon pepper
    marinade

1 teaspoon chopped chives
4 rainbow trout
Salt and pepper

Cream the butter, add the sheep sorrel leaves, lemon pepper, and chives. Mix well. Let stand in the refrigerator overnight, at least, before using.

Clean the trout and pat dry with absorbent paper. Sprinkle each fish with salt and pepper, inside and out. Spread a generous amount of softened sorrel butter over the entire fish and inside the body cavity. Wrap each fish in heavy aluminum foil and place in a baking pan. Bake in a hot oven (400° F) for 10 to 20 minutes, depending upon the size of the trout, until the fish begin to get tender. Open the foil, baste the fish with the sorrel butter, and finish cooking under the broiler, being careful not to have the pan too close to the heat.

Blanching Dandelions Outdoors

Tie together the leaves of a young dandelion plant growing in the lawn when the growth is just beginning. Invert a large clay flower pot over the plant. As the plant grows, the leaves will blanch from lack of sunlight and the plant will not develop its normal bitterness.

Forcing Wild Greens Out of Season

Poke sprouts can be forced indoors in a flat in wintertime. In late autumn, dig the roots of at least two dozen pokeweed plants. Chop off each large root about six inches from the crown and plant in a large, earth-filled box with the crown portions barely covered. Take the box indoors to the cellar after freezing weather has set in, and keep it watered. Or place in a garage or on a porch where the temperature does not go below freezing, and invert a cardboard box over the top. In a few weeks, each crown will produce several crops of blanched poke sprouts which can be cut for use as soon as they have reached a height of about eight inches. Do not let the sprouts grow tall enough to develop purple coloring in the stalks. After the sprouts are cut, another crop will grow. Prepare the poke sprouts according to the directions given on page 79, or use them in recipes calling for asparagus.

Dandelions and chicory can be forced by the same method. The blanched greens are very tender and mild.

DANDELION JELLY

1 quart dandelion blossoms	1 package powdered fruit pectin
2 quarts water	(1¾ ounces)
2 tablespoons lemon juice	5½ cups sugar

Pick bright, fresh dandelion blossoms. Rinse them quickly in cold water to remove any insects that may be on the petals. Snip off the stem and green collar under each blossom.

In an enamel saucepan, boil the dandelion petals in water for 3 minutes, or a little longer, until the water takes on their color. Cool and strain, pressing the petals with the fingers to extract all of the juice. Measure out 3 cups of dandelion liquid. Add lemon juice and powdered fruit pectin. Stir to combine. Bring the mixture to a boil, using a large jelly kettle. Add the sugar, stirring to mix well. Continue stirring and boil the mixture for 2½ minutes. Pour into hot, sterilized jelly glasses and seal with self-sealing lids, according to the directions of the manufacturer. If the jelly is to be used within a short time, pour into small glasses and cover with melted paraffin.

This jelly tastes like honey.

PART II

Summer's Bounty

WILD STRAWBERRIES

My best-loved memory is of the morning my father came home jubilantly carrying his straw hat lined with sweet fern and filled with new-found bounty, calling to us:

"Come, see! Wild strawberries! All over Havill Hill!"

Wild strawberries are not commonly found in southern Indiana, so this was a once-in-a-lifetime discovery. We left our morning chores undone without a twinge of conscience, hurriedly collected an assortment of small tin pails and berry baskets, and set out at once, clanging down the pathway for the hill.

The wild-strawberry vines were strewn down the steep hillside in front of a tumbledown log cabin where a family named Havill had lived before I was born. All I knew of them was from stories I heard, told by neighbors and my parents, but I always felt the presence of the mistress of the cabin very plainly whenever I explored the abandoned cabin or visited the hillside to pick bouquets for my mother from the flourishing remnants of Gail Havill's old-fashioned flower garden:

"Easter flowers," iris, peonies, sweet peas, hollyhocks, lilacs, and roses.

On that morning we settled down at the threshold of Gail Havill's cherished flower garden, where a drift of white field daisies were abloom, and filled our baskets with bouquets of little scarlet strawberries. Each dew-washed berry was a glistening red, a minikin of wild flavor that released a fragrance so entrancing I could both smell and taste it. The delectable breath of the sun-warmed berries wafted up to my face when I knelt on the grass and parted the daisies above the strawberries. The teasing aroma permeates the entire being, for after the first taste of wild strawberries, the strawberry aroma and the strawberry flavor—and the strawberry days—become inseparable. Even the fingers, reddened with the juices of crushed wild strawberries, are imbued with the delicious fragrance of wild strawberries.

But the fragrance and flavor of wild strawberries—and the berries, themselves—are ephemeral things. Plucking the small fragile berries from their stems is a painstaking task not to be hurried lest the fruit be crushed into a pulp by careless fingers. It takes all of a June morning to fill baskets and berry pails with tiny wild strawberries. But there was never a task more captivating nor one that immerses its doer so completely in summer itself.

The whole atmosphere of the wild strawberry field invites, entices, welcomes. There are the bees at the greenish-white heads of clover; butterflies and winged insects hovering over the first heavy-scented milkweed blossoms. The air is hot and moist; it resounds with an undertone of gentle buzzings and the fragmentary calls of songbirds wheeling overhead in the perfect sky of June, in search of bugs for their noisy nestlings in nearby trees. Then there are the white field daisies all about, like so much cream poured into a bowl nature has filled with ripe fruits. We are closer to June on our knees in the ground-hugging wild strawberry vines than we ever are in our everyday outer world. Here, in the space of a morning, at least, we can feel the rapport with nature that is instinctive to the plants and animals but is alienated from us in our usual surroundings.

That year, Mother said she knew what James Whitcomb Riley meant by "knee deep in June, strawberries melting off the vine." We were knee deep in the patch until all the tiny sweet berries were jarred up and labeled Wild Strawberry Preserves or put down in a brown stone jar with sugar and brandy to start the tutti-frutti. We were immersed in the wild strawberry harvest every summer's morning until the last of the exquisite berries melted off the vine and, ultimately, in our mouths. Mother rewarded our diligent hours among the glossy leafed vines with a procession of fresh strawberry desserts; immense pies filled with the miniature scarlet berries, lusciously enfolded in whipped cream and cool gelatin; bowls brimming with sun-ripened wild berries, sweetened with their own sugar and drenched with cream; mounds of frosty pink ice cream, flecked with bits of berry pulp and extravagantly flavored with the truest essence of strawberry one could imagine; and *shortcake!*—flaky biscuits, split, with a crimson layer of plump, juicy berries reposing in their warm, buttery middles and peaks of wild strawberries adorning their tender, sugar-sprinkled, crusty tops, and torrents of red juices streaming over their sides.

These were the riches of our simple table. But we thought nothing of its sumptuousness in those earlier days. We savored the rewards of the meadow with the natural directness of rustic children without a notion of our mother's culinary artistry. It was not until much later that we recognized our simple bowlful of wild strawberries with thick cream as the epicure's celebrated *fraises du bois,* or Mother's everyday "good cooking" as *cordon bleu.*

The perfection of Mother's wild strawberry desserts—and of her cookery—lay not only in her kitchen expertise but, to a degree, in the plenitude of fresh foodstuffs she had to work with. To Mother, fresh meant creamy milk from the morning's milking; eggs taken, still warm, from the nest; chickens dressed in the morning and fried for the noonday meal; ears of sweet corn pulled from the stalk, shucked, silked, and plunged into boiling water only minutes later; light bread baked and eaten oven-warm, or at least on the same day of baking . . . or wild strawberries picked in the dew of early morning and eaten by noon. That was *freshness*, an evanescent, treasured quality in the flavor of foods my mother prepared in those earlier days.

It is this fleeting freshness that is so intense in the vivid flavor of just-picked wild strawberries. If it escapes, the lively wild strawberry fragrance and flavor also diminish. The euphoric sense of time's endlessness that came of leisurely mornings spent berrying on Havill Hill was short-lived in those remembered strawberry days. The instant we reached the farmhouse kitchen, Mother whisked the blue-patterned damask cloth off the round kitchen table, uncovering the serviceable oil cloth beneath it, and said, "Hurry, now! We have to tend to these berries before they lose their taste."

She put empty bowls and empty pie tins around the table at each of our mealtime places and urged us into our chairs. The brimful berry pails and baskets sat in the middle of the table. The pie tins were for the green stems we would remove from the tiny red berries and the empty bowls were for the stemmed strawberries.

Picking wild strawberries is one thing; stemming them is another. Small children are ideally suited to the first task and its infinite pleasures, while only their nimble fingers are suited to the latter task. Sitting on a kitchen chair, pinching off the tiny green caps of too many little berries to count, being very careful not to squash the tender, ripe fruits, is a chore lacking all the freedoms and the delightful distractions that captivate the young strawberry picker in the meadow. But slowly, the pyramid of strawberries to be stemmed disappears and fidgety children are freed from their chairs. And, at last, the reward of eating luscious wild strawberries is near.

If the fragile wild fruits have been picked clean, with no dirt and trash included in the baskets, wild strawberries are best used at once, *without* washing. My friend Dolores Blount, after painstakingly gathering and stemming a trove of wild strawberries from a field near her house, told me, "When I finished with them, there was nothing left but pulp. They went all to pieces in the wash water—it was as red as juice. After all that work!"

There is nothing unclean about wild berries picked in a grassy meadow, anyway. No sprays sully their purity. Only the fingers of those who will eat the berries touch them. And they have already been washed by the morning's dew. Seldom is there need for additional washing; but if there is, one should hold only a few firm berries at a time in the palm of the hand and spray them lightly with water to avoid leaching out their flavor, color, and aroma. Their utter delicacy makes me think it could really be true that some cooks (French?) rinse wild strawberries that need cleansing with a shower of white wine. Next to dew-washed wild strawberries, I like the capricious idea of bathing wild fruits in wine.

At our farm in Vermont, wild strawberries border the pathway up the mountain and carpet the high meadow. In June, when we were there, we saw the pretty clusters of white-cupped blossoms on the vines with little nubs of fruit beginning to form where the earliest blooms had faded. In early July, Pat Ruddick and her two children, our tenants on the farm, began harvesting the bounty of wild strawberries from our mountain meadow.

"They're tasty, but a little tart still," Pat said that evening, "and minute! It took me forever to pick only a cupful."

The wild strawberries have been her daughter Victoria's excitement this year as they were mine when I was Victoria's age.

"She keeps running up to the meadow to check on them," Pat told me. "Saturday, when I have the morning free, we're going up to pick them."

Now I am thinking of them on a Saturday, wishing I could be in Vermont with Victoria and Max and their mother, to share with them the very special excitements of gathering wild strawberries.

There will be a quick breakfast—toasted English muffins with orange marmalade and tea, probably—with Victoria and Max asking their mother again and again, "How soon are we going?"

Soon, after what seems an interminable time to the children, Pat will have put the kitchen in order, Victoria will have collected the berry baskets, Max will have located his socks, and they will be off to the meadow. How I envy them! I can visualize them walking away from the red farmhouse, past Mr. Heath's beloved trout pond, past the weathered-gray pony shed, to the hidden path beyond that leads to the footbridge over the stream above the waterfall. They step very carefully on the old mossy boards of the narrow footbridge, crossing only one at a time over the boulder-filled rushing stream, and then begin the steep ascent to the meadow through the most enchanting woods I know. They climb a rocky overgrown path beside which lie rotting sleighs and sleds left there from an earlier day when Mr. Heath's horses pulled the sleighs over snowy winter roads. The woods are dense and shadowy. There are paths to explore, mushrooms to find, porcupines to see, and flattened places in the ferns where deer have lain, but today Victoria and Max have other enchantments on their minds. They fly up the rough path ahead of their mother, scrambling over the huge fallen tree that blocks the pathway, and burst out of the dark woods into the sunshine of the high meadow.

Max runs directly to the awesome granite boulder at the edge of the meadow, and when his mother emerges from the woods, he greets her with triumphant shouts from its summit. But Victoria turns to a corner of the high meadow where orange-red hawkweed blooms with white field daisies, where the muted sound of water stepping down the rocks in the stream can barely be heard, where the song of a white-throated sparrow punctuates the quietness now and again—this is Victoria's summer realm where a colony of wild strawberries is ripening.

The wild strawberry plants grow barely six inches above the ground. They are connected to each other by their own red runners, which take root and send up miniature sprigs of leaves at each node. The broad leaflets, in sets of three, sit atop hairy reddish stems that spring

directly from the roots. The small white flowers, pale replicas of wild rose blooms with fragrant centers full of golden stamens, are borne on shorter stems of their own, so that when the tiny, round berries develop, they are secluded under canopies of saw-toothed leaves. The ripening berries are spread over the meadow floor as if the earth were a great table on which a feast is laid before the chipmunks from the woods, the meadow mice, the wild partridges, and the chickadees.

Victoria is as knowing of the meadow's delicious secrets as the bold little chipmunks that shrill to her *"chit-te-rie! chit-te-rie!,"* from the tumbled stone wall or as the grayish brown mouse that vanishes into its secreted burrow under a grassy tussock when she kneels nearby. The strawberries here in the meadow, the common field strawberries of Vermont, are as wild as the partridge and as keen-flavored as only native strawberries slowly coaxed to ripeness in the cooler temperatures of mountain altitudes can be. Excessive heat, whether it be from the sun or the cooking kettle, destroys something of the delicate fillip of wildness in them. For that reason, wild strawberries that are destined for the table should be used in recipes that do not require the berries to be cooked.

Some summers, particularly in Indiana, I have found so few wild strawberries that the harvest never makes the acquaintance of cream or cupboard shelf; indeed, the best berries never leave the meadow. Sometimes, even in the midst of Vermont abundances, we are content just to sink into the thick mat of strawberry plants and consume handfuls of sweet wild strawberries right there on the mountaintop. While we eat our fill in leisure, we look alternately at the inner meadow, into which we must look closely to find the tiny red fruits, and the mountaintops that spread out in front of us beyond the treetops of our own woods below us. Later, when we leave the meadow, like John Greenleaf Whittier's barefoot boy, with fingers and lips "redder still, kissed by strawberries on the hill," we carry another harvest with us, a regenerative one that comes of strawberrying in quiet meadows of thought and savoring the enriching flavors of all of nature's feasts.

Tutti-Frutti

The mystique of the tutti-frutti jar begins with wild strawberries. Take the first quart of tiny, wild strawberries and cover them with an equal amount of sugar. Let the strawberries plump up with sugar for about an hour, then pour one quart of the best brandy over the sugared fruit. Put the brandied fruit down in a stoneware jar with a close-fitting cover and place it in a dark, cool corner of the cellar. As the fruits of summer ripen, add a quantity of each (no more than a quart) along with an equal amount of sugar, in the same manner. No more brandy will be needed. Stir the tutti-frutti every day after adding the new fruit until the sugar in the bottom of the jar dissolves; this takes a week or more after each addition to the stone jar. Between times, stir the sauce as often as you think of it—daily, if you remember.

A stone jar is best for making tutti-frutti. It must be covered closely, but it cannot be airtight. If the stone jar does not have its own lid, cover the top of the jar with a china plate and fit a piece of heavy aluminum foil down over the plate. Tie a string around the jar top to keep the foil in place. When a stoneware container is not available, use a large, wide-necked glass jar with its own clamp lid. Cover the outside of the glass jar with aluminum foil to keep the light from fading the fruits.

As they come into season, these fruits may be added along with equal amounts of sugar: red or black cherries, stemmed and pitted; red raspberries; currants; gooseberries; sliced and peeled peaches, pears, apricots, nectarines, and fresh pineapple; green-gage, purple, and red plums, peeled and seeded.

Fruits with tough skins, such as grapes and apples, do not brandy well; neither do very soft fruits such as bananas and melons. Too many small seeds are objectionable; I omit black raspberries and blackberries for that reason and because they darken all the other fruits.

The tutti-frutti may be spiced. Stick cinnamon, whole allspice, whole cloves, finely grated orange peel or lemon peel may be added as the jar fills, to one's taste. The flavor of almonds is given by adding a few blanched peach kernels.

The tutti-frutti makes its own wine each time new fruits and sugar are added. The last of the fruits go into the stone jar around September. In about a month, when the tutti-frutti stops fermenting after the last addition of peaches and pears, it can be sealed tightly in sterilized jars and put aside to mellow until Thanksgiving or Christmas. Then the dark, elegant tutti-frutti is ready for a grand debut on the festal board as the finishing touch to puddings, cakes, chiffon pies, and ice cream, or as a rich, winy sauce to accompany the fat Christmas goose.

MOTHER'S BONNYCLABBER SHORTCAKES WITH STRAWBERRIES

2 cups unbleached white flour
2 tablespoons sugar
½ teaspoon salt
2 teaspoons baking powder
¼ cup pure lard
½ cup clabbered milk (see below)

¼ teaspoon baking soda
3 tablespoons butter
½ cup granulated sugar
1 quart wild strawberries,
    sweetened with ½ cup sugar
Sweet cream

Sift together into a mixing bowl the flour, sugar, salt, and baking powder. With the fingers, work in the lard until the mixture is the texture of coarse crumbs. To the clabbered sour milk, add baking soda and stir, then add at once to the flour mixture, stirring in the clabbered milk with a fork. Turn the shortcake dough out onto a lightly floured board and knead gently, not more than a dozen punches with flour-dusted hands. Roll the dough out to ⅜-inch thickness and cut into 2-inch rounds.

In the bottom of the baking pan in the preheating oven, melt 1 tablespoon of the butter, but do not let the butter heat any longer than necessary to melt it. Remove the pan from the oven. Dip each unbaked shortcake in the melted butter on one side, then turn it over and lay it in the pan with the buttered side up, thus buttering both the top and the bottom of the unbaked shortcakes. Do this until half of the shortcakes are arranged in the baking pan. Then sprinkle a small amount of granulated sugar over the shortcakes, using a teaspoon or two of sugar. Take the remaining shortcake rounds, dip them in the butter at the side of the pan as before, and top each buttered, sugared shortcake round in the pan with a second round. Sprinkle the tops of the shortcakes with sugar, as before. Bake in a very hot oven (450° F) for 12 minutes.

Split the hot shortcakes, rebutter the insides with 2 tablespoons of additional butter, and spoon the sweetened wild strawberries in the middle and over the tops of the shortcakes. Serve the strawberry shortcakes in individual bowls and pass a pitcher of sweet cream to pour over them. The shortcakes should go directly from the oven to the table. Makes 8 or 9 double shortcakes.

To Make Clabbered Milk

Clabbered milk, or bonnyclabber, is thick, sour milk which has separated into curds and whey. The curds are the bonnyclabber and they are used in the shortcakes.

To get clabbered milk, fresh, skimmed milk is allowed to sour at room temperature until it thickens. This will take 36 hours or more. The milk cannot be homogenized, pasteurized milk from the grocery; it must be fresh milk, straight from the cow. The sweet cream can be skimmed off before the milk sours and saved to pour over the shortcakes.

The sale of unpasteurized milk is controlled by stringent regulations so clabbered milk is not readily available to everyone. Thick dairy sour cream may be substituted, ¾ cup to ½ cup of clabbered milk. Or substitute ½ cup of buttermilk.

Old-fashioned Strawberry Shortcake

2 quarts wild strawberries	1 egg, beaten
2 cups flour	½ cup milk
4 teaspoons baking powder	1 tablespoon melted butter
2 tablespoons sugar	Additional sugar and butter
½ teaspoon salt	1 cup heavy cream, whipped
⅓ cup shortening	

Sweeten strawberries to taste and set aside for at least 1 hour before the shortcake is ready.

Sift flour, baking powder, sugar, and salt together. Cut in the shortening until the mixture resembles coarse meal. Combine the egg and milk and stir into the flour mixture to form a soft dough. Turn out onto a lightly floured board and divide the dough in halves; pat each half out into a round to fit a greased 8-inch layer-cake pan. Place 1 round of dough in the pan and brush it with the melted butter; top with the second round of dough. Sprinkle the top round of dough with additional granulated sugar (about 2 tablespoons). Bake the shortcake in a very hot oven (450° F) for 15 to 18 minutes, or until the top is lightly browned.

On a large round platter, split the hot shortcake apart and rebutter the middle with additional butter, then fill the interior with a portion of the sweetened wild strawberries. Cover with the top layer of shortcake and spoon the rest of the wild strawberries and their juice over it. Cut into pie-shaped portions and serve at once, while warm, topped with whipped cream. Or pass a pitcher of rich cream to be poured over each portion. Serves 8.

OLD-FASHIONED SUN PRESERVES

3 pounds ripe wild strawberries   3 cups water
6 cups sugar

Clean the strawberries and weigh them. Combine sugar and water and cook until it spins a thread (228° F). Remove from heat. Add the strawberries to the syrup and let stand overnight. The next morning, skim the berries from the syrup and place them in deep platters in a single layer. Again cook the syrup to 228° F, and pour it over the berries. Cover the containers with a pane of glass, propping an edge open on one end with a wedge of paper or other small object to allow the moisture to evaporate. Cover the platters with a layer of cheesecloth to keep insects out. Let the berries stand in very hot direct sunlight for 3 or 4 days, or until the syrup thickens and the berries become translucent. Stir the preserves twice a day. Bring the berries inside each evening at sunset. When the preserves finish, pour them into hot, sterilized jars and seal. Makes 12 jars.

NOTE: When there is no sunshine, or if it rains, bring the preserves indoors and finish them in a very slow oven (110° F) or under a 100-watt electric light bulb. Place the light bulb so that it is directly over the pan of preserves with the glass pane removed, no more than 18 inches above the berries. Cover the light bulb and preserves with a tent of cheesecloth, as before. A gooseneck lamp works very well for this purpose. Stir the preserves every 6 hours until the berries and syrup are waxy, then seal in jars.

UNCOOKED STRAWBERRY JAM

1 quart wild ripe strawberries   ¼ cup water
2 cups sugar   1¾ oz. powdered fruit pectin

Crush the strawberries and stir in the sugar. In a small pan, combine the water and the pectin. Bring to a boil and boil hard for 1 minute, stirring constantly. Add boiled mixture to berries, and stir until sugar dissolves (about 3 minutes). Pour jam into clean glasses or freezer jars. Let stand 24 hours. Store jam in refrigerator to be used within three weeks, or store in freezer for later use. Makes 6 jars of jam.

FRESH STRAWBERRY PIE

9-inch baked pie crust (page 44)   3 tablespoons cornstarch
2 pints wild strawberries   1 tablespoon lemon juice
1 cup sugar   Whipped cream

Fill the pie crust with fresh, whole wild strawberries. Crush enough additional strawberries to make 1½ cups of berries and juice. Combine crushed berries with the sugar, cornstarch, and lemon juice. Bring to a boil and cook, stirring constantly, until mixture thickens and clears. Cool, pour over the strawberries in pie crust, and chill. Serve with whipped cream. Serves 6 to 8.

WILD STRAWBERRIES CHANTILLY

1½ quarts wild strawberries   2 tablespoons confectioners'
1 cup superfine granulated sugar   sugar
2 cups heavy cream   ⅓ cup kirsch

Sweeten the strawberries with the granulated sugar. Whip the cream stiff and sweeten with the confectioners' sugar. Fold the kirsch and strawberries into the whipped cream. Pile in the center and on the top of a sponge cake (recipe below).

SPONGE CAKE

5 egg whites   1 cup superfine granulated sugar
1 teaspoon cream of tartar   1 cup cake flour
½ teaspoon salt   1 teaspoon vanilla extract
5 egg yolks   1 teaspoon lemon extract
5 tablespoons cold water

In a large bowl, beat the egg whites until foamy. Use medium speed with an electric mixer. Add the cream of tartar and salt and beat until stiff. In another large bowl, combine the egg yolks, cold water, and the superfine sugar, and beat at medium speed until the mixture is light yellow and fluffy. Sift the cake flour three times and add it to the yolk mixture along with the flavoring extracts. Beat until well blended, using low speed on the mixer. Then fold in the beaten egg whites and blend well. Pour the batter into a large, ungreased 10-by-4-inch tube cake pan and bake in a slow oven (300° F) for 70 minutes. Turn upside down to cool. Makes 12 portions.

Wild Strawberries in Meringue Shells

Sweeten 1 pint of wild strawberries with ½ cup of superfine granulated sugar. Put a dip of French vanilla ice cream or strawberry ice cream in the center of each of 4 large or 6 small meringue shells (recipe below), then spoon the sweetened wild strawberries over the ice cream. Serves 4 or 6.

Meringue Shells

4 egg whites   1 cup superfine granulated sugar
⅛ teaspoon salt   ½ teaspoon vanilla extract

The egg whites should be at room temperature. Beat the egg whites with an electric mixer until frothy, add the salt, and continue beating until the egg whites are stiff but moist. Then add ½ cup of the sugar, very gradually, sprinkling only 2 tablespoons at a time over the egg whites while the mixer runs at medium speed. Add the vanilla and beat well. Then gradually beat in the rest of the sugar, beating thoroughly after every addition. Drop the meringue by spoonfuls into mounds on a brown-paper-covered cookie sheet. (Run the brown paper under cold water, briefly, before putting it on the sheet, to keep the meringues from sticking.) Make a depression in the center of each meringue so that it has the shape of a bird's nest. Bake in a slow oven (250° F) for 45 to 60 minutes, or until the meringues will lift off the paper easily. Remove the meringues from the paper while they are still warm. Makes 4 large or 6 small meringues.

Coeur à la Crème

2 teaspoons unflavored gelatin
3 tablespoons cold water
2 cups cottage cheese
8 ounces cream cheese, softened

1 cup thick, heavy cream
1 tablespoon confectioners' sugar
1 quart wild strawberries,
   sweetened to taste

In a bowl, soften the gelatin in the cold water. Place the bowl in a pan containing hot water and stir until the gelatin dissolves. Put the cottage cheese through a fine sieve or food mill. Put the softened cream cheese in a bowl of the electric mixer and beat on low speed until it is smooth and creamy. Add the heavy cream and blend, using low speed. Add the confectioners' sugar. Then stir in the gelatin and the cottage cheese. Line a 1-quart coeur-à-la-creme mold, or 8 individual heart-shaped molds, with squares of cheesecloth that have been dipped in cold water and squeezed as dry as possible. Pour into molds and chill overnight. Unmold and serve topped with the wild strawberries. Serves 8.

Strawberry Ice Cream, Country Style

2 cups ripe wild strawberries
6 eggs
2½ cups sugar
1 quart milk

1 quart light cream
½ teaspoon salt
2 tablespoons vanilla extract

Crush the strawberries thoroughly, sweeten to taste, and let stand at room temperature for an hour or so to draw out the juice. Beat eggs until light, add sugar gradually, and beat until mixture thickens. Add milk, cream, salt, and vanilla. Pour into container of a 1-gallon ice-cream freezer and stir in the strawberries and juice. Churn until ice cream stiffens, using 1 part salt to 8 parts ice. Makes 1 gallon.

NOTE: Don't skimp on the cream; at the farm, we use *all* cream.

Tapioca Creams with Wild Strawberries

1 egg, separated
4 tablespoons sugar
⅛ teaspoon salt
1½ teaspoons unflavored gelatin
2 cups milk

3 tablespoons quick-cooking
   tapioca
½ teaspoon vanilla extract
1 pint wild strawberries,
   sweetened

Beat egg white until foamy, add 2 tablespoons of the sugar, and beat until stiff but not dry. Set aside. Combine remaining 2 tablespoons sugar with salt and gelatin; add ½ cup of the milk and the egg yolk. Blend well. Add remaining milk and tapioca. Cook over medium heat, stirring constantly, until mixture comes to a boil. Remove from heat, stir hot mixture into the beaten egg white, and add vanilla. Cool for 20 minutes. Pour into 6 fancy molds and chill until firm. Unmold and serve with wild strawberries spooned over the top. Serves 6.

STRAWBERRY BAVARIAN CREAM

1 cup crushed wild strawberries	½ cup hot water
¾ cup confectioners' sugar	1 tablespoon lemon juice
1 tablespoon unflavored gelatin	1 cup heavy cream, whipped
¼ cup cold water	Whole strawberries for garnish

Sweeten the crushed wild strawberries with the confectioners' sugar. Soften the gelatin in the cold water, then add the hot water and stir until the gelatin dissolves. Add the lemon juice and excess juice from the crushed wild strawberries. Chill the gelatin mixture in the refrigerator until it is partly set, then beat it until it is frothy. Add the crushed strawberries and fold in the whipped cream. Chill in individual molds until set. Unmold at serving time, and garnish with whole strawberries. Serves 4.

STRAWBERRY ROLL

5 egg yolks	5 egg whites
¾ cup superfine sugar	2 cups ripe wild strawberries
¼ cup flour	2 cups whipped cream

Grease a jelly-roll pan; line with waxed paper and grease again. Beat the egg yolks well, then add ¼ cup of the sugar gradually and continue beating until yolks are light. Add the flour and mix well. Beat egg whites until stiff but not dry, and fold into the egg yolk mixture. Spread batter in the jelly-roll pan and bake in hot oven (400° F) for 10 to 12 minutes, or until cake tester comes out clean. Sprinkle top of cake with sugar and turn out onto a piece of waxed paper. Peel off paper which lined the bottom of pan during baking and roll cake up carefully. Cool. Sweeten wild strawberries with the remaining ½ cup of sugar (or more, to taste, if needed) and fold berries into the whipped cream. Unroll the cake and spread with berries and cream. Reroll and chill before serving. Serves 6 to 8.

STRAWBERRIES IN THE SNOW

1 cup milk
1 cup cream
3 egg yolks
4 tablespoons sugar
1 tablespoon flour
¼ teaspoon salt

½ teaspoon almond extract
3 egg whites
6 tablespoons sugar
2 cups wild strawberries
¼ cup toasted slivered almonds

On the day before this dessert is to be served, prepare the custard. Scald milk and cream together in a double boiler. In a small bowl, beat egg yolks with sugar, flour, and salt. Gradually add the milk and cream mixture to the bowl, stirring constantly. Return to double boiler and cook over hot (not boiling) water, stirring constantly, until thick enough to coat a spoon. Remove from heat immediately and pour into a cool bowl. (If you happen to cook it too long, causing curdling, place the pan of custard over cold water immediately and beat with a rotary beater until smooth; do not reheat.) Add almond extract when custard has cooled, cover bowl and chill thoroughly, preferably overnight.

The next day, fill a skillet half full of water. Heat almost to simmering point. Beat egg whites until they form soft peaks, then gradually add sugar and beat stiff. With a wet tablespoon, drop beaten whites onto hot water; cook 3 to 4 minutes on each side with water continually below simmering. Remove meringues with a slotted spoon and place on paper towels to drain. Chill meringues on paper toweling until needed. To serve, spoon wild strawberries into 6 glass serving dishes or sherbet glasses; top with meringues and pour custard over all. Sprinkle each dessert with toasted slivered almonds. Serves 6.

MULBERRIES

To savor the simple tangy flavor of sweet ripe mulberries, eaten out of hand under the wide-spreading branches of the native American red mulberry tree, the *Morus rubra*, is joy enough for me. But, ah ... later! Even tastier rewards are promised the summer-tanned children who stain their fingers purple gathering the fruit of this handsome tree of roadsides and fencerows. Lofty chiffon pies, light and airy as a June breeze; juicy, crusty cobblers served steaming from the oven with cream to pour over; luscious, fruity jams and jellies, rich with the concentrated essence of red mulberries.

In early summer, when red mulberries ripen, I invite two agile, youthful climbers (my sons) to go with me to the neighborhood mulberry tree. The best mulberries always hang high, like the reddest apples and the juiciest peaches, and I have outgrown the sport of tree climbing, at least beyond the lower branches. We carry pails, an old blanket, and a plastic sheet. I spread the coverings under the tree while the boys scramble upward, each climbing to dizzying heights where he chooses a spot daring enough to make good picking.

"Look out!" Bob shouts. "Here they come!"

There is a great rustling of leaves as the boys shake the branches and a purple shower of mulberries rains down, pelting the coverings under the tree. The shower stops and I dash under the branches to fill the pail with dark purplish-red berries that resemble blackberries. Each mulberry develops from a long cluster of pistillate flowers rather than from a single blossom, as the blackberry does.

There is a slight rustling above, a subdued giggle, and then the mulberries rain again. This time they smash down on my back and polka-dot my white shirt with stains.

"Whoops! Sorry," Jim says. "My foot slipped."

I look up to check the situation above for safety. This time a shower of juicy mulberries pelts my face. The boys laugh.

"How many more do you need, Mom?"

"That's plenty," I answer.

While I pick up the harvest of mulberries, the boys climb around the branches, sampling mulberries and collecting leaves. Mulberry leaves, like sassafras leaves, are not all shaped alike. The same tree bears both heart-shaped leaves and lobed leaves with small blunt teeth.

Mulberry trees grow rapidly and make attractive shade trees within a few years. Having a mulberry tree near our house entices the song-birds, who are as fond of mulberries as my mischievous helpers are. We are doubly rewarded for our hospitality, with quantities of fruit and with serenades.

My pail filled, I settle back against the tree trunk to watch the mulberry harvesters in the branches above. The boys, juice-smeared and daring, are no less natural creatures than the birds who dart brazenly in and out of the leaves, now pecking for a meal, now pausing to trill a birdsong.

Admiring our harvest, I feel like singing, too. "Here we go 'round the mulberry bush," I hum while I make a fat mulberry pie. It will have two flaky, tender crusts, with the design of a mulberry leaf traced on the top crust.

Are we not amply rewarded for our purple-stained fingers?

Mulberry Pie

3 cups ripe mulberries,
  cleaned and stemmed
1 cup sugar
3 tablespoons quick-cooking
  tapioca

⅛ teaspoon salt
1 tablespoon lemon juice
2 tablespoons butter
Pie pastry, 9-inch double
  crust (page 44)

Combine mulberries with sugar, tapioca, salt, and lemon juice. Fill pastry-lined pie plate with fruit mixture, dot with butter, and cover with top crust. Brush crust with milk, sprinkle with a little sugar, prick with a fork, and bake in a hot oven (400° F) 40 to 50 minutes. Serve either warm or cold, with ice cream or with lemon sauce. Serves 6 to 8.

Sour Cream Mulberry Pie

1 cup sour cream
¾ cup sugar, white or brown
1 tablespoon flour
3 cups ripe mulberries

1 tablespoon lemon juice
Pie pastry, 9-inch single
  crust (page 44)

Combine sour cream, sugar, and flour. Fill pastry-lined pie plate with mulberries, sprinkle with lemon juice, and cover berries with sour cream mixture. Bake in a hot oven (425° F) for 10 minutes, then reduce heat to moderate heat (350° F) and bake about 30 minutes longer, until berries are soft and bubbling and crust is browned. Serves 6 to 8.

Mulberry Parfait Pie

1½ cups ripe mulberries,
  cleaned and stemmed
¼ cup sugar
1 package lemon-flavored gelatin
1 cup boiling water

1 pint vanilla ice cream
Baked 8-inch pastry shell
  (page 00)
Whipped cream
Whole mulberries for garnish

Combine mulberries and sugar; set aside. Dissolve lemon-flavored gelatin in boiling water. Add ice cream, cut into pieces, and stir until ice cream melts. Chill in refrigerator until a spoonful of the mixture will hold its shape (about 30 minutes). Fold in the sweetened mulberries. Turn mixture into baked pastry shell; chill until firm. Garnish with whipped cream and ripe mulberries. Serves 6 to 8.

Red Mulberry Cobbler

1 quart ripe mulberries,
  cleaned and stemmed
½ cup sugar
2 tablespoons flour
1 tablespoon lemon juice

1 cup flour
½ teaspoon salt
2 teaspoons baking powder
¼ cup shortening
½ cup milk

Mix berries with the sugar and flour. Add lemon juice and spread in the bottom of a deep, well-buttered pie dish. Sift flour, salt, and baking powder together, and cut in shortening. Add milk all at once. Stir until a dough is formed. Turn out onto a lightly floured board and pat or roll out to a ¼-inch thickness. Cover top of fruit with dough, trim edges, and cut a design in center for steam to escape. Sprinkle a small amount of sugar over top of dough, bake in a very hot oven (450° F) for 15 minutes, then reduce heat to a slow oven (325° F) and bake 20 minutes longer, or until cobbler is browned and berries cooked through. Serve warm. Serves 8.

Mulberry Chiffon

2 cups mulberries, cleaned
  and stemmed
⅔ cup sugar
½ cup water
1½ tablespoons unflavored gelatin
¼ cup cold water

2 tablespoons lemon juice
1 cup heavy cream, whipped
2 tablespoons confectioners' sugar
Cookie-crumb crust (see
  below), ladyfingers, or
  sponge cake strips

Combine mulberries with sugar and water. Heat to boiling. Remove from heat and press through sieve or food mill. Soften gelatin in cold water and stir into the hot mulberry puree. Cool. Add lemon juice and chill in refrigerator until fruit mixture is almost set, then beat until fluffy. Sweeten the whipped cream with the confectioners' sugar and fold in. Pour into a cookie-crumb crust and chill until firm. Or line a large glass bowl or individual serving dishes with ladyfingers or sponge cake strips, pour in chiffon filling, and chill until firm. Serve garnished with whipped cream and fresh mulberries. Serves 6.

CRUMB CRUST FOR PIES

1⅓ cups finely rolled crumbs
  (graham crackers, zwieback,
  vanilla wafers, or ginger snaps)
¼ to ½ cup sugar (depending on the
sweetness of the cookies used)
¼ to ½ cup butter, melted
  (depending on richness desired)

Combine the crumbs with the sugar and pour the melted butter over the mixture while blending it with a fork. Press the crumb mixture into a 9-inch pie plate, distributing evenly. Set an 8-inch pie plate on top of the crumbs and press firmly to make an even layer. Remove the 8-inch pie plate and chill the crumb crust well before adding the pie filling.

If desired, the crumb crust may be baked in a moderate oven (375° F) for 8 minutes to make it crisp.

MULBERRY JAM I

2 quarts fully ripe mulberries
2 tablespoons lemon juice
7½ cups sugar
6 ounces liquid fruit pectin

Crush mulberries thoroughly or grind. Measure 4 cups of the crushed fruit into a large kettle. Add lemon juice and sugar and mix well. Bring to a full, rolling boil over high heat and boil hard for 1 minute, stirring constantly. Remove from heat, and stir in liquid pectin at once. Stir and skim for 5 minutes and pour into glasses. Seal with paraffin. Makes about 11 six-ounce glasses.

Mulberry Jam II

8 cups crushed mulberries   6 cups sugar
  (wash and stem before crushing)   ¼ cup vinegar

Combine crushed mulberries, sugar, and vinegar. Bring to a boil and cook until thick, stirring often to prevent burning. Pour into hot sterilized jars and seal at once. Fills 10 jelly glasses.

Mulberry Jelly

2½ quarts fully ripe mulberries   7 cups sugar
2 tablespoons lemon juice   6 ounces liquid fruit pectin

Crush mulberries thoroughly. Place in jelly bag and squeeze out juice. Measure 3½ cups mulberry juice into a large kettle. Add lemon juice and sugar and mix well. Bring to a boil over high heat, stirring constantly. Stir in liquid pectin at once. Bring to a full rolling boil and boil hard for 1 minute, stirring constantly. Remove from heat, skim, pour quickly into hot, sterilized glasses. Seal with paraffin. Makes 11 six-ounce glasses.

ELDERBERRIES

The tide of summer begins to ebb in August. Suddenly wild sunflowers are bending their yellow heads and joe-pye weed is turning purple in untended fields. The lush fruitfulness of last month's vegetation gives way to the slightly bedraggled, weedy look of late summer. One day, as if in chorus, everyone remarks that summer is ending. Plumes of goldenrod, whose name in old herbals is "farewell summer," and clusters of ripening elderberries hanging over the roadbanks, tell us that summer is spent. The graceful sweet elder bushes fairly bend with heavy clusters of purplish black fruit. We gather them by the basketful—and still there are abundances of berries left for the birds to feast upon until frost.

Kurt and I went to the elderberry hedge before breakfast this morning to get a basketful of the ripe elderberries. When the days are hot and humid, as they are now in the dog days of August, we like to get out early, at sunrise, before the sun burns away the morning's blue haze and while the refreshing dew is still on the parched grass. There were no farmers in the roadside fields this morning—the hayfields are mown and the corn is well on its way to ripening—and we met no one on the road to stir the dust or to spoil the stillness in passing by. Usually we must go much farther afield than this well-traveled country road to find such quiet and privacy.

We always find a bounty of elderberries here, right by the roadside. Although the elderberry is relished by birds, and an ardent wild-foods hunter would never miss its harvest, the average cook—save for an occasional jellymaker or winemaker—ignores them. Quantities of nutritious, delicious elderberries, free for the taking, go to waste at the side of the road. The elder (*Sambucus*) is largely neglected as a food plant, although it was not always so. There are at least twenty species of elder widely distributed throughout the north temperate and subtropical regions of the world, with eight or more species native to the United States. Several of these are useful for culinary purposes. In past centuries, especially in Europe, the elder was valued and had many uses for food, wine and beverages, cosmetics, and medicine. At our house, we use the bounties of the sweet elder (*Sambucus canadensis* of the honeysuckle family), both blossoms and fruits, in some of the same ways it was used in years gone by, as well as in our own original ways.

The elder, or elderberry, is a common, plentiful shrub along country roads and railroads, in overgrown fencerows, and in untended places. Almost everyone who is familiar with the outdoors recognizes the plant. The elderberries and elder flowers, called elderblow, are easily picked; there are no briars on the moderately tall shrubs, and all but the uppermost clusters can be reached while standing on the ground. Each cluster of fruit contains hundreds of the dark, beady berries. This morning Kurt and I picked a half-bushel of elderberry clusters in less than fifteen minutes, taking them all from one shrub, about ten feet tall, growing by the side of the road.

"What I like about elderberries," Kurt said, "is that they are so easy to get, for a change. We usually spend half a day just *looking* for mushrooms or pawpaws or wild grapes."

Although elderberries are plentiful here and easy to harvest, the inevitable expenditure of time necessary to most worthwhile projects comes after we bring the elderberries home. My sons, Jim and Bob, and Sandra Oxley, my helper, spent all morning stripping the tiny berries from their stems while I mixed up a rich pastry dough and peeled apples for an elderberry apple pie, to be spiced with mace and flavored with lemon peel. There were apples left over, so I cooked a

gingery chutney with the apples, some of the elderberries, pineapple, raisins, dates, and elder-flower vinegar. We will open the jars of chutney later, one at a time, when we have roast duck, or pork, or a curry.

Today the rest of the elderberries from our early morning harvest are dripping their juices through the jelly bag. Tomorrow I will make the dark sparkling jelly with the distinctive flavor that all of us fancy on crusty hot rolls made with sour dough. Then, the next day, on my birthday, I will receive my annual gift from my neighbor—a basketful of larger-than-usual, sweetly flavored ripe elderberries picked along a creek bank he claims is inaccessible to all but himself. These special elderberries are for a small keg of ruby-colored wine. We made a bargain one year: he would provide the keg and the wild elderberries, and I would make the wine. Of all the country wines, we both thought elderberry the most delicious and beautifully colored. Besides, older people we knew swore it was a very healthful, tonic beverage. He and I thought we ought to have a kegful on hand, and so the bargain was made.

I had never made wine before and was anxious to try my hand at it. I remembered my father, who was almost a teetotaler, making a small keg of elderberry wine every summer—sometimes grape or blackberry, too—only for gifts or "medicinal purposes." Whenever anyone in the family had a winter cold, Dad drew off some of the elderberry wine, squeezed into it the juice of lemons and oranges, and sweetened it with a spoonful of sugar. If the toddy was for any of us children, he weakened the wine with a dip of well water. When there was a fire in the parlor stove, he would put the poker into the hot coals and heat it until the end was fiery red; then he would put the end of the red hot poker, with a great sizzling, directly into the mug of wine. The ailing one was put to bed with the hot toddy and an extra comforter.

My recollections of the actual winemaking were very pleasant. Sketchy as to proportions and methods, but vivid with impressions of overflowing baskets of dark glistening elderberries picked from Grandpa's fencerows; of sitting all afternoon in the shady backyard around the baskets of elderberries with my father and mother and grandparents, endlessly stemming the berries for the wine; of the dark, swirling pool of purple juice in the huge white pan; of the long streams of white sugar disappearing into the hole in the side of the wooden keg; and later, the strange fermenting-smell that pervaded the cellar and lingered faintly on into the winter, reminding me of the autumnal winemaking every time I was sent there to bring up apples or potatoes or vegetables for my mother.

With such pleasant remembrances of winemaking, I agreed without hesitation when my neighbor said, "I'll get the elderberries and the keg, if you make the wine."

It was not until later, as I sat alone on my birthday stemming a million elderberries for our wine, that I had second thoughts about the bargain I had made. The recipe called for *two gallons* of the tiny, stemmed elderberries!

We put the elderberries into a large ten-gallon stoneware jar and crushed them with a clean new length of two-by-four lumber, following specific directions given to us by a friend of my husband who specializes in making folk wines. For five days, while the elderberry juice fermented in the brown stoneware jar, winemaking dominated our kitchen; the juice had to be stirred daily and the brew protected from the tiny, ubiquitous wine flies that appear out of nowhere when fruit sours. I washed out the borrowed wine keg daily and aired it in the sunshine until it no longer smelled of last year's wine.

Finally, we were ready to strain the fermented juice and pour it, with the sugar, into the clean, fresh keg. The big jar and the keg were unwieldy, so my husband took care of this task while I weighed out the great quantity of sugar we would need, wiped up the dark fruit-stains that were everywhere, washed cups and funnels, and disposed of the purple-stained cheesecloth we had used to strain the fermented juice. I was really delighted to see the juice going into the keg; I wanted to get the large stoneware jar and the wine flies and the fermenting odor out of my kitchen. But my delight was short-lived. I turned from the sink to see Kurt carefully pouring the fermented juice into the bung hole at the side of the keg while, unseen at the bottom side of the keg, the juice was leaking out between the staves. A puddle of purple juice spread over the cabinet top and was already streaming down the cupboard doors.

We salvaged the juice that had not yet leaked out of the wine keg and mopped up the mess. I telephoned my father, hoping to borrow his wine keg to replace my neighbor's leaky one.

Dad laughed when I described the chaos in my kitchen. He said the wine keg had dried out during its disuse, causing it to shrink and loosen at the joinings.

"Sink that keg in a tubful of water for a few days," he said, "and the staves will swell tight again."

So back into the kitchen went the brown fermenting-jar, with attendant wine flies, while the keg swelled in the water. We added the sugar and water to the juice, according to the recipe, so now the wine was working furiously in the stone jar. We could hear it churning and fizzing. The kitchen smelled like a winery for another few days, but at last the wine was snug in its tight keg with a water seal and I had only to tend it once or twice a week until Thanksgiving. Then the ruby vintage was ready for sampling. It was clear and sparkling red, a beautiful, heady beverage with its own fragrant bouquet. When we toasted the success of our project, our neighbor, Kurt, and I, we laughed at our mishaps and decided to make the wine again. It was worth all the trouble.

Except for that first attempt, our winemaking has been free of mishaps. There is another wine that we brew from the elder—a pale, delicate brew of the blossoms, called elderblow, that is reminiscent of champagne and as rustic and romantic in flavor as only a folk drink called elderblow wine could be.

I think I look forward to the harvest of the elder flowers in early summer even more than to the elder's fruiting in August. An elder-berry hedge in flower is a charming thing. Lacy, creamy white clusters of blossoms spread over the branches like crocheted doilies spread over a bush to dry. Zephyrs of honeyed fragrance spill out into the air at the slightest stirring of the breezes. The countryside is a veritable per-fumery, with a delightful sweetness falling on it like June's gentle dew.

"You can smell them blooming even before you get there," my son Jim remarked this spring when he pulled down a tall elderbush for me so that I could break off the clusters of flowers. "It smells like our whole apple orchard in bloom and it's all coming from this one bush."

Each fragrant flat-topped cluster of elder flowers is called a cyme, or sometimes, a corymb. The cyme is made up of smaller clusters of flowers, each growing upward from five various points on the main stem to approximately the same height. Hundreds and hundreds of tiny flowers make up each cluster of elderblow. The exquisiteness of the tiny, individual flowerettes may go unseen, like snowflakes in a snowbank, until one is immersed in them—as I am later, while strip-ping elderblow from their stems. Every lovely elder flower has five minuscule petals, called corollas, and between the petals lie diminu-tive pollen-tipped stamens. The elder flowers to be used for cookery should be picked just after the cluster has opened fully, when the flowers have a fresh, sweet fragrance—not after the cluster has been in full bloom for several days, with the corollas beginning to turn brown at their edges.

Cooking with flowers always reminds me of making mud pies. It is a kitchen diversion that I thoroughly enjoy. Besides, elder-flower con-coctions are as delicious as they are whimsical. My husband likes the pleasant, subtle, flowery flavor of elderblow; he is especially fond of elderblow fritters and orange-elderblow muffins. The boys still think that eating flowers is slightly eccentric, but I remind them that they once ate mud pies, too.

The most delicious fun of all is making a large, lacy pancake around one whole corymb of elderblow. We discovered this one August in Vermont when we were making wild blueberry pancakes, using a soapstone griddle on our ornate old wood-burning range. One of the boys was out looking things over before breakfast and spied a very-late-blooming cluster of elder flowers hanging out over the waterfall. He waded across the stream to get it for me and brought it into the farmhouse kitchen. The hot griddle was on the stove and a bowlful of pancake batter was on the table. The idea was unavoidable.

"Let's make a pancake out of it," I said when I saw the pancake-sized cluster of elderblow.

I dipped the cluster of flowers into the pancake batter, holding it by its main stem, and when I lifted it out again, I saw that the weight of the batter on the delicate flower clusters made them all hang together. I called Bobby to get a spatula, and between us we spread the batter-dipped cluster out over the hot greased griddle, stem up. Then I spooned additional pancake batter over the flower cluster to fill in the spaces between the flowers. As the pancake was baking, I took the kitchen shears and began snipping off all the stems sticking up out of the batter. There was not a moment to spare.

"Hurry!" Bobby urged when bubbles began to appear on the top of the pancake and I was still snipping stems. "It's almost ready to turn."

The finished pancake was delicious. Its delicate flower flavor was enhanced even more by the maple syrup we had helped our friends, the Azarians, make at their sugar shack during the sugaring season.

Now when the elder flowers are in bloom, we often make elderblow pancakes, but we always have two nimble cooks at the griddle.

I use the flowers, too, to flavor vinegars, and I dry them to brew for tea. I drink the tea—really a tisane—only for its flavor and the novelty of the beverage, but perhaps I receive benefits from the brew of the elder that I am not even aware of.

In times past, elder flower tea was a standard remedy for colds, even in fairy tales. Hans Christian Andersen writes about the little boy who had a cold because he got wet feet. His mother put him to bed; "Then she had the tea-kettle brought in to make him a good cup of elder-tea—that would be sure to warm him!"

All parts of the elder were used, in one form or another, to benefit health. "There is hardly a Disease from the Head to the Foote but it cureth," wrote William Coles in 1656. A fountainhead of healing powers sprang from the elder, according to the herbalists, and many of them were magical.

Reading old herbals reveals that the elder formerly had great value outside the realm of cookery and home remedies. Elder was thought to have supernatural powers for warding off evil spirits and witches.

"The common people formerly gathered the Leaves of Elder upon the last day of Aprill, which to disappoint the charmes of Witches they had affixed to their Doores and Windowes," wrote William Coles in *The Art of Simpling*.

Similar superstitions crossed the ocean with early settlers of our country. In early New England, elder bushes were planted in the garden to protect the house from witches. It was also believed that whoever burned elderwood on Christmas Eve would learn the identity of all the witches and sorcerers in the neighborhood.

But in Germany, long ago, ghosts were believed partial to elder and a branch of it placed in the house caused one to awake in the night to see a specter standing by the bed. Men doffed their hats in the presence of the elder and believed it could not be struck by lightning.

The most intriguing elder folklore comes from Denmark. There the spirit of the elder, *Hyldemoer*, or "Eldermother," lives in the elder tree. She protects all of the herbs and avenges any injury done to an elder. A Danish woman would not break off a sprig of elder without asking permission of the spirit of the tree: "Eldermother, give me some of thy wood and I will give thee mine when it grows in the forest." Elder flowers were never plucked without the leaves. The Danes believed it to be bad luck to have elderwood in the house for furniture or floorboards, and it was never burned for firewood. If a baby was laid in a cradle made of elderwood, the Eldermother would pull the child out of the cradle, or fairies might come and pinch the baby. The Eldermother in Hans Christian Andersen's fairy tale seems more benevolent:

> The little boy looked over at the tea-pot. The lid was lifting higher and higher, and the elder-flowers were coming out fresh and white; great long branches were shooting forth, even from the sprout, spreading out on all sides and growing bigger and bigger until there was a lovely elder-bush, a whole tree. . . . Oh, how it blossomed and what a perfume it had! In the middle of the tree sat a kindly old woman in a strange dress, perfectly green like the leaves of the elder tree and covered with large white elder-flowers—you couldn't tell at first glance whether it were made of cloth or of real live leaves and flowers.

I have not yet stood under the blooming elderberry bush at midnight on Midsummer's Eve and seen the King of Elves and all his train go by, nor carried a magical elderberry in a bag tied around my neck, nor seen an elderbush sprouting out of my pot of elderblow tea with Eldermother perched in its branches—but perhaps I shall, one day. There is an elderberry bush in my dooryard and, so far, I have had no trouble with witches.

Gooseberry–Elder Flower Tart

3 cups fresh gooseberries,
 cleaned and stemmed
½ to 1 cup fresh elder flowers
1¼ cups sugar
¼ teaspoon salt

3 tablespoons tapioca
2 tablespoons butter
Pastry for 9-inch double-crust
 pie (page 44)

Combine cleaned, stemmed gooseberries, elder flowers, sugar, salt, and tapioca. Line a 9-inch pie tin with pastry and fill with the gooseberry mixture. Dot with butter and cover with a round of pastry or with latticed strips of pastry. Flute the edges of the pastry and brush the top with milk; then sprinkle the top pastry with sugar to make it brown nicely. Bake 10 minutes in a very hot oven (450° F), then reduce the heat to 400° F and bake for an additional 35 minutes. Serves 6 to 8.

Elderblow Fritters

Clusters of elderblow
Brandy or Grand Marnier
1 cup flour
1 teaspoon baking powder
¼ teaspoon salt
2 tablespoons sugar
2 eggs, separated

⅔ cup rich milk
1 tablespoon melted butter
1 tablespoon lemon or
 orange juice
1 tablespoon grated rind of
 lemon or orange
Confectioners' sugar

Pick the clusters of elderblow when they have just bloomed out fully. Rinse the flowers briefly in salted water, shake off the excess water, and place the clusters, flowers down, on paper toweling to drain dry. Then break each cluster of elderblow into smaller clusters, leaving each section attached to as little stem as possible. The sections should be about the size of a tablespoon. Put them, flowers down, on a plate and pour over them enough brandy or Grand Marnier to immerse the flowers. Let the elderblow clusters soak in the liquor while the batter is being prepared:

Sift together the flour, baking powder, salt, and sugar. In a bowl, beat the egg yolks and add the milk. Then stir in the sifted dry ingredients and mix together. Add the melted butter and fruit juice, using lemon if brandy is used to soak the elderblow and orange if Grand Marnier is used. Blend well. Beat the egg whites stiff and fold into the fritter batter.

Dip each brandy-soaked elderblow cluster into the batter, drop the cluster into deep hot fat (350 to 375° F) and fry until light brown on both sides. Drain the fritters on absorbent paper. Combine the confectioners' sugar with the grated lemon or orange rind, dust over the fritters, and serve at once. Serves 4 to 6.

ELDERBLOW WINE

1 quart elderblossoms,
  firmly packed
3 gallons water
9 pounds granulated sugar

3 pounds seedless raisins,
  chopped fine
½ cup lemon juice, strained
1 cake compressed yeast

Remove elderblossoms from stems. Pack a 1-quart measure full, pressing down firmly. Boil together the water and sugar for 5 minutes. Add the elderblossoms and mix well. Cool to lukewarm. Then add the raisins, lemon juice, and yeast. Let the mixture stand in a large crock, covered with cheesecloth, for 6 days, stirring 3 times daily. Strain and let stand in a jug or a cask with a water seal (see elderberry wine recipe on page 130) until the wine is still, then bottle and cork tightly. Age several months before drinking. This wine keeps well for several years. Makes about 3½ gallons.

ELDERBLOW CUSTARD

2 clusters of elderblow
2 cups milk
2 eggs, beaten
⅓ cup sugar

⅛ teaspoon salt
1 tablespoon semolina
1 egg white
2 tablespoons sugar

Strip the flowers off the stems of two clusters of elderblow. Put the flowers in a pan with the milk and heat to scalding; hold just below boiling point for several minutes to extract the flavor from the elderblow. Strain the milk and discard the flowers. Mix the beaten eggs, sugar, salt, and semolina, and add the hot milk. Return to low heat, or cook over hot water, until the custard coats a metal spoon, stirring constantly. Remove from the heat instantly and set the pan in another pan containing cold water to stop the cooking. Cool slightly, then pour into four dessert dishes. Chill in the refrigerator. At serving time, make a meringue of the egg whites beaten stiff with the sugar. Float a spoonful of meringue in the center of each dessert dish and garnish with a bit of elderberry jelly or a sprinkling of cinnamon. This dessert has a subtle flowery flavor that is pleasant. Serves 4.

NOTE: If the semolina is not available, 1 tablespoon of tapioca may be used instead.

ORANGE–ELDERBLOW MUFFINS

1 cup flour
3 teaspoons baking powder
⅛ teaspoon salt
4 tablespoons sugar
½ cup fresh elderflowers
1 egg, beaten

¼ cup sweet milk
3 tablespoons melted butter, cooled
⅓ cup orange juice
1 teaspoon grated orange rind

Sift dry ingredients together and combine with elderflowers. Combine beaten egg, milk, and butter. Add all at once to dry ingredients and stir lightly until just blended. Quickly stir in orange juice and grated orange rind. Fill greased muffin wells ⅔ full and bake in a moderate oven (375° F) for about 25 minutes. Serve hot with orange marmalade. If desired, drop a spoonful of orange marmalade on top of each muffin before baking. Makes 12 muffins.

ELDER FLOWER MUFFINS

1¼ cups flour
2½ teaspoons baking powder
2 tablespoons sugar
¾ teaspoon salt

½ cup fresh elder flowers
1 egg, beaten
¾ cup milk
⅓ cup melted shortening

Sift the flour, baking powder, sugar, and salt together. Add the elder flowers. Make a well in the center and add the egg, milk, and shortening, all at once, and stir quickly until the ingredients are just blended. Do not overbeat; the mixture should be slightly lumpy. Fill greased muffin wells two-thirds full and bake in a hot oven (400° F) for 25 minutes. Serve with elderberry jelly. Makes 12 muffins.

TO DRY ELDER FLOWERS

Gather clusters of elderblow when they are in full bloom. Strip the blossoms from the stems onto a cookie sheet, picking out any bits of stems that fall into the pan with the blossoms. Spread the blossoms in a thin layer on the cookie sheet. Dry them in the oven, set at the lowest possible temperature with the door ajar. Or, dry the elder flowers outdoors in the shade on a warm sunny day when the humidity is low.

I sometimes dry elder flowers or petals for a potpourri in my attic, spread out on a table close under the eaves, where it is very warm on sunny days.

When the elder flowers are dry, store them in covered jars or canisters.

ELDERBLOSSOM TEA

Use 1 to 1½ teaspoons of dried elder flowers for each cup of tea. Place the dried elder flowers in an earthenware teapot which has just been rinsed with hot water to warm it. Bring fresh water to a boil, pour it over the elder flowers, and cover. Steep for 5 to 10 minutes, keeping the teapot over gentle heat, but do not allow the tea to boil. Strain the tea (actually a "tisane") into a teacup and serve with a twist of lemon and with honey or sugar to sweeten.

Elderblossom tea was a grandmothers' remedy for an ordinary cold. The teakettle was put on to boil at the first sniffle and the patient was put to bed after drinking very hot elderblossom tea, which was supposed to induce perspiration. Present-day herbalists still recommend it for cold discomforts and, with mint added, for dyspepsia as well. To make elderblossom-mint tea, use equal amounts of dried elder flowers and dried mint, preferably peppermint, when making the infusion, or add a leaf or two of fresh mint for each cup of tea being brewed.

Dried elder flowers may be mixed with any of the ordinary teas to add their muscatel flavor and fragrance. The tea is then steeped only 3 to 5 minutes rather than the longer time required to extract flavor from the flowers alone.

ELDER FLOWER VINEGARS

Dried or fresh elder flowers will give an interesting flavor to vinegar for fruit-salad dressings or elderberry chutney. Twice as many fresh elder flowers must be used as dried flowers to obtain the same strength of flavor. White wine vinegar should be used, because cider vinegar will mask the subtle elder-flower flavor.

In a glass jar with a glass lid, combine ½ cup of dried elder flowers or 1 cup of fresh elder flowers with 1 pint of white wine vinegar. Set the vinegar on a window sill where the sun will shine on it, and leave for 10 days. Shake the jar gently each day. When the vinegar has taken the flavor of the elder flowers, strain and bottle it.

For a sweet vinegar, add ½ cup of sugar to the jar.

To hasten the flavoring of the vinegar, bring the vinegar to boiling before pouring it over the elder flowers; then set the jar in the sunshine for 3 or 4 days before using.

ELDER FLOWER LEMONADE

In a saucepan, combine 2 cups of sugar and 2 cups of water. Bring to a boil, then simmer until the liquid clears and the sugar is dissolved. Remove from the heat and add 1 pint of fresh elder flowers. Let stand for 24 hours, until the flavor is extracted from the elder flowers. Strain and refrigerate the elder flower syrup. Use as needed to sweeten and flavor lemonade.

ELDER FLOWER PANCAKES

Fresh elder flowers, removed from their stems, can be stirred into pancake batter. Substitute them for up to one half of the amount of flour called for in the recipe, or add them to a thin pancake batter without changing the ingredients. They will add flavor and lighten the pancakes.

ELDERBERRY APPLE PIE

3 cups ripe elderberries
3 cups sliced apples
3 tablespoons flour
1 cup sugar
½ teaspoon mace

½ teaspoon grated lemon rind
2 tablespoons butter
Pastry for 9-inch double-crust
  pie (page 44)

Combine the elderberries, apples, flour, sugar, mace, and lemon rind. Pour into a 9-inch pastry-lined pie pan. Dot the pie filling with butter and cover the top with pastry. Flute the edges of the pastry and cut a vent in the top crust to allow steam to escape during baking. Sprinkle a little milk on the top of the pastry, followed by a sprinkling of sugar, to make the crust brown prettily. Then bake the pie in a very hot oven (450° F) for 10 minutes; reduce the heat to 400° F and bake for 1 hour longer, or until the apples are tender and the crust is browned. Serve the pie warm. Serves 6 to 8.

Elderberry Pie

4 cups elderberries
1 cup sugar
1 teaspoon cinnamon
2 tablespoons lemon juice

3 tablespoons tapioca
Pastry for 9-inch double-crust
   pie (page 44)
2 tablespoons butter

Combine elderberries, sugar, cinnamon, lemon juice, and tapioca. Line a 9-inch pie plate with pastry, pour in the elderberry mixture, dot with butter, and cover the top with pastry. Sprinkle the top of the unbaked pastry with a small amount of milk, then with sugar, to make the crust brown while baking. Flute the edges of the pastry, cut a vent in the top to allow the steam to escape, and bake for 10 minutes in a hot oven, 450°F, then finish baking at 400°F for about 50 minutes. Serves 6 to 8.

Sour Cream Elderberry Pie

1 egg
1 cup sour cream
1 cup sugar
1 tablespoon flour
1 teaspoon cinnamon

2 tablespoons lemon juice
2 cups elderberries
9-inch pastry shell, unbaked
   (page 44)

Beat the egg well, stir into it the sour cream, sugar, flour, cinnamon, and lemon juice. Mix with the elderberries and pour into an unbaked 9-inch pastry shell. Bake for 10 minutes in a 400° F oven, then finish baking in a moderate oven, 350° F, for 40 minutes, until the crust is browned and the center of the pie is set. Serves 6 to 8.

Elderberry Chutney

6 cups tart apples,
   peeled and sliced
2 cups elder flower vinegar
   (page 126)
2 cups ripe elderberries
3 cups seedless raisins
1 cup chopped dates

1½ cups diced pineapple
4 cups sugar
2 tablespoons salt
½ teaspoon cayenne pepper
1 tablespoon ground ginger
1 stick cinnamon

Put the peeled, sliced apples through a medium-blade grinder or chop them in an electric blender. Cook the apples with the vinegar until they boil, stirring often. Then strain the vinegar into another pan, and place the apple pulp in a crock. To the hot vinegar, add the remaining ingredients and boil for 10 minutes, stirring often. Pour over the apples in the crock and let stand in the refrigerator for 24 hours. Then cook the chutney down, stirring frequently, until it is thickened (about 30 minutes). Seal in hot, sterilized jars. Makes 4 pints.

How to Extract Elderberry Juice

Stem the ripe elderberries immediately after picking. Elderberries left on their stems too long may take on some of the stem's rank flavor.

Put the elderberries in a pan and barely cover them with water. Bring the berries to a boil, crushing the berries slightly with a wooden mallet as they heat. Then reduce the heat and simmer the berries, covered, stirring frequently, for 15 minutes.

Strain the juice through a jelly bag if it is to be used for jelly-making, or through a double thickness of cheesecloth for other purposes.

Elderberry Jelly

3¾ cups elderberry juice
¼ cup lemon juice

1¼ ounces powdered fruit pectin
5 cups sugar

Combine the elderberry juice, lemon juice, and fruit pectin in a large kettle. Place over high heat and stir until the mixture boils hard. Stir in the sugar and bring to a full rolling boil, stirring frequently. Boil hard, stirring constantly, until the jelly stage is reached (see below). Remove the jelly kettle from the heat, skim, and pour the jelly into hot, sterilized glasses. Seal with hot paraffin at once. Fills 6 jelly glasses.

Jelly Test for Fruit Juices

The jelly stage is reached at 8° F above the temperature at which water boils at your altitude on that day as registered on a candy, deep-fat, or jelly thermometer, or when the two drops of jelly that run off the edge of a metal spoon slide together and sheet off the spoon in one drop.

Pectin Test for Fruit Juices

To determine if cooked fruit juice contains enough pectin to jell, put 1 teaspoon of cooked juice in a small bowl with 1 tablespoon of rubbing alcohol (70% alcohol). *Do not taste.* Stir the mixture. If there is enough pectin in the juice to make jelly, the mixture will form a gelatinous mass. Juice low in pectin will thicken only slightly. *Discard the mixture.*

If the test indicates a low pectin content, add 1 tablespoon of liquid pectin to each cup of juice to be used to make jelly. Then test the juices again, as before, using 1 teaspoon of the juice with the pectin added and 1 tablespoon of rubbing alcohol in a separate bowl. *Discard the mixture.*

Keep adding liquid pectin to the fruit juice and repeating the test until it shows that the juices will jell.

Then proceed with the jelly making, using ¾ to 1 cup of sugar to each cup of juice.

Elderberry Wine

Pick a basketful of ripe elderberries and remove from stems immediately. Do not wash the berries as the skins contain natural yeast. Put 2 gallons of stemmed berries into a large stone jar and thoroughly smash them with a clean piece of wood such as a length of 2-by-4 lumber. Add 2 quarts of pure cold water (well water is best because no chemicals have been added to it). Cover the crock with a double piece of cheesecloth, tied down around the top to keep insects from entering. Let berries ferment for 5 days. The crushed elderberries will come to the top, forming a chapeau (cap) on the wine. Break up the chapeau every evening with a wooden paddle.

On the fifth day, strain the juice through a cloth, squeezing to remove as much juice as possible from the berries. Measure the juice; there should be about 1½ gallons of fermented liquid. Pour into a 10-gallon wine keg (make sure beforehand that it does not leak), and lay the keg on its side. Dissolve 22½ pounds of sugar in enough pure water to finish filling the keg. Fill to overflowing.

Do not plug up the bunghole in the side of the keg; leave it open for three days so that all the remaining impurities can ferment out over the side of the keg. Add pure water as needed to keep the keg filled right up to the top of the hole. Cover the opening with a tent of cheesecloth to keep fruit-flies from gathering, but keep the cloth out of the wine.

After three days, drill a small hole in the bung and fit a rubber or plastic tube into the hole. Plug up the keg and put the end of the tube into a jar containing water. Change the water in the jar every few days and leave the keg like this in a cool place until about Thanksgiving-time, when the wine will be ready to highlight the harvest feast.

BLACKBERRYING

Berry season is not marked on the household calendar, but those who live close to the land know that it begins with the ripening of the first tiny wild strawberries in daisy-blooming meadows, rises to a peak when glistening blackberries bejewel thorn brakes, and ends after the last bouquets of dark juicy elderberries have been stripped from their stems by eager songbirds. As a devotee of the rustic pleasures of blackberrying since childhood, which is the proper time for one's initiation to the berry patch, I look forward to donning a heavy sweater early every spring and going out to estimate the scope of the harvest, as forecast by the blooming of delicately scented racemes of white flowers among red-stemmed green leaflets on prickly new briars. Later, while picking pokeweed sprouts for dinner, I find little green nubs of swelling fruits where, earlier, the first blooms were.

I recall the times when blackberrying was July's daily—and necessary—routine, rather than the recreational pastime it is for me today. While my hands do the simple task of berrying without mental direction, my thoughts are free to wander in my mind's sunny meadows. I am projected into the most pleasant of remembered days, and all the while my eyes and senses explore the splendors of the blackberry field I am in.

Every summer without fail, Mother used to can at least a hundred quarts of blackberries and fifty small jars of blackberry jam and jelly. She put up, too, a number of half-gallon jars of blackberry juice to make into fresh jelly later in winter when the supply dwindled. Since I picked berries all summer to help Mother can her quota, blackberrying surely would have become something of a chore if it were not for the gay holiday spirit that prevailed whenever we went afield to bring in the wild bounty for Mother's preserving kettles.

When blackberries ripened, we got up earlier than usual—*usual* was daybreak for Mother, six o'clock for slugabeds like me. Chores had to be done so that we could be away from the farmhouse all morning. Mother would pack a lunch for us in one of the berry pails.

"Step lively," Mother encouraged, "or someone will beat us to the biggest berries."

Nothing was more discouraging than arriving at the best berry thickets in the woods pasture and finding the briars tromped down

and the patch picked over. That the brambles were on our land did not make the berries ours—blackberry patches are in the public domain, local custom decrees, and posted land is taken as insult.

Getting dressed for blackberry picking was no small chore. A day in berry briars calls for a special outfit to protect the picker from snags and scratches, chigger bites, and sunstroke. During berry season, or whenever Mother helped my brothers with haying or at the barn, she borrowed a pair of overalls from Grandpa, which fit her neatly. These she wore over a faded blue-denim work shirt with long buttoned sleeves and high buttoned collar. If the shirt had short sleeves, she pulled a pair of cotton stockings, with the feet cut out, over her arms. Thin cotton gloves with the fingertips cut off, oxford shoes and heavy stockings, and a wide-brimmed calico sunbonnet with a deep ruffle covering her neck completed the standard berry picker's gear.

Around her ankles, wrists, and waist she tied cords soaked in coal oil to ward off chiggers. When she tried to deck me out similarly, I insisted that I'd rather have chiggers—which I did. My outfit consisted of a straw hat, jeans, and a long-sleeved shirt. I cheerfully accepted chiggers and scratches for freedom. Freedom was the essence of a day spent berrying. Mother regarded any time away from the farmhouse as "freedom"—a reprieve from ordinary chores, which oppress the creative spirit.

When we reached the blackberry patch the sun had barely begun its climb above the line of green woods surrounding the pasture. The morning stretched out before us, a summer idyll. Here was time to savor the choicest berries, to gather a bouquet of black-eyed Susans, to watch the glint of sunfish in a shallow pool of creek water. Now there was time to talk quietly—and so much time that, for long periods, it wasn't necessary to talk at all.

Again and again we filled the bright lard pails that hung from ropes tied about our waists with juicy, tart-sweet purple berries. We emptied the smaller pails into deep galvanized-metal berry buckets (erstwhile milk pails). With both hands free for picking, we filled the buckets quickly. At midmorning, when the level of dark, glistening berries in our buckets reached the two-gallon mark, we stopped to rest in the shade of a spreading beech tree on the second rise of the hill below the woods. Mother took off her bonnet and fanned herself with its starched brim while I explored the contents of the sack lunch she had packed for us at breakfast time.

Mine was a jelly sandwich: tangy red-plum jelly and freshly churned butter spread on Mother's good "light bread." Hers was a breakfast biscuit, split, with a cold hard-fried egg and a slice of bacon between the halves. A waxed bread-wrapper kept the sandwiches from drying out. The morning's sun had warmed the brown sack; when opened, it released a richness of fragrance, created from the intermingling of several aromas closed in together, that rises from all lunch boxes, sack lunches, and picnic hampers. We carried drinking water in a quart canning jar with raised letters on the side spelling out Ball Ideal. The water looked cool and limpid in the blue-green jar, but it was always lukewarm by the time we let ourselves drink it.

We ate our lunch—the sandwiches, some sugar cookies, a banana—and cooled off in the dappled shade cast by the big beech tree, then started picking again with renewed vigor. Still, the last third of the berry bucket always seemed to fill much more slowly than the larger portion we had picked before lunch, an illusion I often contemplate during the last interminable hour in a berry patch when the sun is hottest, the last trek up the hill to the woods is steepest, and the bucket is not quite full.

"Don't let your eyes deceive you," Mother warned when I grew restless and began appraising our harvest. "Your bucket is a long way from full."

"Full," by Mother's definition, meant a berry bucket not only full to the brim but rising high above it to a lofty dark peak on top of which not one additional blackberry could be balanced without the whole mound tumbling down.

Not until the last enormous gallon of blackberries gleamed high above the rim of the bucket—full to the utmost—did we head for home. Even then Mother couldn't resist picking berries along the way. Every so often we stopped to take still another handful of berries, too large and beautiful to pass by, hanging within arm's reach along a fencerow like black jeweled pendants.

"It always seems," Mother mused, "that we find the best picking after our buckets are full."

When we reached the barn lot, even the lard pails we wore at our waists were filled with glistening dark berries. We felt well satisfied with the morning's picking.

And so the peaceful interlude of blackberrying came to an end. We reached the farmhouse kitchen at noon—faces heat-flushed, fingers scratched and stained, berry pails *full*. The tranquil morning slipped beyond reach, as unattainable as a cluster of huge blackberries hanging high over Yellow Banks Creek. The serious business of canning was now at hand.

I prepared the blackberries for the canning kettle while Mother served a noon dinner to the men. I washed the berries outside under the backyard apple tree in a spot handy to the cistern. I pumped water into a spacious round enameled pan and tumbled the fragrant, sun-warmed blackberries into it. Although we had "picked clean," bits of grass and leaves and various small insects floated to the top of the water when the berries were turned. Mother's rule was to rinse the berries quickly through three waters, skimming off the trash and "looking" the berries during each transfer from one pan to another.

In the kitchen Mother lifted hot sterilized jars out of boiling water and set them to drain on the oilcloth-covered kitchen table. As soon as the jars were cool enough to handle (but while still hot) I slipped a rubber ring around the rim of each jar, making sure its edge rested precisely on the glass ledge where it belonged. Next, using a tin canning funnel, we filled each jar to the neck with glossy damp black-berries. Then the simple sugar syrup, which Mother had stirred to a boil on the kitchen range, was poured in to cover the berries. We wiped the rims of the jars clean with a damp cloth so that not a drop of sticky syrup remained to spoil the seal. Mother prided herself on seldom losing a jar of canned goods through spoilage, so no step in the canning process was carelessly done. She passed a finger around the rim of the jars to be sure they had not chipped when we filled them, then tightened on the zinc lids with her strong hands. She put the jars of berries inside the canning kettle on a rack, poured hot water around the jars until they were neck deep, and put the canning kettle on the stove to heat for the prescribed number of minutes. Then she removed the scalding hot jars one by one from their boiling water bath and deftly completed the seal with a slow, steady turn of the canning wrench gripping the zinc lid. The jars cooled on a rack on the kitchen table the rest of the afternoon.

After Mother was sure the jars were sealed—she turned them upside down to test for leaks—we added another dark row of fruit to the growing store of provisions that Mother cached on rough board shelves, floor to ceiling, against one wall of the cool cellar. Cherries, plums, gooseberries, green beans, peas, corn, blackberries and dew-berries, tomatoes, peaches, elderberries, sauerkraut, richly colored jellies and jams—these were truly the fruits of her labors. I understood Mother's quiet pride when she invited visitors down to the cellar in the farmhouse to view the impressive store of canned goods there. Though her friends admired her industry and complimented her skill ("They look fresh as just-picked!"), I knew Mother's shelves of filled jars meant more to her than mere hard work. Each sparkling cluster of jars marked another treasured, sun-filled morning of freedom spent gathering in summer's bounty. Who could ever again see blackberries as common things after those halcyon days of berrying on the hillside?

Blackberries can only be considered common in that they abound in many states. There are hundreds of species of blackberries (*Rubus*), of which the inveterate berry picker gathers several in a day's outing without needing to discriminate among them by any classifications other than the practical ones of size, ripeness, flavor, and color. The sweet, soft, round-shaped blackberries of one species go into the pail with the tart, firm, oblong ones of another, without a thought. Here in southern Indiana only the nature of the briars leads to a general differentiation. An early-ripening variety of low-vined, trailing blackberry is called a dewberry; all later species, which have upright thorny canes, from waist-high to towering heights, are called blackberries. Few Hoosiers think of blackberries and dewberries as different varieties of the same berry but rather of the dewberry as a berry in its own right.

Dewberries begin to ripen two weeks before blackberries, which is, when Indiana weather runs true to form, in mid-June. The first blackberries are ripe on the Fourth of July; for many families, a blackberry cobbler is as traditional as the fireworks and homemade ice cream that liven backyard picnics on Independence Day.

The tart-sweet flavor of dewberries is quite easily distinguished from that of blackberries, especially in jellies, and the glossy drupelets that compose them are big, fat, and juicy. I consider them choicest of the blackberries, not only because their rich tangy flavor is distinctive, but because they are rare and hard to find in this area. A good-sized patch of running dewberry vines is a prized find, and not one likely to be shared.

Dewberries are usually larger than blackberries, often nearly an inch long and about as wide, or as Dad used to describe those he found in our back pasture, "as big as the end of my thumb." When comparing a shiny black dewberry with an equally beautiful blackberry, to say that the dewberry is rounder, plumper, and juicier looking is quite specific. In subtle contrast, blackberries are leaner-looking, oblong or conic in shape, and often twice as long as they are broad. But these wild beauties are as wonderfully varied as sisters in a large family.

After the supreme enjoyment of wild blackberries and cream—which is surpassed only by that of blackberries alfresco leisurely eaten out of hand in the bramble patch while the harvest of berries is being methodically plucked—I serve my family a blackberry cobbler. I follow Mother's recipe carefully, simple as it is, but I suspect that its most important ingredient is not one I measure out and stir into the dough. Lest my cobbler lack it, I rouse my children early on a hot July morning, get them busy at their chores, pack a picnic lunch for us, gather up an assortment of berry baskets, supervise a thorough dousing of ankles and arms with insect repellent, and off we go across the meadow to the bramble patch for a carefree morning of berrying.

We have a good day, and we are duly proud of our wild harvest. A brief chore at the sink and the berries are rinsed clean, ready for the ceremonial blackberry cobbler.

It must bake before our noses, wafting out into the kitchen a tantalizing aroma that makes it impossible *not* to look behind the oven door where the pale raw-dough blanket over our prized berries is turning into a sugary, puffy, crusty, browned pastry flooded with the bubbling tide of juices underneath. At last the blackberry cobbler is drawn from the oven. I serve it up in generous portions and pass around the pitcher of cream. Springing from its crusty topping and sweet tangy filling are amazing reservoirs of flavor that recall a thousand associations: swaying summer fields and whistling bobwhite calls; jelly sandwiches; strange insects clinging drunkenly to overripe blackberries; Mother's serenity in the heart of a thorn patch; hot, steamy, summer kitchens and pealing dinner bells; sagging cellar shelves lined with dark jars; a fragrant procession of jams and jellies, cobblers, pies, dumplings, and savory desserts—the most obvious rewards of a morning in the blackberry thicket, then and now.

MOTHER'S BLACKBERRY COBBLER

5 cups fresh blackberries
1 cup sugar
3 tablespoons flour
2 tablespoons butter
2 cups flour
4 teaspoons baking powder
½ teaspoon salt
½ teaspoon cream of tartar
2 tablespoons sugar
½ cup butter
⅔ cup milk (about)

Butter an oblong baking dish (about 8 by 10 inches) and fill it almost to the rim with ripe blackberries sweetened with 1 cup of sugar (or more, if desired). Sprinkle the 3 tablespoons flour over the sweetened berries and dot with butter. Set aside.

Into a bowl, sift flour, baking powder, salt, cream of tartar, and sugar. Cut in butter until mixture resembles coarse meal. With a fork, stir in enough milk to form a ball of dough (slightly *less* than ⅔ cup of milk). Turn out on a floured board and roll dough to ¼-inch thickness. Cover the blackberries with the dough and trim the edges; cut a vent in the top to allow steam to escape during baking. Sprinkle the top of the dough generously with additional sugar and bake in a hot oven (400° F) about 45 minutes, or until the crust is browned and the juices bubbling. Serve warm with rich cream. Serves 6 to 8.

BLACKBERRY PIE

Pastry for double-crust pie (page 44)	1 cup sugar
	3 tablespoons tapioca
4 cups ripe blackberries	2 tablespoons butter

Fill pastry-lined pie pan with blackberries mixed with sugar and tapioca. Dot top with butter. Cover berries with top crust, cutting a vent in the center to let steam escape. Trim and crimp edges of pastry. Brush with milk, then sprinkle on additional sugar. Bake in a hot oven (400° F) for 10 minutes, then continue baking at 350° F for about 40 minutes more, or until the top crust is browned and the berry juices thickened and bubbling. Serve warm. Serves 6 to 8.

BLACKBERRY DUMPLINGS

1 quart blackberries	Butter
1 cup sugar	1 cup warm blackberry juice,
4 tablespoons flour	sweetened to taste

Make a double-crust recipe of pie pastry (see page 44). Roll it all out at once to ⅛-inch thickness and cut into 6-inch squares.

Toss blackberries in sugar and flour, and place a mound onto the center of each square. Place a chunk of butter in the center, and fold the corners of the dough to the center, pinching edges of pastry together.

Put the dumplings close together in a greased baking pan and pour around them the warm blackberry juice. Sprinkle the dumplings with sugar and bake at 375° F for 35 minutes or until dumplings are browned and juicy. Serve warm with cream or ice cream. Makes 6 dumplings.

BLACKBERRY PANCAKES

4 eggs, separated
1 cup milk
1½ cups flour
2 teaspoons baking powder
2 tablespoons sugar

½ teaspoon salt
3 tablespoons butter, melted
1 cup fresh blackberries
¼ cup confectioners' sugar

Beat the egg yolks, add the milk, flour, baking powder, sugar, and salt, and mix to a smooth batter. Add the melted butter. Beat the egg whites until stiff but not dry, and fold in. Toss the blackberries with the confectioners' sugar and add. Pour the batter onto a sizzling-hot greased griddle and bake the pancakes on both sides, using about ¼ cup of batter for each pancake. Serve the pancakes with Orange Butter Sauce (recipe below). Makes 14 to 16 pancakes.

ORANGE BUTTER SAUCE

¼ cup butter
1¼ cups sifted confectioners'
   sugar

2 teaspoons grated orange peel
2 tablespoons orange juice
   (about)

Cream butter until light and fluffy, gradually add confectioners' sugar and continue beating until the sauce is fluffy. Add the grated orange peel and enough orange juice to make the sauce moist enough to spread easily. Makes about ¾ cup sauce.

LADYFINGERS WITH BLACKBERRY CREAM

2 cups fresh blackberries
1 cup sugar
⅛ cup water
½ tablespoon gelatin

¼ cup milk
2 tablespoons kirsch
½ pint heavy cream, whipped
8 ladyfingers

In a medium saucepan, combine blackberries, sugar, and water. Cook over low heat until soft, simmering gently. Put the mixture through a sieve. Soften the gelatin in the milk in a saucepan over hot water, then blend into the blackberry puree. Stir in the kirsch. Chill until partly congealed, then fold in the whipped cream. Spoon the blackberry cream into 4 dessert dishes lined with ladyfinger halves. Sprinkle the ladyfingers lightly with additional kirsch. Serves 4.

SOUR CREAM BLACKBERRY PIE

1 cup sour cream
½ cup sugar
1 tablespoon flour
3 cups ripe blackberries

1 tablespoon lemon juice
Grated nutmeg
Pastry, 8-inch single crust
  (page 44)

Mix sour cream, sugar, and flour. Spread blackberries in a pastry-lined pie pan, sprinkle lemon juice over berries, and cover with sour cream mixture. Grate a sprinkling of nutmeg over the top. Bake in a hot oven (425° F) for 10 minutes, then reduce heat to a slow oven (325° F) and continue baking about 40 minutes longer, until berries are soft, juicy, and bubbling. Serves 6.

BLACKBERRY FLOAT

2 cups ripe blackberries
1 cup sugar
½ cup water
2 tablespoons butter
1 egg

1 cup flour
1½ teaspoons baking powder
⅛ teaspoon salt
⅔ cup milk

Bring to a boil the blackberries, ½ cup of the sugar, and water. Set aside.

In a mixing bowl, cream the butter and remaining sugar, add the egg, and beat well. Sift together the dry ingredients, add alternately with the milk, and mix until smooth. Put the batter in the bottom of a greased 1½-quart round baking dish. Spoon the stewed blackberries and juice over the top of the batter. Bake at 400° F until the crust is golden and a toothpick inserted into the batter comes out clean, about 30 minutes. The batter rises up through the berries during baking. Serve the blackberry float warm with cream. Serves 6.

BLACKBERRY JAM CAKE

1 cup butter
2 cups sugar
5 eggs
3 cups flour
¼ teaspoon salt
½ teaspoon cinnamon
1½ teaspoons cloves
1½ teaspoons allspice

1 teaspoon baking soda
1 cup buttermilk
1 cup chopped dates or raisins
1 cup chopped hickory nuts
   or pecans
1 tablespoon flour
1 cup blackberry jam

In the large bowl of an electric mixer, cream butter, gradually add sugar, and beat until light and fluffy. Add eggs and continue beating. Sift flour with salt and spices. Dissolve baking soda in buttermilk. To the creamed mixture, add the flour mixture alternately with the buttermilk. Beat well. Toss fruit and nuts with the tablespoon of flour, and blend in. Add blackberry jam. Grease two 9-inch layer-cake pans and line with 9-inch circles of waxed paper. Stir batter well and pour into pans. Bake in a moderately slow oven (325° F) for 40 minutes or until a toothpick inserted into the cake comes out dry. Cool the layers in the pans for 15 minutes and turn them out onto a wire rack. Ice the cake with Caramel Icing (recipe below). Serves 6 to 8.

CARAMEL ICING

3 cups brown sugar
1 cup evaporated milk

½ cup butter

In a saucepan, combine the brown sugar, evaporated milk, and butter. Cook until a soft ball forms when a small amount of syrup is dropped into cold water, or to 238° F on a candy thermometer. Beat until creamy enough to spread over cake layers.

BLACKBERRY JAM WITH ORANGE

6 cups blackberries
½ cup water
¾ cup orange juice
3 tablespoons lemon juice

1 tablespoon grated orange peel
1 package powdered fruit pectin
7 cups sugar

Cook blackberries with water until they are well heated. Put half of the berries through a sieve or a food mill to remove part of the seeds. Combine the blackberries, fruit juices, grated peel, and pectin crystals.

Stir over high heat until the mixture comes to a hard boil. Stir in the sugar and bring to a full rolling boil, then boil hard for 1 minute, stirring constantly. Remove from heat, and stir and skim for several minutes to prevent the fruit from floating. Pour into hot, sterilized jam jars. Cover jam with ⅛-inch melted paraffin. Makes about 6 glasses of jam.

Cantaloupe and Blackberry Salad

1 cantaloupe, chilled	2 cups fresh blackberries,
Lettuce leaves	chilled

Peel and seed the cantaloupe and cut into wedges or rings. Arrange them around a platter lined with lettuce leaves and fill the center of the platter with the blackberries. Serve the salad with a sauceboat of Lime Honey Dressing (recipe below).

Lime Honey Dressing

1 cup salad oil	½ teaspoon paprika
⅓ cup honey	¼ teaspoon salt
⅓ cup lime juice	Grated rind of 1 lime
½ teaspoon prepared mustard	

Combine all the ingredients in the container of a blender. Cover the container and blend until well mixed. Chill the dressing. Makes 1½ cups.

Grandpa's Blackberry Wine

"Mash 2½ gallons ripe blackberries in a 5-gallon crockery jar. Add 15 pounds of sugar and enough water to fill the jar to the rim. Put cheesecloth over the jar and let it work in a dark, cool place for about ten days. Then strain and put into a 5-gallon keg. Lay the keg on its side and fill it up to the bunghole. As the 'pummies' [the pomace or residue of crushed fruit] work out over the sides of the keg, add more water to keep the keg full. When the wine quiets down, close the hole with a cork with a rubber tube through it. Put the other end of the tube in a glass of water. Leave the keg like this until the wine quits sparkling and is still. Then close the bunghole tight with the spigot. Let the wine age for two or three months more. It will be ready to drink by the time cold weather sets in."

Cottage Cheesecake with Blackberry Glaze

1 6-ounce package zwieback
1 cup sugar
¼ cup butter, melted
1½ pounds cottage cheese
¼ cup flour

¼ teaspoon salt
6 eggs, separated
1 cup sour cream
Rind and juice of 1 lemon
Blackberry Glaze (recipe below)

Roll the zwieback and make crumbs. Mix crumbs with ¼ cup of the sugar and the melted butter. Grease a 9-inch spring form and dust the sides with zwieback crumbs; press the remainder of the crumbs onto the bottom of the pan. Bake the crust for 5 minutes in a 325° F oven. Cool.

Press the cottage cheese through a sieve. Add the remaining sugar, except for 2 tablespoons which should be reserved to combine with the egg whites. To the sweetened cottage cheese, add the flour, salt, beaten egg yolks, sour cream, lemon rind and juice. Blend well. Beat the egg whites stiff but not dry, add the remaining 2 tablespoons of sugar, and fold into the cheese mixture. Turn into the zwieback crust and bake for 1½ hours at 325° F. Cool in the pan, spread Blackberry Glaze on top. Chill the cheesecake thoroughly before serving. Serves 10 to 12.

Blackberry Glaze

2 cups fresh blackberries
⅓ cup sugar
1 tablespoon lemon juice

¼ cup water
1 tablespoon cornstarch

Combine blackberries, sugar, and lemon juice and place over medium heat. Stir the water into the cornstarch and add to the blackberry mixture, stirring constantly. Continue to stir and cook until the blackberry glaze thickens. Chill before serving as a topping for plain pies, cakes, and cheesecake.

BLUEBERRYING
IN VERMONT

It was Adele Dawson who introduced us to blueberrying during our first August in Vermont. We had already explored every foot of our newly acquired farmstead and knew we had no blueberries on our forty acres. There were wild strawberries, red raspberries, blackberries, chokecherries, and a forestful of mushrooms—but no blueberries. So we asked Adele, our neighbor who lives across the waterfall, if she knew of any good berrying places.

"Oh, yes! Let's all go berrying this afternoon!" she said with characteristic enthusiasm and hospitality. "I know a marvelous place—but you could never find it alone. Besides, I want to have a blueberry pie when Barry comes to visit."

The blueberry patch was in Owen's Meadow on one of the smaller Vermont mountains, on the old road to Peacham. The bumpy road leading to it curves and winds across the top of the mountain through a densely forested section. The route was circuitous and confusing to us, for we were newcomers to the area, and outlanders at that. But we noted the landmarks as we followed Adele in her jeep: a pink house by the side of the road where we turned off the highway; a barn with its roof caved in by winter snows; a crossroads; a logging-woods. We wanted to learn our way around the backroads of Vermont, to collect a repertory of special places to visit on our own.

Now Adele, who had helpfully supervised our initiation into the pleasures of Vermont living during our first visits here, was leading us to her berrying place. It was a wild ride, for Adele drives as energetically as she lives, and Kurt, in our low sports car, had a hard time keeping up with the tough little Scout jeep as it bounced over the rough road. And only a real Vermonter—or a bear—could know that a blueberry patch lay barely a hundred feet off the road from the place where Adele pulled off the road and parked.

Adele and her grandchildren, Bart and Victoria, and our sons, Jim and Bob, were already out of the jeep and climbing over the low stone wall into the blueberry field when we drove up. We left our car and hurried to catch up. To reach the stone wall, we had to cross a field that was grown up with small chokecherry bushes and late summer's tall grasses. Golden-yellow coneflowers were blooming among the weeds. A well-trampled path leading across the field told us that others picked blueberries here, too.

Beyond the stone wall, the land sloped steeply downward. We could see the low blueberry bushes, acres of them, sprawling down the mountainside. And there were the blueberries!—prolific clusters of them, blue as the Vermont sky, some showing under the shiny green leaves and others, hidden by the foliage, visible when a branch was lifted.

The small blueberry bushes seemed to grow in groupings, like ornamental shrubs, outlined naturally by nicely shaped young pines and smaller trees. A network of well-worn paths threaded through the maze, like paths in a garden. Scattered here and there along the slope were the familiar gray boulders of Vermont hillsides and drifts of white-blooming pearly everlastings. In front of us, another mountain rose alongside our blueberry mountain with no valley between the two, and its evergreen-wooded summit was directly before our eyes.

We admired nature's landscaping, then climbed the low stone wall at the edge of the blueberry patch and, like Robert Frost's berrypickers:

> . . . we took one look round
> Then sank out of sight like trolls underground.

Blueberry (*Vaccinium*)

I came to the blueberry patch with idealistic notions of blueberrying. My expectations were built on the lovely imagery of Robert Frost's poem, "Blueberries" and on the romantic musings of friends who extolled the joys of picking blueberries, to my envy. For years, the simple phrase "blueberrying in Vermont" evoked episodes of pastoral daydreaming. Now I was here, blueberrying on a Vermont mountainside, and it was as poetic an experience as I imagined it to be.

But my imaginings did not prepare me for the flavor of my first taste of wild blueberries, nor did my acquaintance with supermarket blueberries. These wild mountain fruits were tiny, tart-sweet, and firm-fleshed, with a concentrated blueberry flavor. They were not sweet or soft and were never tough-skinned like their tame sisters from the A & P. "The fruits do not yield their true flavor to the purchaser of them," wrote Henry David Thoreau after making a supper of huckleberries and blueberries on Fair Haven Hill. "The ambrosial and essential part of the fruit is lost with the bloom which is rubbed off in the market cart, and they become mere provender," he said.

As with all wild fruits, part of their flavor is connected with the gathering of them, created by one's self out of the sights, sounds,

Huckleberry (*Gaylussacia*)

scents, and feelings that invade the senses as the wild blueberries are eaten, from bush to hand to mouth, on the mountainside. "If you would know the flavor of huckleberries, ask the cow-boy or the partridge," Thoreau wrote. "It is a vulgar error to suppose that you have tasted huckleberries who never plucked them."

There are at least twenty species of blueberries (*Vaccinium*) and huckleberries (*Gaylussacia*) growing in the United States. Often only a botanist could tell exactly which is which. It makes no difference whether you gather blueberries or huckleberries, lowbush or highbush or swamp, whortleberries or hurtleberries, dangleberries or tangleberries or bilberries—all are edible, and several kinds may end up in the same berry basket anyway.

Blueberries or huckleberries, both are delicious. But still the matter is one of curiosity, even argument, among inveterate blueberry pickers. A New England friend wrote to me:

When I was in North Carolina, I got into an argument about blueberries and huckleberries. What we know as blueberries here, they call huckleberries there. Of course, they don't know that extraordinary variant that used to grow in my grandmother's pasture, a fat, juicy, grayish, dusty berry, with whitish meat and not too evident seeds—this one in great contrast to the very shiny black huckleberry, with reddish meat, quite fully packed with very tough seeds. The former was particularly good for pies. And of course neither of these had any relationship to the blueberry, which came in all manner of delicious varieties: high-bush berries, low-bush berries, even one kind that crept on the ground in vine-like bushes. The swampberries grew on bushes more like trees, much higher than one's head, and then there were the waist high, delicious, pale blue ones called sugarberries. The sour swampberries were almost black, but nothing remotely like a huckleberry.

In general, there is one consistent, discernible difference between blueberries and the true huckleberries: blueberries have many fine, soft seeds but they are not especially noticed when the blueberries are eaten; huckleberries have ten larger hard seeds that leave the distinct impression that huckleberries are "seedy." Huckleberries are usually almost black and they may not have the silvery bloom on their skins that blueberries have.

The blueberries growing on our mountain in Vermont are lowbush. The frosty bloom veiling their blackish-blue skins give them the blue-sky color that comes to mind with blueberries. Robert Frost describes them:

> And after all, really they're ebony skinned:
> The blue's but a mist from the breath of the wind,
> A tarnish that goes at a touch of the hand.

Finally, at the touch of my hand, the blueberries I had envisioned, like the poet's were

> . . . ready to drum
> in the cavernous pail of the first one to come!

The sound of the first berries drumming noisily on the bottom of a battered tin berry-pail is a sound dear to the memory of an incurable berry picker. Like one familiar chord struck on the keys, it brings back a whole melody of impressions.

Adele, who has a propensity for unique possessions, had her own special berrying pail. It was a tin can of some sort, not so small as an ordinary number 2 can and not so large as a fruit juice can, but just the right size to hang at her waist on the wire hook she had devised to fit onto a loop of her belt. Both hands are needed for picking, one to hold the cluster of bluish fruits, the other to coax the ripe ones off the bush. The ripest fruits will almost fall into one's hand at a touch, but the less ripe ones, for jelly and tartness, must be carefully separated from the cluster. Not all of the blueberries in one cluster ripen at once, as do so many fruits whose seasons flash by, so the delightful pastime of blueberrying may stretch over the period of a month or more.

Since this first blueberrying expedition was impromptu, the rest of us were not fitted out so handily as Adele. We had various small saucepans and handleless shortening tins that we put down nearby on the grass or on rocks, emptying our pickings into them when our hands were full. More than once someone lost sight of his pick-dish, and berrying was interrupted until the misplaced blueberry container was found—like a chewink's nest hidden in the meadow, its bounty would be camouflaged by the deep grasses.

Victoria's pick-dish was an old pint measure of tole finish, with a handle. Some time after the blueberries stopped drumming in our cavernous pails as they filled, Victoria began to feel that picking blueberries was, somehow, competitive—a race to see who could pick the most berries. She began to go from one to the other of us in the blueberry patch, comparing her hoard with ours. Since she had picked a bouquet of pearly everlastings, surveyed the mountainside for bear tracks, walked the stone wall, spied a bird's nest, picked up pine cones, tasted unripe chokecherries, and discovered a rotting branch growing a mossy crop of the enchanting little British soldiers, Victoria had not picked many blueberries.

"You have so many more than I do." Victoria sounded unhappy when she looked into my pail.

"I'll share with you," I said, pouring a few of my blueberries into her tin cup—a small token to give in exchange for her smile.

Victoria darted off, happy with her easy harvest, and ran to her grandmother who had settled down in a blueberry thicket near the tumbled stone wall.

I watched Victoria running from one blueberry picker to another, like a pretty butterfly flitting from flower to flower, until she disappeared from sight behind a stand of pine trees below us on the steeply sloping mountain side. Kurt and one of the boys had also gone farther down the mountain to pick blueberries.

When Victoria reappeared only a short time later, she was carrying her pint measure very carefully, holding it level as she trudged up the incline toward me.

"Want to see my blueberries?" Victoria held up the tin pitcher for me to see. It was brimming with blueberries.

"They're beautiful," I agreed. "Now you have more than I have."

"Yes," Victoria said proudly. "I have more blueberries than anybody."

Not everyone can fill a blueberry pail so quickly and easily as Victoria did. The tiny wild blueberries are difficult to pick and it takes at least an hour to fill a quart container. None of our pails, except Victoria's, was completely filled when we took our leave of the blueberry thicket at sunset.

But when we gathered our family's harvest together, back at the farmhouse kitchen, it filled a roasting pan. We had a wealth of wild blueberries! What would I do with all of them?

"Bake a pie," Kurt suggested.

"Let's have muffins," Jim said.

"Make pancakes!" Bob ordered.

I decided to make blueberry pancakes for supper. I could make them on the wood-burning cookstove, using my soapstone griddle. Kurt had already made a fire in the kitchen range. The air felt chilly soon after the sun went behind the mountains, which is usual in northern Vermont where summer is a short, cool season. The fire took away the uncomfortable chill and made the kitchen cozy.

I like to cook on the old wood-fed range in my Vermont kitchen. There is a gas range in the roomy pantry, or "butt'ry," that I use whenever I want to, so cooking on the wood stove is purely for the fun of it. My husband enjoys splitting the wood and tending the fire, and the cookstove puts out enough heat to keep the chill out of the house on cool evenings and damp mornings so that we do not need to start the furnace. Besides, the boys like to sit in the kitchen rocking chairs beside the stove, warming themselves like the cat, while I prepare their food.

Although my family enjoys the warmth and cheer of a fireside, the wood-burning range in our Vermont kitchen is mainly a vacation novelty to my sons and my husband. The black range, with its curving legs and shiny nickel ornamentation, the raised curlicues embellishing its cast-iron sides, might soon lose its charm if it were the only cooking stove we had available for our use. Its demanding firebox would make filling the woodbox and emptying the ashpan daily, unrelenting chores for young boys to remember. Its steady, soothing warmth would require cords of split wood and constant fire-tending.

But for me, cooking on the old wood-burning range is a nostalgia-filled pastime. A high backed Home Comfort range was the heart of my grandmother's comfortable kitchen. Whenever I arrange the thin strips of bacon in my skillet, I remember thick meaty slices of home-cured bacon that sizzled in another heavy-iron frying pan and sent smoky couriers of fragrance up the open stairway to my bedroom to awaken me on the mornings when I had spent the night at Grand-mother's house. Whenever I put our coffeepot on to perk, I remember the huge blue-speckled enamelware pot that sat at the back of Grandmother's range all day, into whose boiling, steaming depths she dumped the dark coffee-grounds fresh from the grinder that hung on the kitchen wall behind the stove. Whenever I pour a stream of pancake batter onto my hot soapstone griddle, I remember the steaming stacks of hotcakes keeping on the lowered door of the high warming closet that was mounted to the back of the Home Comfort until the menfolk came in from the barn for their breakfast. And whenever I heat the panful of pale Vermont maple syrup for pouring over our blueberry-studded pancakes, I think of the pitchers of greenish-gold sorghum molasses and the plates of home-churned but-ter that my grandmother used so freely in Indiana.

There are lovely dreams wafting on the tantalizing odors from my coffeepot and skillet, fragrant remembrances that are as warming to me as the flames flickering behind the open grating of the wood stove in my Vermont kitchen.

And the crisp-browned blueberry pancakes—stacked on plates that were warmed on the grilled shelf over the back of the stove, spread rim to rim with butter, dribbled generously with delicate maple syrup—these are gone in a twinkling!

Just as quickly, my sentimental reveries give way to the pleasant realities of the evening. Days such as this one are the far-off irrespon-sible days of tomorrow's memoirs.

"Want to go blueberrying again tomorrow?" Kurt asks, pushing back his plate.

"Let's slip in quietly," Jimmy says. "Maybe we can surprise a bear."

The planning continues. We sit around the kitchen table with a sense of completeness settling on us as gently as the soft light from the hanging lamp. From now on, the simple phrase "blueberrying in Vermont" will have real meaning for all of us.

Blueberry Pancakes

2 eggs
2 cups buttermilk
1 teaspoon baking soda
2 cups flour
1 tablespoon sugar

1 teaspoon salt
2 teaspoons baking powder
⅓ cup melted butter
1 cup fresh blueberries

Beat the eggs until they are light. Combine the buttermilk and baking soda, add to the eggs, and blend well. Sift together the dry ingredients and add gradually to the egg mixture. Melt the butter and stir in gently. Pour the batter, about 3 tablespoons at a time, onto a hot griddle (greased, if necessary). Sprinkle a few fresh blueberries on each pancake and bake on the first side until bubbles pop on the surface, then flip the pancake and bake on the other side. Serve with butter and hot maple syrup. Makes about twelve 4-inch pancakes.

Blueberry Pie

3 cups blueberries
1 cup sugar
1 tablespoon lemon juice
3 tablespoons flour

⅛ teaspoon salt
2 tablespoons butter
Pastry for double-crust pie
   (page 44)

Combine the blueberries, sugar, lemon juice, flour, and salt. Pour into a pie tin lined with pastry and dot the top with the butter. Cover with a top crust, with a decorative slit cut in it for a vent, and crimp the edges. Brush the top of the crust with a small amount of milk, then sprinkle it with sugar to make the crust brown nicely. Bake for 10 minutes in a hot oven (400° F), then reduce the heat to 350° F and bake for 40 to 50 minutes longer, until the crust is browned.

Blueberry Chiffon Pie

9-inch vanilla wafer crust
   (page 113)
4 eggs, separated
¾ cup sugar
½ cup milk

¼ cup lemon juice
½ teaspoon salt
1 tablespoon unflavored gelatin
¼ cup cold water
1 pint fresh blueberries

Beat the egg yolks slightly and mix with ¼ cup of the sugar; add the milk, lemon juice, and salt. Cook over hot water until thickened, stirring constantly. Soften the gelatin in cold water; dissolve in the hot egg mixture and cool. Beat the egg whites until foamy; gradually beat in the remaining sugar and continue beating until soft peaks are formed. Fold into egg mixture and pour into prepared vanilla wafer crust. Let the pie chill in the refrigerator until firm, or overnight. Just before serving, add the blueberries.

NOTE: This recipe may be used with red or black raspberries, with blackberries, dewberries, or red mulberries.

BLUEBERRY CREAM CHEESE PIE

9-inch graham cracker crumb
  crust (page 113)
8 ounces cream cheese
1 cup sugar
2 eggs
1 teaspoon vanilla

2 cups blueberries
1 cup sour cream
½ teaspoon vanilla
1 tablespoon sugar

In the small bowl of an electric mixer, beat the cream cheese (which should be at room temperature) with ½ cup of the sugar until the mixture is creamy. Add the eggs one at a time, and beat well after each addition. Add the vanilla. Pour the mixture into a graham cracker crumb crust and bake in a moderate oven (350° F) for 25 to 30 minutes, until the custard does not stick to the finger when touched lightly. Cool the pie, then chill for several hours. Sweeten the blueberries with the remaining ½ cup of sugar, and the sour cream with the tablespoon of sugar and vanilla. Pour the blueberries on the pie, and top with sour cream. Serves 6 to 8.

SPICED BLUEBERRY JAM

2¼ cups blueberries, crushed
  thoroughly
1 teaspoon grated lemon rind
1 tablespoon lemon juice

¼ teaspoon allspice
3½ cups sugar
½ cup liquid fruit pectin

In a large pan, combine the blueberries, lemon rind, lemon juice, allspice, and sugar. Mix well and place over high heat. Bring to a full rolling boil, stirring constantly, and boil hard for 1 minute. Stir in fruit pectin, return mixture to a boil, then remove from the heat. Stir and skim for several minutes, to remove the foam and to prevent the fruit from floating. Pour into hot, sterilized jelly glasses and cover with hot paraffin. Makes 6 glasses.

NOTE: To make plain blueberry jam, omit the allspice and the lemon rind.

BLUEBERRY MUFFINS

2 cups flour	½ cup butter
2 teaspoons baking powder	2 eggs
½ teaspoon salt	½ cup rich milk
⅛ teaspoon mace	2 cups blueberries, damp but
1 cup sugar	well drained

Sift the dry ingredients together, including the sugar. Sift 3 tablespoons of the flour mixture over the blueberries and roll the blueberries until they are coated. In the bowl of an electric mixer, cream the butter, beat in the eggs, then the milk. Stir the flour mixture into the egg mixture, then gently fold in the floured blueberries. Fill buttered muffin wells ⅔ full with the batter. Bake in a hot oven (450° F) for 10 minutes, then reduce the heat to 350° F and bake for 10 minutes longer, or until a toothpick inserted in the middle of a muffin comes out clean. Makes 16 muffins.

OLD ENGLISH SUMMER PUDDING

¼ pound butter	½ cup sugar
1-pound loaf of white bread	¼ cup water
1 quart blueberries	Cream

Generously butter a 1-quart glass bowl. Remove crust from good white bread, slice, and butter on one side. Cut the first slice into a round to fit the bottom of the bowl, buttered-side up, and shape the rest of the slices to line the slope of the bowl so that they dovetail together tightly. Also prepare the additional slices of buttered bread, shaped to fit the bowl, that will be needed to alternate with the stewed sweetened blueberries when the pudding is assembled.

When the bowl is prepared and the additional slices of bread are ready, sweeten the blueberries with the sugar and slowly heat and simmer in ¼ cup of water, until the berries are tender and plumped up and their juices are flowing. Then, using a slotted spoon, dip out enough berries to fill the bottom half of the bread-lined bowl. Cover the berries with a layer of buttered bread. Spoon the rest of the berries onto this layer of bread and cover them with the last layer of bread, buttered-side in. Pour the juice from the pan over the pudding, keeping it away from the edge of the bowl. If the bread slices lining the bowl are cut carefully, the pudding will stay white on the outside. Fit a plate over the pudding and weight it down. Chill in the refrigerator for 24 hours.

To unmold, slip a spatula between the bread and the bowl and loosen the pudding, then turn it over on a platter. Cut the pudding in slices and serve with cream to pour over it or with whipped cream. Makes 8 portions.

STEAMED BLUEBERRY PUDDING

2 cups flour
4 teaspoons baking powder
½ teaspoon salt
3 tablespoons sugar
2 tablespoons butter
¾ cup milk

3 tablespoons maple syrup
1½ cups blueberries, damp but
    well drained
2 tablespoons flour
⅛ teaspoon freshly grated nutmeg

Sift the flour, baking powder, salt, and sugar together into a bowl. Cut in the butter until the mixture is crumbly, then stir in the milk and maple syrup. Blend well. Shake the blueberries in a bag with the 2 tablespoons of flour and the nutmeg. Fold the berries into the pudding dough and pour the mixture into a greased and floured pudding mold or into a 1-pound coffee can. Steam for 1½ hours. Serve warm with blueberry sauce. Serves 6 to 8.

BLUEBERRY SAUCE

2 teaspoons cornstarch
1 tablespoon water
¼ cup sugar
⅓ cup water or blueberry syrup

⅛ teaspoon salt
1 tablespoon lemon juice
2 cups blueberries

In a saucepan, blend the cornstarch and water. Add the sugar, water or blueberry syrup, salt, and lemon juice. Cook over medium heat, stirring constantly, until clear and slightly thickened. Add the blueberries and boil for 2 minutes. Serve warm or cold over cakes and puddings. Makes 2 cups.

BLUEBERRY CUSTARD DESSERT

5 egg yolks	2 teaspoons vanilla extract or
½ cup sugar	2 tablespoons Grand Marnier
1⅔ cups light cream (half-and-	3 cups blueberries
half), scalded	1 cup heavy cream

Beat the egg yolks with ¼ cup of the sugar in the top of a double boiler. Add the scalded cream gradually, beating constantly. Cook over simmering-hot water, stirring constantly, until the custard coats a spoon. Remove the top of the double boiler from the heat at once and set it down in a pan containing cold water to stop the cooking instantly. If the custard cooks too long, it will curdle. (If it does curdle, see page 108.) Cool the custard, then add the vanilla or the Grand Marnier.

Sweeten the blueberries with the remaining ¼ cup of sugar and spoon into 6 sauce dishes. Whip the heavy cream until it forms soft peaks but not until it is very stiff. Fold the whipped cream into the cooled custard sauce. Just before serving, pour the custard over the berries in the individual dishes. Serves 6.

NOTE: This custard sauce is also good with fresh raspberries, blackberries, mulberries, or strawberries. If a liquor is used for flavoring, adjust it to the fruit being served, substituting kirsch, or cognac, or rum, as preferred.

BLUEBERRY-PEACH DESSERT

1½ cups fresh peaches,	2 cups water, boiling hot
peeled and sliced	1 cup dairy sour cream
½ cup sugar	1½ cups miniature marshmallows
1 teaspoon powdered ascorbic acid	1 cup heavy cream
1 box strawberry-flavored gelatin	2 cups fresh wild blueberries
(family size)	

Combine the peaches with sugar and powdered ascorbic acid. Set aside.

Dissolve gelatin in the boiling hot water. Chill until it thickens, then add the sweetened peaches with their juice. Pour into a 1½-quart rectangular oven-proof glass dish and chill until set.

Combine sour cream and marshmallows. Whip the cream and fold into the marshmallow mixture. Spread the marshmallow mixture over the chilled gelatin mixture. Top with the wild blueberries. Cut into 6 or 8 portions and serve.

BLUEBERRY-APPLE CRISP

2 cups blueberries
2 cups tart apples, peeled
    and sliced
Juice of one lemon
1 teaspoon grated lemon rind
½ cup brown sugar, firmly packed
1 cup flour

¾ cup granulated sugar
1 teaspoon baking powder
¾ teaspoon salt
3 tablespoons butter
1 egg, slightly beaten
¼ cup chopped pecans (optional)
½ teaspoon cinnamon

In a bowl, combine blueberries, apples, lemon juice and rind, and brown sugar. Spread in a greased 1½- or 2-quart baking dish. In another bowl, combine the flour, sugar, baking powder, and salt. Cut in the butter with a pastry blender until the mixture is crumbly. Stir in the beaten egg, then the nuts. Spread this mixture over the fruits in the baking dish. Sprinkle the cinnamon over the top. Bake in a hot oven (400° F) for 30 to 35 minutes, or until the topping is browned and the apples are tender. Serve warm with cream or ice cream. Makes 6 portions.

BLUEBERRY CRISP

4 cups fresh blueberries
½ cup granulated sugar
1 tablespoon lemon juice
4 tablespoons butter

⅓ cup brown sugar
⅓ cup flour
¼ cup Crunchy Granola

Spread the blueberries in a rectangular 1½-quart baking dish. Sprinkle with the sugar and lemon juice. Cream the butter and add the brown sugar; mix well. Blend in the flour and the Crunchy Granola. With your fingers, spread the topping over the blueberries. Bake the pudding in a moderate oven (375° F) for 35 to 40 minutes. Serve plain or with ice cream or whipped cream. Makes 6 to 8 servings.

NOTE: This recipe may be used with apples in place of blueberries.

BLUEBERRY GINGERBREAD

½ cup butter or margarine
½ cup sugar
1 egg
1 cup sorghum molasses
2½ cups flour
1½ teaspoons baking soda
½ teaspoon salt

1 teaspoon ginger
1 teaspoon cinnamon
1 teaspoon cloves
1 cup hot water
1½ cups fresh blueberries, damp
    but well drained

Cream the butter and the sugar, using an electric mixer. Add the egg and beat well. Then add the molasses and beat until well blended.

Sift together the flour, baking soda, salt, and spices. Take out 2 tablespoons of the flour mixture, sprinkle it over the blueberries, and toss. Set aside while finishing the batter.

Add the sifted dry ingredients to the creamed mixture alternately with the hot water, adding about 1/6 of the dry ingredients each time, and beat until smooth after each addition. Fold in the flour-coated blueberries.

Grease a 9-by-13-by-2-inch pan and dust with flour. Pour in the batter. Bake in a moderate oven (375° F) for 40 to 45 minutes, or until a toothpick inserted in the center comes out clean.

Serve hot or cold, with or without whipped cream or ice cream. Serves 12.

NOTE: This is an old family recipe that makes a good plain gingerbread without the blueberries.

BLUEBERRY BUCKLE

½ cup margarine
1 cup sugar
1 egg
2½ cups flour
3 teaspoons baking powder
¼ teaspoon salt

½ cup milk
2 cups fresh blueberries
2 teaspoons lemon juice
½ teaspoon cinnamon
¼ cup butter
½ cup chopped pecans (optional)

With an electric mixer, cream the margarine and ½ cup of the sugar together until fluffy, then add the egg and beat well. Sift 2 cups of the flour with the baking powder and salt. Add to the creamed mixture alternately with the milk. Pour the batter into a well-greased baking pan (7½-by-11½-by-2-inches) and sprinkle the blueberries and lemon juice over the top. Combine the remaining ingredients until crumbly and sprinkle over the blueberries. Bake in a moderate oven (350° F) for 55 minutes, or until a toothpick comes out clean when inserted in the middle of the buckle. Cut into squares and serve warm for breakfast or dessert. Makes 8 to 10 servings.

BLUEBERRY-FILLED MERINGUE CAKE

⅓ cup shortening
⅔ cup sugar
4 egg yolks
1 teaspoon vanilla
1⅓ cups flour
2 teaspoons baking powder
¼ teaspoon salt

⅓ cup milk
4 egg whites
½ cup sugar
2 cups blueberries, sweetened with
   ⅓ cup sugar
1 tablespoon lemon juice

With an electric mixer, cream shortening, add sugar gradually, and beat until fluffy. Beat in egg yolks and vanilla. Sift the dry ingredients together and add to the creamed mixture alternately with milk. Blend well. Lightly grease and flour two 8-inch layer pans, pour in the batter, and bake in a moderate oven (350° F) for 15 minutes. During this time beat the egg whites until fluffy, add the ½ cup sugar gradually and continue beating until the egg whites are stiff but not dry. At the end of the 15-minute baking period, spread the meringue quickly over the top of the hot layers, reduce the oven heat to 300° F and bake 20 minutes longer, or until the meringue is lightly browned. Cool. Remove from pans. Put one cake layer on a plate, spread the meringue top with half of the blueberries, top it with the other cake layer, and spread the remaining berries on top of the cake. Chill until serving time. Serves 12.

BLUEBERRY CUP CAKES

½ cup butter
1½ cups sugar
2 eggs
3 cups flour
¼ teaspoon salt
3 teaspoons baking powder

1 cup milk
1 cup blueberries, barely damp
   but well drained
1 tablespoon flour
1 teaspoon vanilla

With an electric mixer, cream the butter and sugar until fluffy. Add the eggs, one at a time, beating well after each addition. Sift the dry ingredients together and add to the creamed mixture alternately with the milk. Toss the blueberries in the tablespoon of flour, then fold in and add the vanilla. Pour the batter into muffin wells lined with paper or foil baking cups. Bake in a moderate oven (350° F) for 25 minutes. When cool, frost with a simple white icing such as Lemon Butter Frosting (see below).

LEMON BUTTER FROSTING

½ cup butter
1 tablespoon lemon juice
Grated lemon rind

1 pound confectioners' sugar
6 tablespoons cream (about)

Cream the butter until fluffy, using an electric mixer. Blend in the lemon juice and a small amount of grated lemon rind. Add the confectioners' sugar gradually along with enough cream to make a frosting of the right spreading consistency. Run the beaters long enough to make the frosting very fluffy. Garnish the top of the frosted cake with a grating of lemon rind.

JELLED BLUEBERRY SALAD

1 package lemon-flavored gelatin
1 cup boiling-hot water
½ cup pineapple juice
2 tablespoons lemon juice
¼ cup mayonnaise

¼ teaspoon salt
1 cup fresh blueberries
½ cup cottage cheese
½ cup drained crushed pineapple

Dissolve gelatin in hot water; add pineapple juice. Chill until the gelatin begins to set, then fold in the remaining ingredients. Pour into a 1½-quart oven-proof glass dish, rectangular in shape, and chill until firm. Cut into 6 squares. Serve each square on a lettuce leaf with additional mayonnaise. Serves 6.

COLD BLUEBERRY SOUP

2½ cups blueberries
¼ cup sugar
1 tablespoon lemon juice

1 tablespoon flour
1 tablespoon cold water
½ cup heavy cream

Combine the blueberries, sugar, and lemon juice in a saucepan and bring to a boil. Mix the flour and water into a smooth paste and add to the blueberries. Cook over low heat for 5 minutes. Puree the cooked blueberries in the electric blender, then strain through a sieve. Chill. (The blueberry puree may be kept in the refrigerator for several days.) Add the heavy cream just before serving. Serve in white lotus bowls. Serves 4.

CHANTERELLES

Our first summer in Vermont was one of continual discovery. We alternated between sightseeing in the area and exploring our own acreage. One day we would drive along the winding roads beside green mountains, browsing in antique and craft shops and dining at old inns; the next day we would stay at home, on our own small mountain, exploring the nooks and crannies of the woods, the high meadow, the waterfall and stream, and the red-clap-boarded farmhouse.

My favorite place of discovery is the sunny mountain meadow with its wildflowers, huge gray granite boulders, and wild berries. I soon came to feel that no day could end until I climbed to its highest point to gather berries or flowers or just to look out over the trees at the mountains and the sky.

The boys are irresistibly drawn to the stream and the Great Falls. They explore them day after day, stepping upstream from one slippery wet stone to another until they find the place, over a thousand feet

above the foot of the falls, where white water begins its frothy tumble downward.

But the old fern-filled hardwood-spruce woods is where that summer's most exciting—and transitory—discovery was made. One morning, after a hard rain had fallen during the night, hundreds and hundreds of mushrooms sprang up on the forest floor. We were surprised by their sudden appearance and amazed by the number of them. We went around the woods excitedly, like children on an Easter egg hunt, picking up one here and finding one there, until we had a basketful of exotic fungi that we wanted to identify.

We took the mushrooms back to the farmhouse and spread them out on the porch floor—some of them looked much too ominous to take into the house. But we were in total confusion, turning the pages of our mushroom field guide, until our neighbor, Adele, an amateur mycologist, came up the hill to help us with the identification.

"Oh, it's too bad there weren't more like this one," Adele said,

164 THE WILD FLAVOR

picking out a bright yellowish-orange trumpet-shaped mushroom from our collection. "It's a chanterelle, and they're absolutely marvelous!"

There were more of the chanterelles up in the woods, and Bob remembered where. So we left our collection lying on the porch floor, still unclassified, and went back to the woods with Adele to fill our basket with the marvelous chanterelles.

The chanterelles we found on that wet July day were growing in a scattered group under the evergreens. Adele pointed out to us the characteristics that make *Cantharellus cibarius* a readily recognizable mushroom for beginners to collect. Their caps and stems are an egg-yolk yellow that is easily seen against the pine-needle background from which they spring in our Vermont woods. Chanterelles are vase- or trumpet-shaped, with the cap not separable from the stem. Their size varies from small, with a cap measuring about two inches across, to quite large, with a cap measuring as much as five inches across. The cap of the chanterelle has ruffled edges; its top surface is smooth, sloping inward toward a depression in the center. The shallow, blunt-edged gills under the cap are connected by forked, interlacing veins. The gills are decurrent, running down the flared part of the trumpet-shape toward the stem but not all the way to the bottom of it. The stem may be three to five inches in length.

Chanterelles have a pleasing, apricot-like fragrance that is easily detected. Their flesh is firm and requires slow cooking. While our mushrooms simmered slowly in butter and their own juices on Adele's stove, we stood around the kitchen, sipping glasses of white wine and keeping an eye on the skillet. There was a tantalizing, nutty odor rising from the pan that compelled us to stay near.

Presently Adele lifted the lid from the skillet and poured the contents of her wineglass into the pan with the mushrooms.

"This wine is so good!" she said. "Let's try it on our chanterelles."

When the mushrooms were ready to sample, we gathered around the stove and speared them onto the tines of our forks, savoring every bite straight from the skillet. Now we look for the chanterelles every summer and fall when a flush of mushrooms appears in our woods. Every time we find them, something of the excitement of our first summer of discovery in Vermont comes back to us, as miraculously as the rain brings back the chanterelles.

ADELE'S CHANTERELLES

2 cups chanterelles	½ teaspoon salt
4 tablespoons butter	¼ cup dry white wine

Clean the wild chanterelles and cut both the stems and caps into pieces. In a pan, sauté the chanterelles in the butter for 5 minutes. Sprinkle lightly with salt, then pour the wine in the pan. Cover and let simmer for about 10 minutes more, or until tender. Serve at once. Serves 4.

CHICKEN CHANTERELLE

2 broiler chickens, halved
Juice of 2 lemons
1 teaspoon salt
½ teaspoon pepper
¾ cup butter
2 cloves garlic, minced

1 cup chanterelles
2 teaspoons marjoram
½ teaspoon salt
⅛ teaspoon nutmeg
Brandy

Rub both sides of the halved chickens with lemon juice, salt, and pepper. In a small saucepan, melt ½ cup of the butter, adding the garlic to it. Place the chicken skin side down on the broiler rack and brush with the garlic butter. Then broil in a preheated broiler for about 15 minutes, basting often with the garlic butter. Turn the chicken and broil for another 15 minutes, basting often.

While the chicken is broiling, melt the remaining ¼ cup of butter and add the chanterelles and seasonings to it. Cook slowly for 5 minutes. When the chicken halves are golden brown, remove the rack and place them in the broiler pan. Baste with the pan juices, then pour the mushroom mixture over the chicken and bake in a slow oven (300° F) for 20 minutes, or until the chicken is very tender. Arrange on a warm platter and pour warmed brandy over the chicken; ignite and let the flame burn out before serving. Serves 4.

CHANTERELLES AND CHICKEN LIVERS

1 pound chicken livers
8 to 10 fresh sage leaves
3 tablespoons flour
¼ cup butter

1 cup chanterelles, sliced thin
4 tablespoons white wine
1 cup cream
4 slices buttered toast

Rinse the chicken livers in cold water and drain. Place them on a pie tin. Snip the fresh sage leaves into tiny pieces with scissors and sprinkle over the chicken livers. Then sprinkle the flour over the livers and toss until coated. Melt the butter in an electric skillet. When the butter is sizzling hot, add the chicken livers. Sauté until the livers are browned and crisp. Add the chanterelles, stir, and continue cooking gently until the chanterelles are tender, about 10 minutes more. Lower the heat to simmer, add the wine and cream, cover and heat until the cream is hot, stirring as needed. Serve on buttered toast. Garnish with parsley. Serves 4.

Chanterelles and Eggplant Casserole

1 large eggplant	chopped fine
2 cups seasoned croutons	1 cup tomato puree
3 eggs, beaten	1 cup water
¾ cup safflower oil	½ teaspoon pepper
1 cup chanterelles, cut into pieces	1 teaspoon salt
1 tablespoon flour	½ teaspoon oregano
3 tablespoons butter	1 teaspoon sugar
3 scallions, chopped	1 cup shredded mozzarella cheese
2 tablespoons green pepper,	

Pare the eggplant and cut into ¼-inch slices. Crush seasoned croutons to make 2 cups of fine crumbs. Dip each slice of eggplant first in the eggs, then in the crumbs. Sauté in safflower oil until crisp and browned. Set aside on absorbent paper to drain.

Dredge the chanterelle pieces in the flour and sauté in a skillet in 1 tablespoon of the butter. Sprinkle with salt and pepper. Cook gently for about 5 minutes and remove from the skillet.

Add 1 tablespoon of butter to the skillet and sauté in it the chopped scallions and green pepper. Add tomato puree, water, pepper, salt, oregano, and sugar. Simmer gently for 5 minutes. Add the chanterelles.

In the bottom of a rectangular baking dish, 1½-quart size, arrange a layer of the sautéed eggplant slices. Spread one half of the tomato sauce over the eggplant, then sprinkle ½ cup of shredded mozzarella cheese over the sauce. Arrange another layer of eggplant slices in the pan, cover them with the remainder of the sauce, and sprinkle the remaining mozzarella cheese on top of the dish. Bake for 20 minutes in a moderate oven (350° F). Serves 4 to 6.

BEEF PAPRIKASH WITH CHANTERELLES

5 tablespoons butter
4 scallions, chopped fine
2 cloves garlic, minced
2 pounds beef tenderloin,
  cut into 1-inch cubes
1 teaspoon salt
½ teaspoon pepper

1 cup chanterelles, cut
  into pieces
2 tablespoons flour
1 tablespoon Hungarian paprika
2 cups beef stock or bouillon
½ cup dry white wine
1½ cups sour cream

Melt 2 tablespoons of the butter in an electric skillet set on low heat, about 260°F. Add scallions, garlic, and beef tenderloin. Sauté very gently for about 10 minutes, or until the meat is tender and just cooked through, adding the salt and pepper while the meat is cooking. Remove the meat and juices from the pan. Add 2 tablespoons of butter to the pan and sauté the chanterelles for 5 to 10 minutes. Remove from the pan.

Add the remaining butter to the pan, stir in the flour and paprika. Blend well and cook for a minute or two while stirring. Add the beef stock, stirring well. Reduce the heat and cook slowly, stirring as required, until the paprika sauce thickens (about 15 minutes). Add ½ cup of a good, dry white wine. Stir in the meat and the chanterelles and heat gently—do not boil. Then stir in the sour cream.

Serve hot over buttered noodles (cook them in stock or bouillon) and garnish with 1 tablespoon of dried dill or with lots of fresh dill, minced fine. Serves 4 to 6.

NOTE: The meat and sour cream mixture may be cooled after cooking and stored in the refrigerator overnight. The next day, warm it again in the electric skillet or in a shallow casserole in a moderate oven (350° F) until it is just hot. It must not boil. The flavor of this dish is better when left for a day and reheated.

If any meat other than beef tenderloin is used, it must be sautéed, then covered and simmered until tender.

PART III

Autumn's Wild Harvest

PAWPAWS

In springtime, when we roam our favorite nearby woods in search of wildflowers and fungi, the main focus of our attention is underfoot. The shy wildlings we seek then are on the woodland floor, pushing through the camouflage of old fallen leaves, unfurling at the base of rotting tree stumps, and springing up in mossy crannies at the edge of a tiny brook that runs through the middle of the woods.

We must look carefully and with the greatest concentration, for spring's best surprises are well hidden. We hurry along with heads bent and eyes searching the damp humus for the elusive morel, the rare showy orchis, the exquisite wild iris, the pink sprouts of pokeweed. The welcoming woods are open and sunlit. Pin-oak leaves are not one whit larger than the proverbial mouse's ear, and our pathway is free of the hindering underbrush that comes later. We make our way quickly and easily from prize to prize, filling our baskets with ferns and wildflowers and mushrooms and the crisp green stalks of spring. We are in step with the season.

By and by, the daily miracles lessen. The wild blue phlox fades, trees and poison ivy leaf out fully, and mosquitoes invade the damp woods. We have used up the joys of our springtime woods, and we abandon them, for a time, for the pleasures of open meadows.

We do not return again until September. Now even the borders of the woods look strange and changed. Our old path is overhung with honeysuckle, and we must part the vines to find our way into the shadowy woods. At once we are in a jungle of poison ivy and stinging nettle. The mosquitoes are vicious, and prickly catbriers tear at our clothes. Where we walked so freely only a few months before, we must now fight our way through underbrush. I go ahead, carefully tromping down a pathway, but Bobby, charging on impatiently, is immediately and painfully caught in a tangle of briers.

"Mother!" he hollers. "Get me out!"

It is not easy to stay cheerful. It is hot and humid in the woods; the temperature is an unseasonable 90 degrees. We are dressed too warmly in long pants, socks, and long sleeves, which we had hoped would protect us from scratches and stings.

In spite of discomforts, even small dangers, we wade on into the woods. As a precaution, we wear bright yellow shirts and make lots of noise to announce our presence should there be squirrel hunters lurking under the hickory trees.

Instead of rifles, we carry shallow baskets. Our hunt for wild bounty is a gentler pursuit which we enjoy more than questing after the wild flavor with guns. In the dense overgrown woods of late summer, we will hunt the odd, pendulous, green fruits of the native pawpaw tree, lush custardy prizes which are well worth enduring stings and scratches to obtain.

This time we do not look downward at the woodland floor to make our discoveries as in springtime, but overhead for the glossy lanceolate leaves of the curious pawpaw tree. The pawpaw, *Asimina triloba*, is an improbable tree to be found in our southern Indiana woods. With its luxuriance of large, drooping, spear-shaped green leaves and strange tropical fruits, the pawpaw is far too exotic for Indiana. Somehow, long ago, the hardy pawpaw strayed northward from the tropics, leaving behind all its relatives of the custard-apple family, Annonaceae, and established itself in the rich river bottoms and uplands of the Ohio and Mississippi river valleys.

Here on the banks of the Ohio River, we are in pawpaw country. Pawpaw thickets are not uncommon along winding creekbanks and in river bottomlands; occasionally, larger well-shaped trees are found growing singly in open places. Although the pawpaw is usually a small tree or large bush, under twenty feet in height, old-timers of this area still recollect the granddaddy of all pawpaw trees hereabouts; it was found fifty years ago by the U.S. Department of Agriculture in Boonville, Indiana, only a few miles from here. This celebrated pawpaw tree was twenty-five feet high and measured five feet around its trunk. Even though it sometimes grows to much grander proportions in the retelling of the tale, the actual record is testimony enough to the superiority of pawpaw trees in this region.

Pawpaw trees grow profusely throughout our neighbor's woods where Bobby and I brave the small dangers to reach the delicious "custard apples" of which we are so fond. The entire southern margin of the twenty wooded acres has an undergrowth of limber, large-leafed pawpaw shoots and bushes, as well as good-sized trees, growing under the shade of the taller trees of the woods. Our bountiful springtime woods become a veritable pawpaw patch in autumn. Bushels and bushels of delicious pawpaws wait in its depths, ours for the picking.

Though the woods are well hunted for mushrooms during squirrel season, and still later for hickory nuts, black walnuts, and wild grapes, we have yet to meet a fellow forager in the harvest of pawpaws. Pawpaws are a neglected delicacy of the woods, foolishly ignored by most *Homo sapiens* but feasted upon by wiser creatures of nature. Now Bobby and I come hungrily to the wild board with them—the birds, opossums, foxes, and raccoons—to take our share of untamed fruits.

We head on into the woods, picking our way through the briers and poison ivy, then stopping to look overhead for the unmistakable spear-shaped leaves. We have gone only a few hundred feet when I see the distinctive leafing on a small plant in the underbrush which blocks our path. It is only knee-high, with a few large leaves at the top of a single stem, but it is certainly a pawpaw plant.

"Look, Bobby." I point at the young pawpaw sprout. "They're here somewhere."

We look up and around us, hoping, and yes! there are pawpaw plants on all sides. Some of the sprouts are only a few feet tall; others are young saplings, twice as tall as we are. We are in the middle of a pawpaw patch.

Then, both at the same time, we see the fat silhouette of one of the funny green fruits hanging under the drooping leaves of a small pawpaw tree.

"I see one!" Bobby shouts.

All of the elements of a wild-foods hunt crystallize in Bobby's excited shout and echo through the woods. His sudden, youthful exuberance distracts me from my own private reverie of the hunt and now I begin to enjoy, more than the hunt itself, my son's high spirits.

"I'll get it!" Bobby crashes toward the young tree where the green prize hangs high. Pesky briers and mean mosquitoes are forgotten now that the wild reward is in sight. He stretches for the pawpaw and finds it far beyond his reach, but the limber sapling bends down easily to yield its fruit to his hand.

Triumphant, Bobby holds the plucked fruit high above his head and sounds a gay tantara: "Ta! Ta!"

The pawpaw is shaped like an enormous green peanut which fits his palm. Its smooth skin is lightly speckled with brown.

"Is it ripe enough to eat?" he asks, bringing the pawpaw to me.

I press the pawpaw gently with my thumb in the middle of the indented side. It is still quite firm but beginning to soften. When it has ripened to perfection, the inside will become very soft and the fragile skin will yield to the slightest pressure.

"No," I answer. "It's too green."

I can see his disappointment. After all, the only joy tantamount to that joy of finding the rare wild fruit is feasting on it, then and there.

"Don't worry," I say. "Put the first one in your basket and we'll soon have more ripe ones than we can eat."

The first-found fruit is always special by virtue of being first, but for us it takes on a pseudomagical aura. By tradition, it goes into Bobby's basket. When we fail to find more of the wild bounty quickly, or when our luck runs out for a time, we take the first-found talisman out of Bobby's basket. With great ceremony, we look at it and hold it to our noses. This refreshes the image in our minds of the object we are trying to see in its own protective habitat and gives us the scent of the quarry. It was Bobby's uncle, who is wise in woodlore but given to the fabrication of convenient folktales, who first advised us to do this. We go along with his woods magic tongue-in-cheek, but we cannot deny that chance favors the alerted senses.

But we do not need magic or heightened sensitivity to find pawpaws in the woods on this day. There is no scarcity in our hunting grounds. Some of the young sprouts bear a single fruit and others have a cluster of several fruits on a single stem. The older trees, which are scattered about in the thickets, bear more and larger pawpaws.

We put all the pawpaws we gather into Bobby's basket and he delights in the growing weight of our plenteous hoard. Then, on a mature tree, among the crop of firm, green-colored, underripe paw-paws, we find the first large, fully ripe one. Its green skin is tinged with yellow and speckled heavily with brown. It is squashy-soft to touch and rich with the fragrance of ripeness.

"Let's eat it," Bob says.

The flavor of a choice pawpaw ripened to perfection rivals that of any fruit. It is luscious and tropical, like a sweet, fruity, tree-grown custard. It is a surprising, full-bodied, exotic flavoring, completely unlike the light, juicy, tart-sweet tastes of most fruits of the North Temperate Zone.

The ultimate in enjoyment of the pawpaw is to devour it in the woods an instant after it is plucked from the bough, squeezing the lush, custard-yellow pulp from its skin into one's mouth. For pawpaw buffs, this is the feast of the year.

Bobby breaks the perfect ripe pawpaw into halves and gives a pulpy half to me. We stand facing each other in the pawpaw patch, our enjoyment audible and unrestrained by decorum. Who minds sticky fingers and a juicy dribble on the chin when the reward is so delectable? Let the seeds fall where they may!

The honest pleasure of a young boy relishing a ripe pawpaw in the woods is marvelous to see—and to remember. I like having my son with me, enlivening the hunt with his enthusiasms. He shows me how to enjoy the simplest pleasures more fully.

The delicious pawpaw flesh is packed with shiny brown seeds, shaped like large flattened beans, and we make much ado over counting the seeds as we spit them out. There are eighteen pretty seeds in the first pawpaw. We are challenged! We must find, among all the pawpaws, the superpawpaw which has a greater number of seeds than eighteen.

Nearly everyone who has heard its name delights in the pawpaw although only a comparative few are aficionados of the flavor or realize how exotic it is. Rather, the pawpaw is regarded as an amusing back-woods folk fruit, relished mainly by hungry barefoot boys and 'pos-sums. And why not? The idea of the pawpaw as the country bumpkin of our native fruits comes to us, ready-made, through song and poem. Who could resist thinking of the pawpaw in the Hoosier dialect after James Whitcomb Riley's verse recalling his boyhood in "Up and Down Old Brandywine"?

> And sich pop-paws!—Lumps o' raw
> Gold and green,—jes' oozy th'ough

> With ripe yaller—like you've saw
> Custard-pie with no crust to.

And many remember, too, with warm feelings, the old standard campfire song of scouting days:

> Where, oh, where, oh, where is Susie? . . .
> Way down yonder in the pawpaw patch.
> Come on boys, and let's go find her . . .
> Way down yonder in the pawpaw patch.
> Pickin' up pawpaws, puttin' 'em in a basket . . .
> Way down yonder in the pawpaw patch.

The pawpaw patches in several states have been honored in the naming of towns, creeks, and lakes. Michigan, West Virginia, and Illinois have towns named "Paw Paw," and Hoosier fishermen know where to find Pawpaw Creek. Even the sound of the name is amusing, with its two short, popping syllables—*paw paw* (po po)—and Bobby and I laugh over it as we go through the woods singing gaily, "Where, oh, where, oh, where is Susie?" But poke fun at the misunderstood pawpaw? Never!

Besides having a taste for the singular flavor of the sweet "lumps o' raw gold," eaten in the woods *à la* barefoot boy, I have discovered the marvelous culinary possibilities of the pawpaw.

Some years ago, one enticing sentence about pawpaws in Fernald and Kinsey's book *Edible Wild Plants of Eastern North America* sent me rummaging through my cookbooks. "It is eaten either raw or baked or as a filling for pies, or is combined with eggs, cornstarch and gelatine for a dessert," said Drs. Fernald and Kinsey. But where were the recipes? All of my cookbooks ignored the native pawpaw as food.

So I began to experiment, first by combining pawpaw pulp with the basic ingredients of a cooked cream custard, the food that raw pawpaws most resemble. The result was delicious, a fortunate blending of rich complementary flavors. It was truly our beloved Hoosier poet's "custard pie with no crust to." Inspired, I added a flaky pie crust and a fluffy meringue to enhance the pawpaw flavor even more. At dinner, when I served it, my family was startled by the idea of pawpaw pie (even Bobby!), but they ate it and loved it.

Encouraged by success, a pawpaw chiffon pie was next (excellent!), then, less sure of the prospects, a freezerful of pawpaw custard ice cream.

"I don't know, Bobby," I said, hesitating to add the cupful of pawpaw pulp to the canister of rich, expensive cream and fresh-from-the-nest eggs. "We might spoil the whole batch."

"Oh, go ahead," Bobby urged, eager to get on to the crushed ice and the coarse salt and the tantalizing drone of the ice-cream freezer.

"Let's try a little, mixed together, first." I was cautious, used to thinking of ruined food in terms of dollars and cents and wasted effort. After all, if pawpaws worked so well in cookery, as it appeared, why were they ignored by chroniclers of culinary art?

I offered the tasting-spoon to Bobby. He tasted, then smacked his lips.

"Put it all in!" he exclaimed. "It *has* to be good!"

Twenty minutes later, we pulled out the dasher and lauded ourselves, with every frosty spoonful, for our successful creation of pawpaw ice cream.

Our first rule of thumb was: *Pawpaws work beautifully in desserts with a custard base.* Now our repertoire included three delicious ways to enjoy pawpaws after that memorable feast in the pawpaw patch, but still our appetites were questing.

"Make something else," Bobby urged.

Bobby and I pondered the few paragraphs of description of pawpaws which we had at hand, but there were no more easy clues, like

those of Drs. Fernald and Kinsey, to the culinary possibilities of pawpaws. It was the plethora of local "banana" names for the pawpaw—False Banana, Backyard Banana, Poor Man's Banana, Prairie Banana, as well as Indiana Banana, Kentucky Banana, Michigan Banana, Missouri Banana, Kansas Banana, and so on—that led us to the *pièce de résistance,* pawpaw cake, and our second rule of thumb: *Pawpaws work beautifully in banana recipes.* My favorite banana recipes needed only slight adjustments to change them into the delectable pawpaw cake and pawpaw bread recipes that I share here with you.

If it were not for the "banana" names of pawpaws, which I think are actually misnomers when applied to the raw fruits, I might not have come upon my discoveries so easily. Although some pawpaw observers compare the flavor of raw pawpaws to the flavor of raw bananas, I fail to detect any similarity in taste beyond the likeness that both taste "tropical." This tropicalness of flavor may account, in part, for the local "banana" names. After all, which tropical fruit would a barefoot boy of bygone days be most likely to think of if he found an exotic green fruit with a strange, faraway flavor growing along the banks of the Brandywine or Wabash or Ohio rivers? Would he relate a fruit so foreign in flavor to red haws or wild goose-plums or purple fox-grapes? More likely, he would compare it with the most common exotic fruit from a faraway place that he knew, a fruit which found its way to the country stores of the hinterlands. There the proprietor hung the entire cluster of bananas at the end of a chain suspended from the ceiling, making a boy's mouth water with longing.

That pawpaws resemble stubby bananas in appearance, as other observers note, requires an even greater stretch of the imagination. I find their shape far more suggestive of smooth green potatoes or gigantic green peanuts. But in cookery, bananas and pawpaws are very much alike indeed. They are almost interchangeable in function, it seems, although each gives its own inimitable flavor to the recipe.

Though pioneer wives cooked everything from buffalo tongue to squash blossoms, our ingenious countrywomen left no recipes for the homely pawpaw. But, earlier, Indians and explorers made greater use of them, at least as a raw fruit eaten out of hand on the wilderness trails.

Sergeant John Ordway, in his journal of the Lewis and Clark overland expedition to the Pacific Coast, following the Missouri and Columbia Rivers, mentioned several times the "pappaws" which the exploring party gathered for food near the end of the homeward journey in September 1806. Ordway noted locations in the river bottomlands of southern Nebraska and in Missouri where the explorers "Camped at Sunset on N. Side an emence Site of pappaws" and "gathered Some pappaws which our party are fond of and are a kind of fruit which abound in these bottoms and are now ripe." Earlier, Spanish and French explorers also found pawpaws in the Mississippi valley, where they grew abundantly. Hernando De Soto and his conquistadors first discovered pawpaws, as well as the great "Misisipi" of the Ojibwa Indians, in 1541. It was from a now-forgotten Indian name for pawpaws that French explorers of the "Father of Waters" later derived the name *asiminier*. Botanists subsequently Latinized *asiminier* to *Asimina triloba*, the technical name for the native American pawpaw. The term *triloba* refers to the petals of the pawpaw blossom, which grow in two whorls of three. The veined petals of the lower whorl are larger and flatter than those of the upper whorl, which forms a cup around the center of the flower. The pawpaw blossom is large and exquisite, as exotic looking as the fruit of the tree. It is pale green when blossoming but turns maroon-colored when full blown. Its fragrance is not typically flowerlike but seems more reminiscent of a wine's bouquet.

To be most accurate in describing the pawpaw scent, flavor, and appearance, whether it be blossom or fruit, one really must say that a pawpaw is only like a pawpaw. And to be most truthful, I must admit that not everyone shares Bobby's and my great enthusiasm for the raw fruit. The pawpaw stirs controversy even among wild-foods enthusiasts. Apparently there is no middle ground in pawpaw enthusiasm; everyone seems either to love it or hate it.

"It's a taste you have to grow up on, to appreciate," says a since-childhood enthusiast. "The older I get, the more I crave them."

"Can't learn to like pawpaws," insists an outdoorsman. "Makes no difference if you eat a bushel of pawpaws or one. You know if you like them, first taste you get."

"Only fit for pigs," comments a farmer.

"A turned-on flavor!" exclaims my long-haired friend who hears a different drummer.

But the remark my father made last autumn pinpoints one valid reason for the ambivalence of feeling about pawpaws.

"I used to find the finest 'pap-paws' on Kamman's Bluff," he said. "They were big yellow ones. I don't want any of those white ones. No, sir!"

As with all wild fruits, there is a wide variation in all qualities from one pawpaw tree to another. The size of the fruits, the number of seeds, and the time of ripening varies. The color of the fruit pulp ranges from white to custard-yellow to a delicate orange. By the same token, the pendulum of pawpaw flavor swings from insipid to delicious. To me, this is one of the joys of the wild flavor; in its infinite variety lies much of its charm. But for others, an encounter with one of the poorly flavored varieties might be enough to set one against pawpaws for life.

Generally, the white-fleshed varieties are less delicious than the yellow-fleshed pawpaws, and even a delicious yellow pawpaw must be ripened perfectly to develop its best flavor. Most pawpaw prejudices would disappear, I think, if more attention were paid to the variety of pawpaw gathered and the degree of its ripeness when eaten. When the pawpaw is choice and well-ripened and of the yellow-fleshed variety, there is nothing objectionable about the flavor. There is a faint, sweet aftertaste which lingers after eating raw pawpaws; it is noticeable, but not at all unpleasant.

The flavor of pawpaws in cookery, that untasted delight still awaiting most pawpaw fanciers, is above controversy. It is subtle, but still surprising; it is unique, but thoroughly delicious. The culinary flavor of pawpaws is so completely acceptable that even the most conventional palates will be captivated by it.

Most pawpaws are harvested underripe from the tree. Dead-ripe pawpaws fall to the ground and perish in a short time. The gentlest shaking dislodges pawpaws that are almost ready to fall, and these are prime for eating at once. More vigorous shaking brings down the heavy underripe fruits, which may be ripened for later use.

To ripen the pawpaws after picking, put them in the shade on a table outside the house, or on a porch, and cover them with cheesecloth. When the green skin becomes speckled with brown, with an undertint of yellow, and dents under the pressure of the finger, indicating a squashy-soft interior, the pawpaw is ripened perfectly for eating raw. A ripe pawpaw breaks apart easily, and the skin of an underripe pawpaw is tough.

The skin of the pawpaw is not edible. It has an astringent quality, more pronounced in the underripe pawpaw, which is unpleasant to taste. If the pulp is squeezed out of the skin, the bitter layer remains in the skin. If the pawpaw is peeled, one must be certain to peel away the thin greenish layer between the skin and the sweet yellow interior.

Another way to ripen pawpaws is to put them into a basket filled with small grain. Wheat is better for mellowing fruits, I'm told, but we find Blacky's oats bin in the barn a perfect place for ripening our pawpaws. Pawpaws buried in grain do not ripen as quickly as those left in the open air and consequently keep longer. But I think the main advantage to covering pawpaws with grain is that fruit flies do not find them.

"I never saw anything draw 'sour flies' like pawpaws," Maude complained when Bobby and I carried our baskets filled with wild bounty into the kitchen. "You can't keep those pawpaws in my kitchen," she warned.

Bobby and I quickly separated the pawpaws into two portions, ripe and underripe. Bobby took part of the underripe fruits out to the barn to bury them in the oats bin, and I stored another portion of underripe pawpaws in the refrigerator where they will keep several weeks without ripening further. Then I prepared the ripe pawpaws for use in cookery, squeezing the sweet, golden pulp out of the skins into the food mill and pureeing it. The large seeds of the pawpaw make this a rather bumpy procedure, but it is easier than rubbing the pulp through a sieve or colander. An ascorbic acid mixture, such as Fruit Fresh, must be added to the pawpaw puree immediately to prevent darkening.

I save out a portion of pawpaw puree to use later in the day for making a loaf of pawpaw bread, and I package the rest in plastic cartons for the freezer. Unlike bananas, pawpaw pulp freezes beautifully. Whole pawpaws cannot be frozen.

Although I would never forego the September tramp through my springtime woods in search of pawpaws, I hopefully throw the pawpaw seeds out by the back fence in a spot where I want my own pawpaw patch to sprout next spring. Once before, under the worst conditions, we transplanted here a dozen pawpaw saplings from the woods, but we gave them too little protection from the sun during the first dry summer and they did not survive to bear fruit. But before they withered we saw the lovely blooms which we always miss during their brief season in the woods, and early in June we saw in our garden several exquisite zebra swallowtail butterflies whose larva feed on pawpaw leaves. Aside from the fruits, could there be better rewards from pawpaw trees in the backyard than blossoms and butterflies?

The Talbott Nursery in Linton, Indiana, which offers pawpaw trees for sale, suggests that pawpaw seeds be planted in a seed bed at a depth of two inches and that the small sprouts, which come up the first year, be shaded under burlap throughout the second summer. After four to five years, the young pawpaw trees will bear fruit.

Some strains of pawpaws in our area bear fruits which ripen as early as late August while other varieties begin to ripen in September and hang on until after the first light frost. Thus we have a season for harvesting pawpaws which extends over two months, from the time we gather the first basketful along Peggy Winterman's property line in August until the last of the preposterous pawpaws in Grimm Woods are touched by October's frost.

Although pawpaws do not need frost to sweeten them, as some believe, there is a resurgence of flavor in the frost-nipped fruits, like the surge of freshness in the air of the new season. It is then that Bobby and I go back to the woods for one more foray into the pawpaw patch before the last heavy fruits fall to the ground. We are reluctant to see the end of plenty in the woods, but thanks to our industry during September's heat, we have our surplus of pawpaws cached in the freezer.

Later, whenever we hanker for the odd, tropical flavor of the sweet, custardy "lumps o' raw gold . . . jes' oozy th'ough," I will bake a spectacular pawpaw cake to surprise my family (especially Bobby) and to remind us of our peaceful pursuits in the pawpaw patch.

PAWPAW CAKE

1¾ cups flour
1 teaspoon baking soda
1 teaspoon baking powder
½ teaspoon salt
½ cup milk
1 tablespoon lemon juice
½ cup shortening

1½ cups sugar
2 eggs
1 teaspoon vanilla
½ cup pawpaw puree
½ cup chopped pecans or
　hickory nuts
3 egg whites, beaten stiff

Sift first four dry ingredients together. Combine milk and lemon juice and set aside to sour. Cream shortening, add sugar gradually, and beat until fluffy. Beat in eggs, one at a time. Add vanilla. Then add dry ingredients alternately with pawpaw puree and soured milk. Fold in the beaten egg whites and the chopped nuts. Pour into two lightly greased and floured 9-inch layer-cake pans. Bake in a moderate oven (350° F) 35 to 40 minutes. Frost with Lemon Butter Frosting (see page 161). Serves 12.

Pawpaw Puree

Use ripe pawpaws only. Squeeze pulp out of skins and puree in a food mill. Sprinkle with lemon juice (to prevent darkening) in the proportion of 1 teaspoon of lemon juice per cup of puree.

Pawpaw Bread

1 cup pawpaw puree (see above)	1¾ cups flour
⅓ cup shortening	2 teaspoons baking powder
⅔ cup sugar	¼ teaspoon baking soda
2 eggs	¾ teaspoon salt

Cream shortening, add sugar gradually, and beat until fluffy. Add eggs, one at a time, beating well after each addition. Beat in pawpaw puree. Sift together remaining dry ingredients and add in four portions, beating smooth each time. Pour batter into a greased, floured loaf pan (8-by-4-by-3-inches) and bake in a moderate oven (350° F) for about 50 minutes, or until a toothpick inserted into the loaf comes out clean. Cool on rack before slicing. Serve slices buttered or with cream cheese. Makes 1 loaf.

NOTE: To vary the above recipe, add 1 teaspoon pumpkin-pie spice, ½ cup chopped pecans, and ½ cup candied orange peel.

Pawpaw Cream Pie

¾ cup sugar	1 cup pawpaw puree
⅓ cup flour or ¼ cup cornstarch	3 egg whites
3 egg yolks, slightly beaten	3 tablespoons sugar
1 cup milk	Pinch of salt
1 cup light cream	1 baked 9-inch pastry shell (page 44)

Combine sugar and flour or cornstarch. Add the beaten egg yolks, milk, and cream. Mix well and add pawpaw pulp. Cook and stir constantly over low heat until thickened. Cool.

Make a meringue by beating the egg whites stiff with 3 tablespoons sugar and a pinch of salt. Pour custard into a baked pastry shell and cover with the meringue. Bake in a moderate oven (350° F) for 12 minutes or until meringue is browned. Serves 6 to 8.

PAWPAW CHIFFON PIE

1½ tablespoons gelatin
¼ cup cold water
½ cup sugar, brown or white
½ teaspoon salt
3 egg yolks, beaten
⅓ cup milk

1 cup pawpaw puree
3 egg whites
¼ cup white sugar
1 cup heavy cream, whipped
Baked 9-inch pastry shell
 (page 44)

Soften gelatin in cold water. Combine the ½ cup sugar with the salt, egg yolks, and milk in the top of a double boiler. Cook over boiling water, stirring constantly, until mixture coats a spoon. Remove from heat and stir in softened gelatin and pawpaw puree. Chill until a spoonful holds its shape (about half an hour). Beat the egg whites stiff with ¼ cup of white sugar. Fold half of the whipped cream into the filling. Pour into the baked pastry shell. Spread remaining whipped cream on top of pie. Serves 6 to 8.

NOTE: Graham cracker crust may be used instead of the pastry shell.

PAWPAW ICE CREAM

1 quart cold milk
6 eggs
½ teaspoon salt
1½ cups sugar
1 cup pawpaw puree, or more

 to taste
Juice of 1 lemon
1 quart heavy cream
2 tablespoons vanilla

Scald 3 cups of the milk in the top of double boiler. Beat eggs well; add salt, sugar, and the remaining cup of milk. Stir egg mixture slowly into the hot milk and cook over a small amount of simmering hot water, stirring constantly, until mixture just coats a clean metal spoon. To prevent curdling, do not have the water boiling vigorously, and take care not to overcook. Stop cooking as soon as the custard coats the spoon and remove from heat at once. Cool pan of custard in another pan containing cold water, then chill thoroughly in refrigerator.

Combine pawpaw puree with the lemon juice and add to the chilled custard along with the cream and vanilla. Pour mixture into a chilled 1-gallon ice-cream freezer canister and fit dasher into place. Freeze and ripen according to directions accompanying ice cream freezer, or see the directions for freezing Hazelnut-Chocolate Ice Cream, page 237. Makes about ⅔ of a gallon.

PAWPAW-PINEAPPLE SHERBET

1½ cups crushed pineapple ¾ cup confectioners' sugar
1½ cups pawpaw puree 2 egg whites
6 tablespoons lemon juice ¼ teaspoon salt
½ cup orange juice

Combine the fruits, juices, and sugar, and freeze in refrigerator trays until nearly firm. Beat egg whites and salt until stiff but not dry, and combine with the frozen fruit mixture. Beat sherbet until it is light and fluffy. Return to trays and freeze firm. Serves 6.

SPICED PAWPAW FRUIT CAKE

3½ cups flour 1⅓ cups shortening
4 teaspoons baking powder 1⅓ cups sugar
1 teaspoon salt 4 eggs
½ teaspoon baking soda 2 cups pawpaw puree
2 teaspoons cinnamon 1 cup raisins
2 teaspoons ginger 1½ cups chopped nuts
1 teaspoon nutmeg 3 cups candied fruits

Sift flour with baking powder, salt, baking soda, and spices. Cream shortening and gradually blend in sugar; beat until light and fluffy. Beat in eggs, one at a time. Add flour mixture alternately with pawpaw puree. Mix raisins, nuts, and fruit and stir into batter. Turn into 2 greased and floured 9-by-5-by-3-inch loaf pans. Bake in a slow oven (300° F) for about 2 hours. Keep a shallow pan of hot water underneath cake throughout baking time. Store cooled cakes in a tightly closed container. Makes about 5½ pounds of fruit cake.

WILD APPLES

A wild apple tree, its gnarled branches bowing low with red-brindled fruit, stands at the water's edge by a lakeside cabin on my brother's farm. The ground under the old tree is strewn with windfalls, and at night raccoons and rabbits come to rummage in the honeysuckle vines for the hardy fruit of the wild apple tree. The shy deer no longer feed there because our cabin encroaches upon their domain, forcing them back into the woods. But years ago my brothers and I used to stand, statue still, on the grassy slope back of Grandpa's barn, spyglass raised, watching the deer family browse in the branches of the wild apple tree.

The apple tree has been a cherished landmark on the hill for as long as I can remember. In springtime it bursts into bloom, swiftly, against the background of the greening hillside. Its dainty pink-tinged white blossoms send out a tart, innocent fragrance that draws us to it, as the bees are drawn. We hardly have time to feast our eyes and noses before the pale petals are scattered to the winds. Then, late in July,

green apples bend the boughs and we test them with the pressure of a thumb to determine how long it will be until their ripening. In August, before the orchard apples begin, the wild apples on the seedling tree blush with ripeness.

There have been many harvests from the apple tree on the hillside, and I remember the excursions to bring in the wild fruits. When Mother wanted more than a bucketful of apples, enough to can or to make into apple butter, Dad hitched the horses to a wagon and took bushel baskets and a ladder to the hill. He drove the wagon under the spreading tree so we could pick apples from the overhanging branches while we stood in the wagon bed. My brothers and I climbed to the top of the tree on the smaller limbs to pick the fruits my father could not reach.

Even though my father had a fine orchard with rows and rows of apple trees in it, my mother always gathered in the wild fruits from the tree on the hillside. The wild fruits had their own virtue, just as Dad's orchard fruits had theirs.

"They came in early," Dad told me when I asked him why they bothered with the wildlings when we had so many orchard apples. "They were good cooking apples and your mother liked them for apple butter."

Making apple butter in the old cast-iron kettle in the backyard was an all-day chore that came up once during the seasonal round of canning, pickling, and preserving that began with the ripening of strawberries and lasted until finally the apple butter, the pumpkin-chip preserves, and the mincemeat were sealed into jars. It was one of the pleasant farmhouse kitchen events that required the efforts of our whole family. First there was the outing to the hill to gather the wild apples. Then, while my brothers carried chunks of wood to the yard where the soot-blackened caldron stood on its own iron tripod over a bed of gray ashes, my father, the hired girl, my grandfather, and I—or anyone who could peel apples with any skill at all—helped Mother peel the russet heap of apples. In the meantime, my brothers scoured out the interior of the huge kettle and laid a fire under it. Then ten gallons of freshly pressed apple cider were poured into the caldron and the fire was lighted. When the cider boiled down to about half, the apples were stirred in, a few at a time so that the slow boiling never stopped, until about three pecks of peeled, cored, and quartered apples were bubbling and sputtering in the apple-butter kettle. All afternoon the apple butter cooked over a slow, even fire. It had to be stirred constantly with a long-handled hoelike wooden paddle, with holes in the end of it, so that the delectable mixture would not stick to the caldron and burn.

Stirring was a chore that fell to my brothers and me, with an adult wisely keeping a watchful eye, but there was a festive air to the apple-butter making that masked its tediousness. Taking turns at the apple-butter kettle—stirring, stirring, stirring—had the feeling of a game, and it was a change from the day-to-day routine. The fragrances rising from the steaming vat were utterly captivating—enough reason to keep one close by. First there was the warming odor of wood smoke, then the tangy, almost vinegary, scent of boiling cider mingled with the winy fragrance of the apples. Then, when the glistening brown mass began to thicken, Mother stirred in a ten-pound sackful of sugar and added the spices—cinnamon, nutmeg, cloves, allspice, and ginger—and the aroma floated deliciously on the air currents, hither and thither, enticing everyone within smelling range to return to the apple-butter kettle.

"Enough ginger!" Grandpa stated, tasting the russet blend.

"Needs to be a little sweeter," Dad was sure to say.

Late in the afternoon, when big bubbles plopped on the surface of the spicy dark butter, and my brothers were thinking once again about starting the inevitable evening chores, Mother would finally declare the apple butter "done."

"Let the fire die, Charles," she would say. "It's ready to be canned."

At suppertime, there were rows and rows of quart jars filled with reddish-brown apple butter, ready for the cellar, and a spicy dishful of the new apple butter on the table. Apple butter has never tasted better than that we made over the wood fire in an open kettle from the wild apples we gathered on the hillside.

The wild fruits have a lively tang and a concentrated appleness in their flavor that surpasses that of tame apples. Whereas the Red Delicious and Jonathans from Dad's orchard trees were large, mild, and unblemished, the fruits of the hillside tree are stouthearted and spirited, like their wildling parent. Over the years, the pruned, tended, sprayed nursery-stock of my father's orchard have fallen, one by one—uprooted by storms, broken by disease, felled for firewood; the doughty wild apple tree that grew from a chance seedling still stands strong on the hillside, showering fruit.

"That tree was good-sized when Laura and I married," Dad told me. "It must be fifty years old, at least. Someone threw apple seeds down and it came up, volunteer."

Nature propagates her apple orchards with the help of the blue jay, the deer, the rabbit, and the squirrel. But out of thousands of seeds that drop to the ground, only one seedling tree may spring up wild and withstand the adversities of weather to bear fruit. "Through what hardships it may attain to bear a sweet fruit," wrote Henry David Thoreau.

I asked Dad if he had pruned the wild apple tree or cared for it as he had tended his orchard trees.

"So far as I know, it never had a limb cut off," Dad said. "The wind took the deadwood out."

The same sharp north wind that prunes the wildling orchards gives the wild apple its very flavor. Wild apples should be eaten in the wind, with the sauce of November air, according to Henry David Thoreau, who wanted his thoughts, like wild apples, to be food for walkers:

> To appreciate the wild and sharp flavor of these October fruits, it is necessary that you be breathing the sharp October or November air. The out-door air and exercise which the walker gets give a different tone to his palate, and he craves a fruit which the sedentary would call harsh and crabbed. They must be eaten in the fields, when your system is all aglow with exercise, when the frosty weather nips your fingers, the wind rattles the bare boughs or rustles the few remaining leaves, and the jay is heard screaming around. What is sour in the house a bracing walk makes sweet.

We seldom take baskets and pails to go apple-picking on the hillside anymore because we would rather harvest the wild pippins by the pocketful. When we are out walking, we stop by a wildling tree and browse among the branches like the deer or rummage in the honeysuckle like the raccoon, and fill our pockets full. We eat the walker's "choicest fruit" on the tramp homeward with all the gusto of an outdoor appetite, with a hunger honed to meet the sharp tang of wild apples by the whetstone of wind. We eat the gnarly apples with an appetite that has something in it that is fierce and aboriginal, something that needs the comfort of wild apples to quiet beating wings of wildness.

The choicest fruits we find are in Vermont along the gray stone walls, by roadsides, at the edges of woods, along the streams. Here the rocky ground seems to offer them stronger footholds than the richer soil of our Indiana homeplace. Last October when my husband and I went to Vermont to take care of things at our farmhouse before winter, we took a back road from Cabot in search of panoramic views. It was early in the morning, after a hard frost, and there was a stillness over the countryside. Straight stems of smoke rose from the chimneys of houses along the lonely road, and no one was to be seen. Vacant summer houses had boarded windows. The feeling that autumn, too, was vacating her seasonal residence made us see and hear and smell as if this were our last chance. On a high hill above Molly's Pond, we stopped and spent a half hour in lovely isolation, looking down on the pond and at the trees aflame with color, storing up impressions to tide us over the winter. The grasses at the roadside and the leaves drifted in the ditches were touched with a delicate, silvery hoarfrost. And at the roadside were two wild apple trees, one with knobby yellow-specked apples and one with ruddy-cheeked apples. We went to the fence and filled our hands and our pockets with the mellow fruit. The apples fairly sparkled in the dark green leaves, all wet and glossy, with the frozen dew on them melting before our eyes in the warming morning sun. They were crisp with cold and when we bit into them they snapped and the frost in them hurt our teeth. But after a moment a pleasant sourness flooded our palates and their flavor was fresh and spicy and unforgettable. Surely we knew wild apples at their perfection that morning when we breakfasted on them by the roadside.

We carried some of the small gamy fruits back to the red farmhouse to eat later. That night, when we sat reading by the fire, I reached into the wooden bowl for one of the apples to eat. It had a pleasing taste, but already it had lost the snap and crispness I relished outdoors with the north wind blowing in my face. It was juicy but I missed the nip of frost in its nectar. It was tangy and spicy, but somehow its flavor was tamed, as if bringing the wilding indoors, from fencerow to kitchen table, had domesticated it.

Or had the indoor comforts of fire and easy chair only soothed my own heightened senses so that I could no longer perceive the keen flavors still in the wild apples?

"In the fields only are the sours and bitters of Nature appreciated," wrote Thoreau, who christened the apples he found on his walks. Like him, we named the wildings we discovered that morning the Molly's Pond Apple and the Farewell Autumn Apple because every seedling apple tree is a unique variety, without name, unlike its parent. Only the snow apple, La Belle Fameuse, comes up true to seed; all others revert to wild, original types. From such chance seedlings, excellent apples as the Wealthy, Newtown, McIntosh Red, and Porter were developed.

So it is that each new wild apple tree we come upon excites our sense of discovery, our expectations. Somewhere along fencerows and creek banks, standing in pastures and on the edges of woods, are unfound, untasted, unsung apples that we have yet to find in our continuing pursuit of the wild flavor.

OPEN KETTLE APPLE BUTTER

3 pecks peeled, quartered, cored
   tart wild apples
10 gallons fresh sweet apple cider
10 pounds sugar (about)
1 ounce cinnamon

1 ounce allspice
1 ounce nutmeg
1 ounce ginger
1 ounce cloves

While preparing the apples, cutting away the waste parts have a wood fire started outdoors and let it burn down to hot embers. Pour the apple cider into a large iron or copper kettle and place over the coals. Boil the cider down to half. Add apples to the boiling cider, a few at a time. Cook slowly and stir constantly for 4 or 5 hours. Keep the fire hot enough to simmer the mixture, but do not let the apple butter scorch. When the butter thickens, stir in the sugar (the amount depends upon the tartness of the wild apples used). Add the spices. Continue cooking slowly, stirring carefully, until the flavor is pleasing and a spoonful dropped on a saucer does not separate. Seal in hot, sterilized jars immediately. Do not allow the apple butter to stand in the kettle. Open kettle apple butter takes about a half-day's cooking. You may use one peck of sweet apples to two pecks of tart wildings instead, if you prefer.

WINDFALL APPLESAUCE

Wash wild apples and cut them into quarters. Remove the cores and cut out the bad places. Put them in a pan with enough water to barely cover the apples. Cook on medium heat, stirring often, until tender (about 20 minutes). Cool, then put the cooked apples through a food mill.

For the table, sweeten with sugar to taste, using about 1 cup of sugar to 1½ quarts of applesauce. Add 1 teaspoon of cinnamon to each cup of sugar if desired.

BAKED APPLE BUTTER

16 cups applesauce
2 tablespoons lemon juice
½ cup cider vinegar
8 cups sugar

1 tablespoon allspice
2 tablespoons cinnamon
1 tablespoon cloves
1 teaspoon nutmeg

Combine all of the ingredients and heat, while stirring, to boiling. Then bake in an enameled pan in a moderate oven (350° F) for about 2 hours, or until no liquid separates from a spoonful dropped on a saucer. Seal in hot, sterilized jars. Makes 6 pints.

FRIED WILD APPLES

4 tablespoons butter or
   bacon grease
6 cups wild apples, cored and
   sliced thin, peeled or unpeeled
½ cup sugar, brown or white

¼ cup water or apple cider
½ teaspoon cinnamon or
   4 strips bacon, crisp-fried
   and crumbled

In a heavy skillet, heat the butter or bacon grease. Add apples, sprinkled with sugar. Lower the heat and let the apples fry, turning often with a spatula, until they are tender (15 or 20 minutes). Add water or apple cider if the pan gets dry. When the apples are tender, sprinkle them with the cinnamon or mix them with the crumbled bacon. Serve with fried bacon, pork chops, or ham. Serves 4 to 6.

DRIED APPLES

Peel and core unbruised wild apples and slice ¼-inch thick in round or wedge-shaped slices.

To dry the apples in the sun, place the apples on a wire rack in the sun and cover them with cheesecloth to keep the insects off them. Turn the apple slices several times each day. Bring them inside at night. It will take several days to dry the apples. (They are dry enough when an apple slice squeezed together in the palm of the hand springs apart when the hand is opened.) Then allow the apples to remain indoors, covered with cloth, for about a week longer. Finally, store them in covered containers.

To dry the apples indoors, thread the apple slices on a long piece of undyed white thread, using a large needle. Leave space between each apple slice so that none of the pieces touch each other. Hang the apple strings near a stove or fireplace. They will dry in two or three weeks.

APPLE PIE

5 cups peeled, sliced apples
⅔ cup granulated sugar
¼ cup brown sugar
2 tablespoons flour
½ teaspoon mace
1 teaspoon apple-pie spice

2 tablespoons lemon juice
1 teaspoon grated lemon peel
2 tablespoons butter
Pastry for 9-inch double-crust
  pie (page 44)

In a large bowl, combine the first 8 ingredients. Line a pie tin with a rich pastry, add the apple mixture, and dot with the butter. Cover the pie with the top round of pastry and seal and crimp the edges. Cut a vent to let steam escape. Brush the top of the pastry with a small amount of milk, then sprinkle with a little sugar to make the crust brown nicely. Bake in a hot oven (400°F) for about 1 hour and 10 minutes, until the apples are tender and the crust browned. Serves 6 to 8.

AMY'S APPLE CAKE

1½ sticks butter
1½ cups sugar
3 eggs
1½ cups flour
1½ teaspoons cinnamon
1½ teaspoons nutmeg

¾ teaspoon salt
1½ teaspoons baking soda
3 cups peeled, chopped apples
1 cup hickory nuts or pecans,
  chopped

With an electric mixer, cream together the butter and sugar. Add the eggs, one at a time, and mix well. Then sift together the dry ingredients, add, and mix until blended well. With a mixing spoon, stir in the chopped apples and nutmeats. Pour into a greased and floured baking pan (13-by-9-by-2 inches) and bake in a moderate oven (350° F) for 1 hour. When the cake has cooled, sprinkle the top with confectioners' sugar. Makes 12 servings.

APPLESAUCE COOKIES

½ cup margarine
1 cup sugar
1 egg
1 teaspoon vanilla extract
1 cup Windfall Applesauce
    (page 192)
2 cups flour

1 teaspoon baking powder
½ teaspoon salt
½ teaspoon baking soda
½ teaspoon cinnamon
½ teaspoon cloves
½ cup hickory nuts or pecans,
    chopped

Cream the margarine and sugar together, add the egg and vanilla, and beat well. Stir in the applesauce. Sift all of the dry ingredients together, then add to the applesauce mixture. Stir in the chopped nuts. Drop the dough by heaping teaspoonfuls onto a greased baking sheet, and bake in a moderate oven (350° F) for 12 to 15 minutes. Makes 24 cookies.

APPLESAUCE-BLACK WALNUT BREAD

2 cups flour
¾ cup sugar
3 teaspoons baking powder
1 teaspoon salt
½ teaspoon baking soda

½ teaspoon cinnamon
1 cup black walnuts, chopped
1 egg
1 cup thick applesauce
2 tablespoons melted butter

Sift the dry ingredients together and add the nuts. In a mixing bowl, beat the egg, add the applesauce and melted butter. Add the dry ingredients and stir until just blended. Pour into a greased loaf pan (8½-by-4 inches) and bake in a moderate oven (350° F) for 1 hour. Cool on a rack.

FRIED APPLE PIES

4 cups dried apples (page 193)
¾ cup sugar
3 cups flour
1 teaspoon salt

1 cup pure lard
⅓ cup water (about)
Fat for frying

Cook the dried apples in water to cover until tender. Sweeten with the sugar.

Make a pastry dough of the flour, salt, lard, and water (see page 44).

Divide the dough into 6 portions. Roll out each portion on a floured board and cut into 8-inch rounds, using a medium-sized plate as a guide. Put a portion of the cooked dried apples onto each round of dough, moisten the edges with water, and fold over to make a half-moon shape. Press the edges together with the tines of a fork. Fry the pies, without crowding, in hot fat, ½-inch deep, in a heavy skillet for at least 5 minutes on each side. Makes 6 pies.

Mrs. Burgess' Kentucky Stack Cake

4 cups dried apples (page 193)
1½ cups sugar
1 cup pure lard, room temperature
1 egg
1 cup sorghum molasses
1 cup buttermilk
1 teaspoon baking soda
3 cups flour
½ teaspoon salt

Cook the dried apples in water to cover until tender. Sweeten with ½ cup of the sugar. Set aside while the cake is baking.

In a mixing bowl, combine the lard and remaining sugar and mix well with a mixing spoon. Add the egg and beat well. Add the remaining ingredients and blend well.

Grease and flour two iron skillets (9-by-2½ inches) and pour the batter into the pans. Bake in a moderate oven (375° F) for 35 minutes, or until a toothpick inserted in the center of the cakes comes out clean. Using a long, thin knife, split each cooled layer crosswise into two layers. Spread the dried apples between the layers and on top of the cake. Serves 12.

Apple Dumplings

Pastry:
4 cups flour
1 teaspoon salt
½ cup milk (about)
1¼ cups pure lard

Filling:
6 cups sliced, peeled apples
1 cup sugar
1 teaspoon apple pie spice
2 tablespoons butter

Syrup:
½ cup maple syrup or ½ cup sugar
¼ teaspoon apple pie spice
3 tablespoons butter
Hot water and syrup from apples

Make a pastry dough of the first four ingredients (see page 44). Divide the dough into two portions and roll each one out on a floured board into a large circle. Square off the edges of the pastry and cut each circle into 4 seven-inch squares, making 8 squares in all.

Combine the ingredients for the dumpling filling and place a portion in the center of each pastry square, burying a lump of the butter in each dumpling. Moisten the edges and points of each pastry square and bring all four corners of the pastry up over the apple filling to the center, forming the dumpling. Seal well and place the dumplings close together in an 8-by-12-by-2-inch baking pan.

Make the syrup by combining the maple syrup or sugar, spice, and butter with the juice left in the bowl in which the apples were mixed with the sugar. Add enough hot water to make a total of 2 cups of liquid. Pour the syrup over the unbaked apple dumplings. Bake for 5 minutes in a very hot oven (500° F), then bake at 400° F for 45 minutes, until the dumplings are brown and the apples tender. Serve warm with cream. Makes 8 dumplings.

PERSIMMONS

In late October there comes a day when the tranquil interlude of Indian summer ends. All at once there is a new feeling of urgency in the autumn air, a crisp reminder that the time for one last pilgrimage into the countryside for wild provender is at hand.

My sister-in-law, Pat, looks out the kitchen window at the darkening sky. Since morning its blue brightness has tarnished to the color of the punched tin panels in the doors of the jelly cupboard in the farmhouse kitchen.

"The persimmons ought to be ready," she says. "If we want a pudding for Thanksgiving dinner, we'd better go to the woods today."

We leave the lunch dishes in the sink and hurriedly round up the simple accoutrements to harvesting the wildling fruits. We find shallow flat-bottomed baskets to carry the fragile, sweet wild persimmons that grow on small trees at the old log cabin site on Havil Hill. We find a thin plastic painter's drop cloth to spread on the ground

198

under the trees when we shake the persimmons down. Then, remembering our need for them, I tuck into my pocket a few roomy plastic sacks to hold our serendipity, that unexpected bounty we always find somewhere along the way.

The preparations for the persimmon hunt are uncomplicated and direct. We find sweaters and in a few minutes we are out of the house and on our way to Havill Hill. We strike out at a brisk gait, for the first half mile is an easy hike over flat land and we are prodded by chilly fingers of wind that flick our cheeks and ankles. As our pace quickens, so do our instincts for squirreling away the wild bounty.

We must have two quarts of ripe wild persimmons to make our own traditional pudding for the Thanksgiving feast. What better fruit to

symbolize the season's abundances and the natural harvest of the land than the native persimmon, that "delicious little plum" described by Hernando De Soto in 1557, that valued *pasimenan* of the generous Indians whose strange, unfamiliar foods became mainstays of early American cookery?

We must also gather quantities more of the luscious wildwood fruits to cache in the freezer until those snowbound Saturdays, much later, when other persimmon puddings, breads, cakes, pies, and cookies baking in our kitchen oven will warm us with savory gusts of spicy fragrance.

"We'll have bad weather by tomorrow," Pat predicts, assessing the lowering gray clouds. "This afternoon we'd better bring in all the persimmons we need."

The children, my sons and their cousins, catch sight of us as we cross the edge of a cornfield where my brother is operating the corn picker. Pat beckons them to join us, and they abandon their pastime of gleaning the scattered ears of corn from the field and run toward us, bounding over rows of blunt cornstalks. They, too, know where to find the farm's wild bounty, and they enjoy nothing more than excursions to its far corners to gather it in.

My brother waves from the tractor but continues down the rows of unharvested corn. On a less foreboding day, he might have joined us in the pleasurable harvest of the farm's untilled fruits, but today he is compelled by the farmer's practicality to gather in the yield of his cultivated field.

As carefully as he gathers in the rewards of his tillage, we will glean the untended acres for the wild fruits that have required nothing of us, neither hoe nor harrow. The bountiful natural harvest is ours for the taking, nature's provision for all denizens of field and woodland.

We cross the fence surrounding the cornfield, holding the tightly stretched strands of barbed wire wide apart; the children scatter out into the next field, running ahead of us through the swaying plumes of dried red sedge grass. Each is eager to find an unexpected trove of wild treasure hidden in the tangled growth of the field.

Every exciting discovery is heralded by gay shouts and laughter. Rebecca walks into a covey of quail hiding in the grasses, and it explodes into flight all about her. Scotty finds the abandoned woven nest of a red-eyed vireo in a small bush along the fencerow. Bobby finds a tortoise's carapace in a shallow ditch, and Jim collects plant galls from the stems of withered goldenrods. I fill a plastic sack with dark purple pokeberries to make red dye for my hand-spun wool yarns. Pat breaks off long tendrils of bittersweet vine, studded with clusters of waxy orange berries, for her Thanksgiving table centerpiece.

By the time we reach the foot of Havill Hill, the plastic sacks are stuffed with our serendipitous discoveries. But the richest prizes of wild treasure wait for the finding at the crest of the hill. Here native persimmon trees grow all about the old Havill homesite, circling the spot where a sturdy log cabin stood for more than a century. A dozen small trees thrive at the edge of a tangled thicket of red plum trees and among aged, gnarled apple trees at the back of the homesite. More young persimmon trees have grown on the eroding slope in front of the homesite where Mr. Havill once tended his peach trees. Now the wildling orchard of persimmon trees, sown by the provident hand of nature, brings new life and fruitfulness to the barren remnants of an old man's orchard.

We can see the persimmons clinging to the crooked branches of the leaf-bare young trees as we approach the wildling orchard. The fruits are like small, frosted-orange ornaments hung there to soften the harsh skeletal outlines of the naked trees.

The children have reached the crest of the hill before us and they run from one tree to the next, discovering persimmons. They are like "'possums after 'simmons," shinnying up trees and pulling down branches, hungrily sampling the wild harvest.

Only Rebecca is not quite willing to take the risk. She runs back to meet us as we walk toward the persimmon trees, holding up a shriveled, dusky-orange persimmon.

"Taste it," she demands. "Is it ripe?"

A green persimmon is not soon forgotten. "If it be not ripe," wrote the doughty Captain John Smith of Jamestown, "it will draw a man's mouth awrie with much torment." An unripe persimmon contains astringent tannic acid and its notorious puckery taste is dreaded by even the most avid persimmon fanciers and, wisely, by Rebecca.

But Rebecca's persimmon is truly ripe. It is a sweet, rich morsel of delightful flavor without a hint of pucker. The pulp is soft and mushy and incredibly delicious, as it should be. Its wrinkled skin, thinly encasing a luscious tawny interior, is a darkened amber color. The pulp is a natural puree laden with a half dozen dark, flat seeds. The flavor is full-bodied and lusty, spiced with the tang of wildness yet reminiscent of ripe apricots and sweet dates tasted together.

We go to Rebecca's tree and begin picking the persimmons from the lower branches. At first Pat and I are like hungry opossums too, stuffing ourselves in a frenzy of eating at the persimmon tree, but soon we begin to collect the fragile golden fruits in our shallow baskets.

"They're small this year because of the drought," Pat says, "but the flavor is good."

Most of the persimmons are about an inch in diameter, only three fourths the usual size of persimmons from these trees. Like all wild fruits, persimmons vary in size from season to season because of weather conditions as well as from tree to tree because of natural variations in wild strains of fruit. Persimmons may range in size from nuggets of less than an inch in thickness to great orange beauties as large as eggs.

The flavor of wild fruits is variable, too. The fruit of one tree is always delicious when ripe while the fruit of another tree is decidedly lacking in flavor, year after year. It is from this natural variability that much of the mystique of the wild flavor arises.

Even the time of ripening varies greatly among varieties of wild persimmons. One tree's fruit requires a touch of frost to bring it to a mellow ripeness while another's fruit ripens to its peak of flavor and falls to the ground during the balmy days of late September, long before the harvest moon rises above the farmhouse. My father always gathered persimmons from a certain tree late in November when he was out shooting quail. I remember the first late-autumn day when he appeared at the kitchen door after the day's hunting, with the happy English setters swirling at his heels and the pockets of his khaki coat bulging with the day's bag. After he unloaded his shotgun and returned it to its place behind the kitchen door, he laid out the limp beautiful birds, one by one, for us to count and admire. Then, promising us a surprise, he unbuttoned the flap of the roomy game bag and revealed the frosty persimmons harvested from the late-ripening tree at the back of the farm.

These Mother stirred into a spicy persimmon pudding which sent fragrant messages to our noses from behind the oven door while the quail spattered and crackled in the frying pan on top of the stove.

The dark, rich pudding cooled on the lowered oven door while we enjoyed the hunter's feast: the platter of golden-fried quail and the delectable milk gravy made of the crusty morsels and drippings left in the frying pan, the mound of fluffy mashed potatoes with melting butter coursing down its peak, the feather-light biscuits made with milk clabber, the savory bowlful of green beans from our summer's garden—celestial dishes, all! But none so heavenly as the persimmon pudding which Mother portioned out at the table and served, still warm, with a sweet whipped cream.

In the years since then, a succession of wild persimmon puddings has entered the oven, cooled on the lowered oven door, and vanished before a circle of appreciative appetites at the farmhouse table, each pudding recalling the one Mother baked from the surprise my father carried home in his game bag. It was a plain, honest pudding, to which was added the spice of the wild flavor of persimmons. It was a dark, moist, shiny-topped, cakelike pudding baked in a shallow pan. The ingredients from which the pudding was made, except for the persimmons, were merely the common staples used in every country kitchen to stir up biscuits, breads, pancakes, cookies, and the like— butter, sugar, eggs, flour, leavening, milk, and spices. Yet Mother's persimmon pudding was Elysian fare, a transcendental experience of taste. She transformed these homely cupboard staples, with only the addition of wild persimmons, into the flavorsome stuff from which yearning remembrances spring.

Pat and I will use Mother's recipe for the first persimmon pudding of the autumn season, and we discuss it now as we spread the drop cloth under the persimmon tree before shaking down the ripe fruits which hang high out of reach on the topmost branches.

"We'll make a pudding for supper tonight," Pat says, "but let's have it with sugar sauce instead of whipped cream, for a change."

What to serve on the persimmon pudding, or whether to serve anything at all on it, is always a subject for friendly argument. At Mitchell, Indiana, where a festival celebrating the native American persimmon has been an annual event for twenty-five years, the persimmon gourmand can indulge in an orgy of pudding eating, going from one booth to the next, sampling puddings until he can eat no more, choosing either sweet sauce or whipped cream for a topping—or even both together. There are, surely, as many kinds of persimmon puddings as there are cooks to make them. Each year the indefatigable judges of the Persimmon Pudding contest taste the hundreds of pudding entries lined up on long tables (an awesome sight!) in the Public Service Building and somehow agree on a champion.

The perennial champion pudding of our family is always made after our mother's recipe, but the festal pudding of the Thanksgiving dinner at the farmhouse is a new tradition of our own generation, a regal steamed pudding stuffed with candied fruits and peels, and with wild hickory nuts and persimmons from the farm. It is carried to the table with great ceremony and flaming brandy, and served with hard sauce. Magnificent! It is symbolic of the wild harvest of the farm, just as the other foods spread on our lavish board represent the plenitude of cultivated fields.

Now the golden harvest rains down on the drop sheet, like the overflow of a heavenly cornucopia, for Jim is shaking the persimmon tree. The persimmons pelt the plastic covering in a gentle barrage of sound: *pllp! pllp! pllp!* The children respond with laughter that echoes across the hilltop. When the bombardment ceases, we scramble under the persimmon tree to retrieve the fallen bounty for our baskets. The saucy Rebecca gaily chants an old folk rhyme:

> 'Possum up the 'simmon tree,
> Raccoon on the ground,
> Raccoon says, "You son of a gun!
> Shake those 'simmons down!"

Everyone is in high spirits. We gather the orange globes of fruit from several trees, amid the shouts and laughter of the exuberant children, and soon our baskets are filled. Reluctantly, we turn away from the wildling orchard on the hilltop and head for home.

This time we take the long way home, following the old dirt road down the hill instead of cutting across the overgrown fields, because the walking is easier. Now our baskets are laden and the older boys are groaning (cheerfully!) under the weight of heavy sacks slung on their backs. By now their faces are ruddy with cold and our clothes are prickly with cockleburs and sticktights, but we are undaunted. We swing along down the long hill, propelled by the exhilaration of our successful hunt. We have collected a wealth of tawny persimmons for puddings and a store for the freezer. We are all immensely satisfied with our flavorful burdens and they seem as light as our spirits.

We spy two more small trees, perched high on the roadbank, loaded with persimmons. Steven climbs up the steep incline to fetch samples.

"They're delicious," Pat says, "but we'll leave these for the 'possums. We can't carry more."

Ripe persimmons are so fragile and easily crushed that we carry only a few layers of fruit in each flat, shallow basket. We separate the layers of fruit with sheets of plastic to protect them even more from crushing. And before putting the persimmons in the basket, we remove each pretty petaled cap, the dried calyx of the persimmon flower. We take great care not to include trash in the basket with the persimmons because the less sorting and rinsing we have to do when preparing the pulp the better. A light rinsing of a few fruits at a time may be necessary, but we think nothing of eating persimmons from the trees on the isolated hilltop *au naturel*. This is truly "organic" food, grown in soil fertilized only by natural compost, watered with rainfall, nurtured by sunrays, tended only by birds, earthworms, insects, and provident breezes. Our wild persimmons have not known sprays or fertilizers or the poisons of smokestacks. And, without the "help" of man, wild persimmons contain rich stores of nutrients; they are richer in vitamin C than oranges and are a good source of potassium, iron, and carbohydrates. The latter is not surprising because persimmons are veritable "sugar plums" to taste, loaded with natural sugars and food energy—127 calories per 100 grams, if you are counting.

Calories are far from our minds as we come to the crossroads and turn up the road to the farmhouse. Crisp leaves scuttle across the lane. The wind has come up stronger and now we face into it. A squirrel scampers up the trunk of a hickory tree, carrying his hoard. Birds dart in and out of the multiflora hedgerow, feeding on scarlet rose hips. The dark cloudbank which hovered on the horizon all afternoon is suddenly surging up the sky, and we hurry to reach the house before it envelops the heavens.

The first cold raindrops spatter as we come into the front yard. We see Uncle Jim on the tractor pulling the wagon, heaped high with corn, under the sheltering roof of the shed. Now the harvest is safely home. The triumph we hear in his shouted halloo is akin to the elation Pat and I feel as we bring in the wild persimmons.

We build up the hearth fire for the shivering children and soon the chilled fingers and toes are tingling with its pervading warmth. Pat begins at once to prepare the persimmon pulp by forcing the fruit through the Foley food mill. She will put it in freezing cartons, adding only a teaspoon of ascorbic acid to each pint portion to protect its bright color, and freeze it for Thanksgiving dessert.

I turn on the oven to preheat and gather together mixing bowls, the flour sifter, measuring cups and spoons, the electric mixer, and the ingredients for our supper pudding. Soon the kitchen is a-buzz with the beater's hum and clattering with dishes and pans. The familiar compelling noises of food being prepared lure the children, straightaway, to the kitchen. They encircle the round oak table, enraptured by the stirring and sifting and beating and creaming. Their eyes—glistening with pure gourmandise—follow the swirling path of the spoon through the tawny batter.

Was ever so much expected of a mere pudding? Will we taste the wildness of the autumn woods in the persimmon flavor while savoring, at the same time, the rare flavor of the day's outing? Will it be truly handsome, befitting the harvest supper, and symbolic of "harvest home"? Will it be unforgettable, as other puddings made by this recipe and stirred in this very kitchen, nourishing us long after supper is over?

MOTHER'S WILD PERSIMMON PUDDING

2 cups sugar	⅛ teaspoon salt
2 cups persimmon pulp	1 teaspoon baking powder
2 eggs	1 teaspoon cinnamon
1 teaspoon baking soda	1 teaspoon vanilla
1½ cups buttermilk	¼ cup cream
1½ cups flour	2 tablespoons butter

In the bowl of an electric mixer, combine sugar and persimmon pulp. Add eggs and beat well.

Add baking soda to buttermilk and stir until the foaming stops. Add the buttermilk mixture to the persimmon mixture.

Sift together the flour, salt, baking powder, and cinnamon. Add to the persimmon mixture gradually and beat well. Stir in vanilla and cream.

In a large baking pan (9-by-13-by-2 inches) melt butter. Pour the melted butter into the pudding batter, leaving just enough in the baking pan to grease the bottom and sides. Beat the melted butter into the batter, pour the batter into the baking pan, and bake the pudding in a 350° F oven for about 45 minutes. The pudding is done when it pulls away from the sides of the pan and the center is set. It will fall after being taken from the oven. Serve the persimmon pudding with whipped cream or Brown Sugar Sauce (recipe below) or both.

Brown Sugar Sauce

1 cup brown sugar   Salt
1 tablespoon cornstarch   1½ cups hot water
4 tablespoons butter   1 teaspoon vanilla

Combine the brown sugar, cornstarch, butter, and a dash of salt with hot water in a saucepan and cook over medium heat until slightly thickened. Remove from heat and cool before adding vanilla. Makes 6 to 8 servings.

Harvest Home Persimmon Pudding

¼ cup butter   ⅓ cup milk
¾ cup sugar   1 cup persimmon pulp
2 eggs   1 teaspoon vanilla
1 cup flour   ½ cup chopped seedless raisins,
1 teaspoon baking powder   or currants
¼ teaspoon baking soda   ½ cup hickory nuts, chopped
½ teaspoon salt   ½ cup candied fruits and peels,
½ teaspoon cinnamon   chopped

In the bowl of an electric mixer, cream butter with sugar until light and fluffy. Add eggs, beating well.

Sift the flour with baking powder, baking soda, salt, and cinnamon. Add sifted dry ingredients alternately to the creamed mixture with the milk and persimmon pulp. Stir in vanilla, fruits, and nuts. Turn the batter into a greased and floured 1-quart pudding mold, filling it about ⅔ full. Fasten cover tightly and steam pudding 1½ hours. Serves 8 to 10.

NOTE: When the pudding is made ahead of time and allowed to cool, or stored in the refrigerator overnight, reheat before serving by steaming for about half an hour.

To flame pudding: Immediately before serving, sprinkle a little sugar over the top of the hot pudding, then pour a jigger of warmed brandy over the pudding and touch brandy with a lighted match. Serve each portion with Hard Sauce (recipe below).

HARD SAUCE

4 tablespoons butter
½ cup heavy cream
2¾ cups confectioners' sugar
⅛ teaspoon salt

1 teaspoon vanilla
  or 1 tablespoon brandy
  or 1 tablespoon lemon juice

Cream the butter in a bowl. In another bowl, whip the cream. Add confectioners' sugar to the butter alternately with the whipped cream, beating well after each addition. Add salt and flavor with vanilla, brandy, or lemon juice. Chill the hard sauce in individual butter molds.

PERSIMMON ICE BOX ROLL

1½ cups persimmon pulp
1½ cups sugar
15 large marshmallows, cut fine
1 cup chopped hickory nuts

  or pecans
1 pound graham cracker crumbs
  (about)

In a bowl, mix together the persimmon pulp, sugar, marshmallows, and nuts. Stir in enough graham cracker crumbs to make the mixture stiff enough to form into a roll. Shape into a roll and chill. Slice and serve with whipped cream or ice cream.

This recipe makes a dozen or more servings. The extra portion may be wrapped in waterproof material and frozen.

NOTE: To vary the flavor slightly, use a half portion of brown sugar to a half portion of white sugar to make up the 1½ cups of sugar called for in the recipe.

Persimmon Cookies

½ cup butter
1 cup sugar
1 egg
1 teaspoon baking soda
1 cup persimmon pulp
2 cups flour

⅛ teaspoon salt
¼ teaspoon cloves
½ teaspoon cinnamon
½ teaspoon mace
1 cup raisins
1 cup chopped pecans

In the bowl of an electric mixer, cream the butter with the sugar until mixture is fluffy. Beat in the egg. Add the baking soda to the persimmon pulp, then add to the creamed mixture.

Sift together the flour, salt, and spices. Add to the creamed mixture in three portions, beating well after each addition.

With a mixing spoon, blend in raisins and nuts. Drop dough by teaspoonfuls onto a greased cookie sheet, flattening each cookie to the desired shape because these cookies do not spread much during baking. Bake 12 to 15 minutes in a 350° F oven, testing with a toothpick to determine doneness. Makes 30 cookies.

Haw Creek Charlie's Wild Persimmon Pudding

2 cups persimmon pulp
¾ cup wild honey
2 cups stone-ground whole wheat
   flour
2 cups milk

1 egg, lightly beaten
1 teaspoon cinnamon
½ teaspoon baking soda
2 tablespoons hot water
2 tablespoons butter

In a bowl, mix together the persimmon pulp, wild honey, flour, milk, egg, and cinnamon, beating well after each addition. Dissolve the baking soda in the hot water and stir in.

Place the butter in a 2½-or 3-quart earthenware baking dish and melt the butter while the oven is preheating. When the butter has melted, tip and rotate the baking dish to coat the sides of the dish. Then pour in the pudding batter and stir with the butter. Cover and bake for 1½ hours in a 325° F oven.

This pudding is very moist, reminiscent of Indian pudding. Serve it with whipped cream or vanilla ice cream. Serves 8 to 10.

INDIANA PERSIMMON PIE

1 cup heavy cream
3 tablespoons confectioners' sugar
2 cups persimmon pulp

Baked 8-inch pastry shell
 or 4 individual pastry tart
 shells
Cinnamon

Whip cream until very stiff. Blend in confectioners' sugar.

In a bowl, combine the persimmon pulp with the confectioners' sugar. Fold in half of the stiffly whipped cream. Turn into a baked 8-inch pastry shell (see page 00) or into 4 individual pastry tart shells. Spread the remaining whipped cream over the top of the pie and sprinkle lightly with cinnamon. Chill thoroughly before serving. Serves 4.

NOTE: Sometimes I add a tablespoon of orange juice to the pie filling and garnish with candied orange peel.

AMERICAN PERSIMMON PIE

2 eggs
½ cup sugar
1 cup persimmon pulp
½ teaspoon cinnamon
¼ teaspoon mace
⅛ teaspoon nutmeg

⅛ teaspoon salt
½ cup evaporated milk
½ cup whole milk
9-inch pastry shell, unbaked
 (page 44)

Separate the eggs. Beat the egg whites stiff and set aside. In a mixing bowl, beat the egg yolks well. Add the sugar, persimmon pulp, spices, and salt. Mix well. Stir in the evaporated milk and the whole milk. Last, fold in the stiffly beaten egg whites. Pour into an unbaked pastry shell and bake in a 450° F oven for 10 minutes, then reduce the heat to 325° F and bake for 30 minutes longer, or until a knife inserted in the center comes out clean. Serve with whipped cream topping. Serves 6.

PERSIMMON BREAD

1 cup persimmon pulp
2 large eggs
1 cup sugar
2½ cups flour

3 teaspoons baking powder
½ teaspoon salt
½ cup cooking oil
1 cup pecans, chopped

In the bowl of an electric mixer combine persimmon pulp, eggs, and sugar, beating well. Sift together the flour, baking powder, and salt.

Add the sifted dry ingredients to the persimmon mixture with the cooking oil. Blend well. Fold in the chopped nuts. Turn into a greased loaf pan and bake at 325° F for 1 hour. Serves 8.

PERSIMMON CHIFFON PIE

1 tablespoon gelatin
¾ cup light brown sugar,
   firmly packed
½ teaspoon salt
1 teaspoon cinnamon
½ teaspoon nutmeg
¾ cup milk
3 eggs, separated

1 cup persimmon pulp
¼ cup granulated sugar
9-inch baked pastry shell (see
   page 44), or graham cracker
   crust (see page 113)
½ cup heavy cream, whipped
1 tablespoon confectioners' sugar

In the top of a double boiler combine gelatin, brown sugar, salt, cinnamon and nutmeg, milk, and the egg yolks, slightly beaten. Cook over gently boiling water, stirring frequently, until heated through (about 10 minutes). Remove from heat and stir in the persimmon pulp. Chill until the mixture mounds when dropped from a spoon. Beat the egg whites stiff with the ¼ cup granulated sugar, and fold in. Pour the mixture into baked pastry shell or graham cracker crust and chill until the pie is firm. Before serving, top the pie with the whipped cream sweetened with confectioners' sugar. Serves 6.

SMOKY MOUNTAIN PERSIMMON PUDDING

½ cup butter
1½ cups sugar
2 large eggs
1½ cups persimmon pulp
½ cup light cream (half-and-half)

2 cups unbleached flour
1 teaspoon baking powder
1 teaspoon cinnamon
1 teaspoon vanilla
1 cup grated raw sweet potato

In the large bowl of an electric mixer, cream the butter and sugar until fluffy. Add the eggs and beat well. Add the persimmon pulp and beat until blended. Sift together the flour, baking powder, and cinnamon, and add alternately with the cream. Mix well. With a spoon, blend in the vanilla and raw sweet potato. Pour the batter into a buttered pan (8-by-13-by-2 inches) and bake for 1 hour at 350° F. Serve hot or cold topped with whipped cream or Brown Sugar Sauce (see recipe on page 207). Serves 10 to 12.

COLD PERSIMMON SOUFFLÉ

3 egg yolks, slightly beaten
½ cup sugar
¼ teaspoon salt
2 tablespoons lemon juice
1 tablespoon gelatin

¼ cup cold water
1 cup persimmon pulp
3 egg whites, beaten stiff
1 cup heavy cream, whipped

In the top of a double boiler, combine the egg yolks with the sugar, salt, and lemon juice. Cook over gently boiling water, stirring constantly, until the mixture thickens. Remove from the heat. Soften the gelatin in the cold water, and add. Stir until gelatin is dissolved. Cool and add the persimmon pulp. Chill in the refrigerator until almost at the setting point. Then fold in the egg whites and the whipped cream. Pile the mixture into 4 individual soufflé dishes and chill thoroughly. Serves 4.

PERSIMMON CAKE

2 cups sugar
1 cup light vegetable oil
3 large eggs
1 teaspoon vanilla
2 cups flour
1 teaspoon salt
1 teaspoon allspice

1 teaspoon cinnamon
1 cup buttermilk
1 teaspoon baking soda
1 cup persimmon pulp
1 cup chopped walnuts, hickory
   nuts, or pecans

In the large bowl of an electric mixer, combine the sugar, vegetable oil, eggs, and vanilla. Mix well.

Sift together the flour, salt, and spices. Combine the buttermilk and baking soda. Add the sifted ingredients to the first mixture alternately with the buttermilk. Add the persimmon pulp and mix well. Stir in the chopped nuts. Pour the batter into a greased and floured baking pan (13-by-9-by-2 inches) and bake at 300° F for 1 hour. Cool and frost with Buttermilk Frosting (recipe below). Makes 10 to 12 servings.

BUTTERMILK FROSTING

2 cups sugar
1 cup buttermilk
1 teaspoon baking soda

2 teaspoons corn syrup
½ cup butter
1 teaspoon vanilla

In a large heavy pan, combine the sugar, buttermilk, baking soda, corn syrup, and butter. Stirring constantly, cook until a soft ball forms when a small amount of syrup is dropped into cold water, or to 235° F on candy thermometer. Remove from heat, cool slightly, and add vanilla. Beat until the frosting is of a spreading consistency.

PERSIMMON ICE CREAM

4 cups light cream (half-and-half)
2 cups sugar
¼ cup flour
½ teaspoon salt
8 egg yolks or 4 eggs

4 cups milk
1½ cups persimmon pulp
½ cup finely chopped pecans, toasted

Scald the light cream in a large saucepan. Combine the sugar, flour, and salt. Beat the eggs until they are light and lemon colored; add them to the sugar mixture and stir until well blended. Gradually add some of the scalded cream to the egg mixture, stirring vigorously, then put all together and cook over medium heat until the custard thickens. Stir constantly to avoid scorching. Cool. If made a few hours ahead of time, the mixture may be stored in the refrigerator until freezing time.

To the chilled custard, add the milk, the persimmon pulp, and the pecans, which have been toasted for about 5 minutes in a moderate oven (350° F). Pour the mixture into a chilled 1-gallon ice cream freezer canister, fit the dasher into place, and freeze according to the directions accompanying the ice cream freezer, or see the directions for freezing Hazelnut-Chocolate Ice Cream on page 237. Makes 1 gallon.

ROSE HIPS

Today I made rose hip jam from the tomato-red fruits of the salt spray rose. They were brought to me as a special favor by my friend Jim Thurston, who gathered the rose hips on Moonstone Beach, New Jersey, along the Atlantic Ocean.

"I found the roses growing right out of the sand only a short distance from the ocean," Jim said. "They were growing up on the dunes above Moonstone Beach—there were no other plants around them except a few tall, bleached grasses. There was a wildlife preserve back of the dunes, and I could see white swans swimming on it while I picked the rose hips."

The rose hips from the salt spray rose (*Rosa rugosa*) are as large as cherry tomatoes and shaped almost like them except that they have a short, prickly stem and a blossom end bearing a withered, star-shaped calyx that earlier held the fragrant pink and white blossom. Rose hips, also called heps, haws, or rose apples, are the seed pods of the rose that form where the rose bloomed.

214

The rose hips called *Rosa rugosa* are the largest of all the rose fruits. They contain unbelievable amounts of vitamin C. The orange-red fruits are tart and fleshy but not particularly tasty when eaten raw. But they make delicious, beautifully colored jams, jellies, and marmalades.

The jam I made today was at first the color of persimmons but as it cooked to thickness, it turned to a lovely, tawny orange. It looks beautiful and mellow in my antique jelly glasses on my cupboard shelf, labeled:

SALT SPRAY
ROSE HIP JAM
from
MOONSTONE BEACH

I did not seal all of the jam into jars but saved out a saucedishful to have at supper with fresh-baked bread. It is exotic! There is a tang and spiciness to the taste of rose hip jam that comes from nature's own hand, not from the cinnamon jar. Its flavor eludes me—is it a little tomatoey? is it like quince?—but its texture reminds me of apple butter.

In my jelly cupboard next to the jams made of Moonstone Beach

rose hips are glasses of sparkling amber-colored jelly. These are labeled:

SWEETBRIER
ROSE HIP JELLY
from
VERMONT

One day last week, Pat Ruddick sent me, via airmail, a boxful of glossy rose hips from the sweetbrier roses that grow on our Vermont farm. I received them the following day, and that night six glasses of delicious jelly were added to my cupboard.

I do not depend on the descriptions of friends to imagine the sweetbrier rose growing in the thickets, pastures, and roadsides of Vermont; I have gathered its pink blossoms in July, along the road to Groton Forest, and in September, its vermilion hips.

"Sweetbrier is thrice crowned: in fragrant leaf, tinted flower and glossy fruit," Henry David Thoreau observed. The glossy orange, red-cheeked fruits of the sweetbrier rose (*Rosa eglanteria*) are the size and shape of an olive. They are smaller than the hips of the salt spray rose and not so tart. Firm, fresh sweetbrier hips have a pleasing hint of apple in their flavor. We pick them from their prickly briers as we are out walking and carry some of the fruits home in our pockets to dry for rose hip tea. Some we split open with a pocketknife, scooping out the white seeds inside with its point, to eat raw as we walk along.

The seeds we scatter along our path may, next year, replenish the wild feast of the fencerows at which songbirds and rabbits will feed, as we have.

Rose Hip Puree

Gather ripe rose hips from the salt spray rose (Rosa rugosa), sweetbrier rose (Rosa eglanteria), or other wild roses with large rose hips, when they are firm and tomato-red, before the downy fibers develop next to the seeds. Cut off the blossom ends and stems and cut the hips in half. Measure the rose hips (with seeds) and put them in a saucepan with an equal amount of water. Cook on medium heat until the rose hips are tender (about 20 minutes). Cool and let stand in a bowl in the refrigerator overnight. The next day, put the stewed rose hips through a food mill to make the puree. Use the puree to make jam or in other recipes.

NOTE: To make 2 to 3 cups of rose hip puree, gather 1 to 1½ quarts of sound, ripe rose hips.

Salt Spray Rose Hip Jam

1 lemon   (recipe above)
½ cup water   3 cups sugar
3 cups Rose Hip Puree

Slice the lemon thinly and simmer it in the water for 15 minutes. Strain the liquid through a sieve, pressing down on the lemon slices to extract all of the juice, and add it to the rose hip puree. Add the sugar and cook over medium heat, stirring constantly, for 20 minutes or until thickened. Seal in 6 half-pint sterilized jars at once.

NOTE: Two-and-a-half cups of prepared rose hips (stems and blossom ends removed) cooked with an equal amount of water yields 3 cups of rose hip puree.

Gingery Rose Hip Jam

1½ cups rose hip puree   2 tablespoons lemon juice
2 cups sugar   1 tablespoon minced crystallized
½ cup pineapple, finely diced   ginger

Combine all of the ingredients in a saucepan and cook over medium heat, stirring constantly, until the jam thickens. Pour into hot sterilized jars and seal. Fills 3 half-pint jars.

PAT RUDDICK'S UNCOOKED ROSE HIP JAM

1 cup rose hips (seeds, stems,
    and blossom ends removed)
1½ cups water

Juice of 1 lemon
3 cups sugar
1¾ ounces powdered fruit pectin

Put prepared rose hips in the blender with ¾ cup of water and the lemon juice; blend until smooth. Add sugar and blend for 5 minutes.

In a saucepan, combine the pectin and the rest of the water. Stir as the mixture comes to a boil over medium heat, then boil hard for 1 minute. Pour the pectin syrup into the rose hip mixture, blend until mixed, and store in the freezer until needed. Fills 2 jars.

ROSE HIP JELLY

1 cup rose hips, stems and
    blossom ends removed
Rose hip seeds
1 cup water

2 tablespoons lemon juice
2 cups sugar
3 ounces liquid pectin

Cut the rose hips in half. Scoop out the seeds with an apple corer; in a saucepan, combine the seeds and the water. Bring the seeds to a boil, then simmer them for 10 minutes, stirring as needed. Drain off the liquid and strain it through a tea strainer. Discard the seeds.

In an electric blender, combine the prepared rose hips and the liquid in which the seeds were cooked. Run the blender until the rose hips are chopped fine, then measure; there should be 2 cups of the rose hip mixture. Add a little water, if needed. Bring to a boil in an enameled saucepan, stirring often, then cover and let simmer for 10 minutes. Strain the juice through a double layer of cheesecloth, squeezing to extract all of the juice. There should be 1½ cups of rose hip juice.

Combine the rose hip juice with the lemon juice and sugar in an enameled saucepan. Stir and bring to a hard boil on high heat. Stir in the liquid pectin and boil, stirring constantly for about 3 minutes more, until the jelly stage is reached (see page 129). Skim the jelly and pour into 4 small jelly glasses and seal at once with hot paraffin. This recipe makes a firm, amber jelly.

Hip and Haw Jelly

Prepare the rose hip juice as directed in the recipe above for Rose Hip Jelly.

To prepare the red haw juice, remove the stems and cut the red haws in half. Measure the red haws, put them in an enameled pan with an equal amount of water and simmer them until they are tender, about 20 minutes. Strain the red haw juice through a cheesecloth.

Combine an equal amount of red haw juice and rose hip juice, then test the combined juices for pectin (see pectin test on page 130). Add as much liquid pectin as is indicated by the test, then add as much sugar as there is juice. (For example, if there are 2 cups of combined juices, use 2 cups of sugar.) Bring the mixture to a boil, stirring constantly, and boil hard until the jelly stage is reached (see jelly test on page 129). Two cups of combined juices will make 4 glasses of jelly.

Rose Hip Tea

2 teaspoons rose hips, crushed
   fresh or dried
6 cloves
6 teaspoons dried lemon balm

or 1 sprig of fresh balm
   (see note)
2 teaspoons honey

Put the rose hips, cloves, and lemon balm in a china teapot that has just been scalded with hot water. Pour a pint of boiling water over the mixture and steep for 10 minutes. Strain and serve sweetened with honey.

A slice of lemon may be added when the tea is served.

NOTE: Lemon balm is a type of mint (*Melissa officinalis*) with lemon flavored leaves. In some areas it is called garden balm or sweet balm.

Hot Spiced Tomato Juice with Rose Hips

To each cup of tomato juice, add 1 teaspoon Worcestershire sauce, ¼ teaspoon salt, ⅛ teaspoon freshly ground pepper, and 2 tablespoons of fresh rose hip puree (or a rose hip beverage-base cube or the contents of a rose hip tea bag). Heat thoroughly but do not boil. Strain, if necessary. Serve in a mug with a slice of lemon. Serve with cheese crackers.

Vitamin C in Rose Hips

Wild rose hips are incredibly rich in vitamin C (ascorbic acid). They all contain at least 25 times more vitamin C than oranges. The amount varies with the species of wild rose, and some have been found to contain almost a hundred times the vitamin content of citrus juices. Since vitamin C is destroyed by heat and is water soluble, these suggestions should be followed whenever possible to conserve as much of the valuable vitamins in rose hips.

Use rose hips as a raw food whenever possible.

After picking keep rose hips chilled until used. This will inactivate vitamin-destroying enzymes.

Add 2 tablespoons of lemon juice or vinegar to each pint of rose hip liquid. The acid helps to prevent enzyme formation.

Gather the rose hips as soon as they are bright red, while they are still firm and before the silky fibers form inside the hip around the seeds.

Cook rose hips quickly but keep the heat as low as possible.

Use a covered container made of enamelware, glass, or stainless steel; do not use copper or aluminum vessels.

After cooking rose hips to extract juice for jelly or extracts, if possible, let the hips stand overnight in the water used to cook them in to draw out more of the vitamins in the liquid.

Dry rose hips for tea in the sun, not in a hot oven, then store in a very tight container if the hips are to be kept for any length of time.

The white seeds inside the rose hips are rich in vitamin E. It is a good idea to boil them in a little water, strain it, then use it as a liquid called for in recipes using rose hips. Grinding the seeds before boiling them also helps to extract the vitamin.

Rose Hip Vitamin Extract

Wash the rose hips of any wild rose with large hips. Cut off the stems and blossom ends. Cut the fruits in half but do not remove the seeds. Or, put the rose hips and seeds through a meat grinder or chop them in an electric blender.

To 1½ cups of boiling water in an enameled pan, add 1 cup of the prepared rose hips. Cover the pan and simmer for about 15 minutes. Let the rose hip mixture stand in the refrigerator, in a pottery crock, for 24 hours. Strain off the extract through a fine sieve. Add lemon juice, 2 tablespoons for each pint of extract, and store in the refrigerator to use as needed to enrich cooked soups, fruit juices, beverages, or any cooked food. The vitamin extract may be frozen in ice cube trays, then stored in plastic bags in the freezer to be used as needed.

NUTTING

Every autumn, when sunny days kindle the foliage of the trees on the rolling Indiana hillsides to the peak of their October brilliance and a light frost tumbles down a crisp layer of leaves to rustle underfoot, my children and I hike to the woods to pick up black walnuts and hickory nuts. When the hazelnuts are ripening, we know it as surely as every chipmunk knows it. When the sweet little wild pecans pelt the ground beneath the tree, we are there to rummage in the grass and leaves. Nutting is the autumn pastime that compels us, on clear, blue-skied October days, to be off for the woods.

We know exactly where to find the trees that drop the best-flavored black walnuts and the largest hickory nuts. We know where a lone pecan tree stands in the middle of a low flat field and where hazelnut bushes are thick on the creek bank, because these are the same woods where I went nutting as a child. Many are the same trees under which I picked up the pungently scented green-hulled walnuts and the bone-white hickory nuts in autumns gone by. These towering black walnut trees and hardy shagbark hickories have changed little with the passing of a quarter of a century, and it is reassuring to see them, stately and enduring, still faithfully showering down their bounty for our family.

Early in October my sister-in-law begins to watch the hazelnut thicket. One day she called me.

"Better plan on coming up this weekend. The hickory nuts are falling and the chipmunks are beginning to work the hazelnuts."

The tiny chipmunks, who are not tree climbers, find most of the low-growing hazelnut shrubs within their range. That weekend, when Pat and I looked in the first clump of bushes for the nuts, we thought we were too late.

"Why, they're all gone!" Pat exclaimed. "These bushes were just full on Monday!"

We looked on the ground in the leaves, and there was the evidence that confirmed our suspicions. Little hollowed-out shells lay scattered under the hazelnut bushes where the chipmunks had feasted on the tiny sweet nutlets.

But as we moved along the creek bank, where hazelnut bushes grow thickly under hickory, elm, dogwood, sassafras, and oak trees, disappointedly searching each clump of shrubs, we found a few remaining clusters of nuts among the yellowing leaves—then more. Soon we realized that the chipmunks had left hazelnuts for us on all of the taller bushes that grew straight up, without many branches, to a height of about ten feet. The tall bushes were too limber to support even the weight of a chipmunk without bending, and the tiny acrophobiacs had not yet become hungry enough to brave the heights.

Pat and I gleaned the thicket and found enough of the hazelnuts (*Corylus americana*) to fill a large grocery sack. Each tiny round hazelnut is encased in a fringed leafy husk. When the pale green husk turns brown and the nut ripens, the dried husk opens and releases the yellowish-brown hazelnut. The nuts grow in beautifully arranged clusters that look almost flowerlike as they hang under the leaves. The clusters contain any number of nuts, from two to ten, although Pat and I picked a few growing singly.

While we were looking overhead through the birchlike leaves to find the scattered hazelnut clusters, we made another of the serendipitous discoveries that are natural to the wild foods hunt. A vine of wild fox grapes (*Vitis labrusca*) twined around the slim trunk and over the branches of a sapling sassafras tree. Some of the long, slender bunches of grapes were hanging within our reach. I tasted one. Frost had not yet sweetened the purplish-black, bloom-frosted grapes and my jaws were set by their tartness. Their flavor was very foxy and wild. They were perfect for the dark jelly our families like, so Pat and I picked all we could reach.

We carried our bounty back to the rustic lakeside cabin that my brother built for us beside the old wild apple tree. Here is where we find the tonic of wildness prescribed by Henry David Thoreau, where we walk out into our own waldens each time we come back to the family farm to rediscover its riches. We spread the hazelnuts out to finish drying, not far from the sandstone fireplace in the cabin's main room, and stored the wild grapes in the refrigerator. A good wind the night before had brought down the hickory nuts and there were several hickory trees, from one side of the farm to the other, where we wanted to pick up nuts.

Of the many hickories (*Carya*) in Indiana, we gather the nuts of the common shagbark hickories that are found all over the farm and the large rounded nuts of a rare big shellbark hickory that stands about a hundred feet tall and is surely as many years old. The shellbark (*Carya laciniosa*) once grew in great abundance in the Midwest river-bottom area as did other towering trees such as sycamores, black walnuts, pecans, and tulip trees. But today the bottomlands are largely deforested, and fields of corn grow where the tall trees stood. Most of the once-plentiful bottom hickories have been searched out by timber scouts. But a few lucky nut gatherers know that here and there may still be found a superior form of hickory bearing a very large round hickory nut with delicious sweet meats. We have one of these shell-barks on the farm and know where several more stand at the edge of a creek in a moist old hilly woods nearby. But we must return to the hickories several times each autumn if we are to find enough fallen nuts for our use. Squirrels attend the hickory-nut trees and indus-triously carry off all the nuts they do not eat.

We carry a burlap sack apiece, for we will come back lugging heavy loads of rich, wild nuts to crack on some early winter day, on the cabin's hearthstone before a crackling fire. Shelling nuts is the perfect fireside task for a housebound day when the sleet tinkles against the windowpane and there is nothing else to do. It takes infinite patience and lots of spare time to pick out the stubborn kernels from their intricate shells. But we keep at it, feeling a little like chipmunks burrowed in for the winter with our hoard, until we have enough nutmeats ready for the Christmas baking and candy-making.

Pat and I picked up only a little more than a gallon of nuts for our hoard under the big shellbark tree at the edge of the woods, but we could see that there were still plenty of green-hulled nuts hanging among the leaflets.

"We'll have to come earlier in the morning to beat the squirrels to these nuts," Pat said. "They begin to feed at dawn."

We walked back into the woods a few hundred feet to a big shag-bark hickory (*Carya ovata*) to gather its long, pointed, bone-white nuts. The shagbark is an old tree, too, and strips of gray, ragged bark warp away from its thick columnar trunk. The shagbark is easily distinguished from all other hickories by its bark alone. This tree has no branches for the first fifty feet or so because it grows in the woods alongside other big trees, but looking up, we can see the large luminous gold leaves, lightened by the October sun shining through its crown, that add much to the early color of Indiana's autumn foliage.

Before carrying them home, we pried off any dry hulls that had already partly fallen away from the chalky thin-shelled hickory nuts. We threw the thick, four-sectioned hull fragments under the shagbark hickory tree where the litter of other years is like nature's kitchen middens. We always examine the natural debris under nut trees with the interest of archaeologists looking for artifacts of another culture:

Hazelnut (*Corylus americana*)

here are the old, gnawed-out shells of squirrel-eaten hickory nuts, and others riddled with wormholes; this thick layer of empty, darkened hulls remains from the harvest of other years; here are the twigs and long shaggy scales of gray bark shed by the slow-growing shagbark; there are some fresh deer tracks; a puffball mushroom turning yellow; some small hickory-nut trees; the ubiquitous poison ivy; and here is the empty red cylinder of a 12-gauge shotgun shell that tells of a hunter who stood under this tree.

Pat cracked a few hulled hickory nuts with a stone and tasted the sweet-flavored kernels, but they were still wet and soft. Our hickory nuts, like the hazelnuts, need to dry for several weeks to develop their splendid flavor and crispness.

After a weekend of foraging, Pat and I had gathered a half-bushel of hickory nuts from the various trees on the farm—as well as the wild grapes, a bucketful of crab apples, a gallon of early-ripening persimmons, a dishful of sheep sorrel, and armloads of autumn-blooming goldenrod and white asters. Our sons had contributed some black

Hickory nut (*Carya ovata*)

Shagbark hickory

walnuts to our nut hoard, a panful of lake fish for our supper, some reindeer moss and bird's nests to wonder at, and long tendrils of bittersweet to drape over the cabin door. The refrigerator was overflowing, the porch floor was spread with wild nuts that were drying, and the cabin was richly adorned with our wild harvests.

When I was growing up in the country, we always gathered in the crops of wild-growing nut trees. In most farm homes then, store-bought nuts were never seen in the kitchen. We used wild pecans, hickory nuts, and black walnuts extravagantly, and hazelnuts whenever we could beat the chipmunks to them. Sometimes there were butternuts, too, but white walnut trees were not plentiful in Grandpa's woods.

In my kitchen today, we keep supplies of the same wild nuts that my family gathers in Grandpa's enduring woods whenever we spend time at the cabin in the autumn, and we have an ample amount of butter-nuts (*Juglans cinerea*) that we are able to get when we vacation in Vermont. We gather the tiny wild pecans close to our home in Newburgh, Indiana. Pecans (*Carya illinoensis*) are southern-growing nuts, and the northernmost part of their natural range is southern Indiana. Living as we do within sight of the Ohio River, we can easily find native pecan trees in our area. The thin-shelled, olive-shaped nuts that grow wild on tall, picturesque pecan trees near our house are about half the size of the pecans from the horticultural varieties, but they are sweeter and better. Of course, we could buy the larger pecans at the grocery the year around, but if we have a choice between a food that grows wild in its natural state and its cultivated, processed, packaged counterpart, my family will choose the wildling we have gathered for ourselves. And when I list my family's favorite dishes made with nuts—candies, pies, cakes, cookies, ice cream—there is no doubt that we need plenty of nuts on hand to last us through the winter.

Butternut (*Juglans cinerea*)

Earlier this fall, when we were lugging a heavy load of black walnuts home from the woods, my sons thought we had been greedy in our harvesting, even though we left the ground under the trees covered with nuts for the squirrels.

"We'll never use this many!" Jimmy said. "Let's dump some—they're heavy!"

But later, when the husks are removed, the bulk of our harvest shrinks greatly. Each sackful of walnuts contains more husks than nuts. The contents of a sack now fill only a pail. And later still, when the kernels are removed from their hard, tough shells, our harvest is concentrated even more: a gallon of uncracked nuts yields only a cupful or so of nutmeats.

Much effort is expended between the pleasant autumn outing to gather "nuts from brown October's wood" and the first delectable taste of black walnuts in the Christmas fudge. With black walnuts

(*Juglans nigra*), the work begins after the heavy load is brought back to the house. The greenish-yellow hulls should dry a bit, until they begin to darken and shrivel, then they must be broken away from the hard, woody shell of the round walnut that is encased within. Handling black walnuts after the leathery hulls are crushed is a messy chore. The same is true of butternuts. Even when partly dried out, the hulls contain a dark oily stain that has remarkable permanence, both on the hands and on cloth. I used to spread unhusked walnuts on our graveled driveway so that car wheels could pass over them and split the hulls. But since I learned to use them to make a warm-brown natural dye for my hand-spun yarns, I value the hulls as much as the walnuts. So now I put the unhusked walnuts in an old burlap sack and pound them, a few at a time, with a heavy stone, or crush them, one at a time, under the heel of my shoe. Then, wearing heavy gloves, I can break the tannin-filled hulls away and save them for the dye pot.

After the brown-staining husks are removed, the walnuts should be washed clean and then allowed to dry for several weeks until the kernels inside are no longer moist and green-tasting, but dry, crisp, and well flavored. The simplest way to do this is to scatter the walnuts on the ground where the garden hose can be turned on them or where the

Pecan nuts and leaves (*Carya illinoensis*)

Black walnut (*Juglans nigra*)

rain can fall on them; then let the rinsed walnuts lie in the sun or in a warm, dry building until they are seasoned.

Each autumn when we return to Grandpa's woods to gather in the wild harvest cast at our feet by the old nut trees, I think how fortunate we are. Such forest abundances have been endangered in many places by unremitting demands upon the butternut, the black walnut, the hickory, and the pecan for their useful and beautiful woods. But my brother, like Grandpa before him, values these trees that are part of our heritage more than the timberman's dollar.

Sometimes my brother joins us when we make an afternoon's outing of gathering in the nuts. His little son Scotty is too young to walk the whole distance and we have the picnic basket to carry, so we bounce along the rough trail through the field toward the woods in a rubber-tired wagon that my brother pulls behind his tractor. As I sit in the jostling wagon, with a few stray ears of corn bouncing around me on the wagon bed, watching my brother up front driving the tractor, I am struck by the similarity of this afternoon to one I remember when my brother and I bumped across these same ruts, twenty-five years ago, in a real wagon pulled by horses and driven by my Uncle Roy.

This day could well be that day: the crispness edging the October air; the laughing, shouting children; the cawing flocks of noisy crows; the sun's gentle warmth on our backs when we search under the trees; little boys pelting saucy red squirrels with walnuts; a patient, indulgent uncle boosting his nephews up tree trunks and warning them of an old well hidden by huge flat sandstones—how clearly our family excursion calls up that long-ago afternoon.

We carried a picnic basket that day, too, and ate our lunch under the spreading, leafless branches of an old black walnut tree on a high hill overlooking Grandpa's house. I remember how it was that afternoon with all of us sitting about on the crisp leaves under the bare tree: my Uncle Roy leaning his back against one side of the thick-trunked, rough-barked walnut tree and Grandpa resting against the opposite side; my mother and Aunt Helen sitting on opposite ends of a fallen log on which the picnic was spread, handing out fried chicken and cookies; and the rest of us scattered around, sitting on rocks, on stumps, and on the lumpy, half-filled gunny sacks that held the harvest of nuts we had gathered before the picnic.

And while we ate, a red squirrel in the tree barked and chattered at us and my brother teased him more by throwing nuts into the branches. Every so often a walnut broke its bond with the tree and plummeted straight to the ground, rolling to rest nearby. This was a game to little cousin Ginger. At each sound of *thump!*, she was off for the fallen walnut, rummaging in the leaves until she found a nut—any nut—to add to her small sack. Another cousin, Buddy, fiendishly ground the pungent husks of fallen walnuts under his foot to split the hulls, then rubbed the dark oily stain on his fingers, then on any of us that he could catch, until his father made him stop the mischief.

Now, as I sit in the bumping wagon, I think, *A poor wagon*, because I remember our wooden wagon, painted green, yellow, and red, pulled by a snappy team of horses. And the noisy red tractor seems a sorry substitute for the spirited chestnut mare and the faithful Tony, who was (we loved to say it) "part Percheron."

But it is plain that the exuberant children enjoy themselves enormously. And twenty-five years from now, their remembrances of nutting in the autumn will surely feature their uncle's red tractor with the same nostalgia I feel today for Uncle Roy's horses.

I want to say to the children: *Remember this!*

For such a day, one so rich in the feeling of family solidarity and so blessed with the riches of nature, deserves to be well-remembered. The bounteous old walnut trees, the beauty of the farmstead dressed in the luminous golds, fiery reds, rich magentas, and warm browns of autumn leaf, the blue haze touching the familiar hills, the unusual charm of dried weeds and grasses, the fallen leaves like trampled flames underfoot, a high-flying skein of honking geese—these images have no chronology. They span the autumns.

Later, when we returned to the cabin, happy with our experiences and our harvest of black walnuts, I talked to my son Bobby about my uncle's horse-drawn wagon. I told him how like that day this one had been.

"Bobby," I asked, lightly, "in what sort of vehicle do you imagine you will take your children to Grandpa's old woods to go nutting twenty-five years from today?"

Bobby liked the question.

"A jet-propelled hovercraft!" he said. "Or a nuclear-powered terrestrial explorer!"

"Yes," I agreed, "but certainly *not* a horse-drawn wagon."

"No. . . . But, Mother." Bobby was serious. "I don't really think there will be any woods left twenty-five years from now."

"Bobby!" I was shocked. "Do you *believe* that?"

"Well, if there are," Bobby said, "we'll all have to line up and pay to get into them."

Bobby has expressed my fear—and that of a whole generation. But such pessimism is not new. In 1862 Thoreau had written:

The era of the Wild Apple will soon be past. It is a fruit which will probably become extinct in New England. . . . I fear that he who walks over these fields a century hence will not know the pleasures of knocking off wild apples. Ah, poor man, there are many pleasures which he will not know. . . . I see nobody planting trees to-day in such out-of-the-way places, along the lonely roads and lanes, and at the bottom of dells in the woods . . . and the end of it all will be that we shall be compelled to look for our apples in a barrel.

Even Henry David Thoreau sometimes had too little faith in nature.

As I sit here, in 1972, writing these words in my own cabin in the woods on the shore of a small lake, the porch floor is spread with wild nuts I have gathered from trees that have endured longer than four men, and the refrigerator is filled with wild fruits, and I can see by my window a wild apple tree with red-cheeked fruits hanging no higher above me than the end of a walking stick.

I want to say to you, Bobby Kluger, *Have more faith! Believe in nature!* Twenty-five years from now you will walk in these same fields and woods in Indian-summertime, rediscovering the same wild flavors.

For someone is planting trees today. In out-of-the-way places, along lonely roads and lanes, in wooded dells, and in your great-grandfather's woods, nature is still planting trees.

Margo's Black Walnut Canapés

½ cup black walnuts, chopped fine   2 tablespoons mayonnaise
4 tablespoons cream cheese, softened   Salt to taste
2 tablespoons sour cream   Angostura bitters

Combine black walnuts with cream cheese, sour cream, and mayonnaise. Mix well. Add salt and a dash of angostura bitters. Spread on toast or crackers. Serves 6.

Black Walnut Cake

⅔ cup shortening   3 teaspoons baking powder
1½ cups sugar   ¼ teaspoon salt
1 teaspoon vanilla extract   ¾ cup milk
3 large eggs, separated   1½ cups ground black walnuts
2 cups flour

With an electric mixer, cream the shortening, add the sugar, and beat until light and fluffy. Add the vanilla and the egg yolks; beat well. Sift together the dry ingredients, then add alternately with the milk. Beat the egg whites stiff in another bowl and fold them into the cake batter along with the nuts. Pour the batter into two 9-inch layer pans, greased and floured lightly, and bake in a moderate oven (350° F) for about 30 minutes, or until a toothpick inserted in the center comes out clean. Cool the layers and frost with Black Walnut Icing (recipe below). Makes 12 servings.

Black Walnut Icing

With an electric mixer, cream 1 stick of butter with 1 box of confectioners' sugar until fluffy, adding enough cream to make the icing a good spreading consistency. Add ½ teaspoon of black walnut extract. Spread the frosting between the layers, on top, and on the sides of the cakes. Then sprinkle the frosted cake with ½ cup chopped black walnuts.

BLACK WALNUT DESSERT

½ cup butter
1 cup confectioners' sugar
3 egg yolks
2 ounces chocolate, melted
½ cup black walnuts, chopped

1 teaspoon vanilla extract
  or 1 tablespoon rum
3 egg whites, beaten stiff
1½ cups crushed vanilla wafers

Cream the butter, add the sugar and egg yolks, and mix well. Add the melted chocolate and blend. Add the nutmeats and flavoring and fold in the stiffly beaten egg whites. Cover the bottom of a refrigerator freezing tray with half of the vanilla wafer crumbs. Pour the chocolate mixture over the crumbs and sprinkle the remaining crumbs on the top. Place the tray in the freezing compartment of the refrigerator and freeze overnight. Serves 8.

BLACK WALNUT PIE

1 cup sugar
1 cup dark corn syrup
2 tablespoons butter
3 eggs, well beaten

1 tablespoon vanilla extract
1 cup black walnuts, chopped
Pastry for 9-inch single crust
  (page 44)

In a saucepan, boil the sugar and syrup together slowly until the mixture thickens, then add the butter. Pour very gradually into the eggs, beating constantly. Add the vanilla. Sprinkle the black walnuts over the bottom of the pastry shell, then pour in the syrup mixture. Bake in a hot oven (425° F) for 10 minutes, then reduce the heat to 350° F and bake 40 to 50 minutes longer. Serve the pie cold with whipped cream topping. Serves 6 to 8.

HICKORY NUT-CORN PUDDING

2 eggs, beaten
2 tablespoons sugar
2 tablespoons flour
1 teaspoon salt
1 cup milk

1 medium-sized can cream-style
  corn (yellow)
½ cup hickory nuts, chopped
2 tablespoons butter

Combine all of the ingredients except the butter and pour into a well-greased casserole. Dot the top of the pudding with butter and bake in a moderate oven (350° F) for 1 hour. Makes 6 servings.

SOUR CREAM HICKORY NUT COOKIES

1 cup butter	4½ cups sifted flour
2 cups sugar	4 teaspoons baking powder
2 large eggs	½ teaspoon baking soda
1 cup sour cream	¼ teaspoon salt
½ teaspoon vanilla extract	½ cup chopped hickory nuts

In the large bowl of an electric mixer, cream the butter; add the sugar gradually and beat until fluffy. Add the eggs, one at a time, beating well after each addition. Stir in the sour cream and vanilla. Sift together the dry ingredients, add, and blend well. Drop the batter by tablespoonfuls onto a greased cookie sheet. Sprinkle the tops of the cookies with additional hickory nuts. Bake in a moderate oven (350° F) for 20 minutes. Makes 3½ dozen large, soft cookies.

HICKORY NUT CAKE

1 cup butter	4 teaspoons baking powder
1½ cups sugar	¼ teaspoon salt
2 egg yolks	1¼ cups light cream
¼ cup maple syrup	1 cup hickory nuts, chopped fine
3 cups sifted flour	5 egg whites, beaten stiff

In the large bowl of an electric mixer, cream the butter, then add the sugar gradually, beating well. Add the egg yolks and beat again. Add the maple syrup and beat well. Sift together the dry ingredients and add alternately with the cream, beating thoroughly after each addition. Then fold in the hickory nuts and stiffly beaten egg whites with a spoon. Pour the batter into three 8-inch cake pans that have been greased and floured. Bake the cakes in a moderate oven (350° F) for 30 minutes, or until a toothpick inserted in the center comes out clean. Cool the cakes on racks; they will fall slightly. Then put the layers together with Hickory Nut Filling between them (recipe below) and cover the top and sides of the cake with Maple Sea-foam Frosting (see page 47.) This delicious cake is doubly rich because of the candylike filling. Makes 12 servings.

Hickory Nut Filling

3 cups sugar
1 cup light cream
1 teaspoon corn syrup

1 tablespoon butter
1 cup hickory nuts, chopped
¼ teaspoon maple flavoring

Combine the sugar, cream, and corn syrup in a heavy saucepan. Cook, while stirring, until a soft ball forms when a small amount of syrup is dropped into cold water, or 235° F on a candy thermometer. Add the butter. Cool, then beat until the filling is creamy. Add the nuts and quickly spread between cake layers.

NOTE: This cake filling can also be served as a fudge. One teaspoon of vanilla extract may be substituted for the maple flavoring.

Quail with Hazelnuts

4 quails
Salt
Pepper
Flour
¼ cup butter
1 tablespoon vegetable oil
1 cup chicken stock or water

2 tablespoons white wine
    or 1 tablespoon lemon juice
1 cup seedless green grapes
½ cup hazelnuts, chopped
1 tablespoon butter
4 slices buttered toast

Sprinkle the quails inside and out with salt and pepper and roll in flour. Melt the butter in a heavy skillet and add the vegetable oil. Sauté the quails in the fat over medium heat until they are well browned. Add the stock, cover the pan, and cook over low heat for 15 minutes, or until tender. Add the wine and the grapes; stir, but do not boil.

Meanwhile, toast the hazelnuts with the tablespoon of butter in a pan in a moderate oven (350° F) for about 5 minutes, stirring and watching carefully to keep the nuts from burning.

Place each bird on a slice of buttered toast and spoon over each some of the grapes and the sauce from the pan. Sprinkle each serving with hot, toasted hazelnuts. Serves 4.

Hazelnut-Mocha Dessert

1½ tablespoons unflavored gelatin
¼ cup cold water
¾ cup strong hot coffee
4 ounces sweet cooking chocolate
½ cup sugar

1 cup hazelnuts
1 cup heavy cream
1 teaspoon vanilla extract
2 dozen ladyfingers

Soften the gelatin in the cold water. Pour the hot coffee over the sweet chocolate to melt it, putting it over low heat if necessary. Remove from the heat and add the sugar and gelatin. Cool, then chill in the refrigerator until almost set.

Meanwhile, chop the hazelnuts fine and dry them in a hot oven (400° F) for about 5 minutes. Cool. Whip the cream until it is stiff, then fold it into the chilled gelatin mixture with the nuts and the vanilla. Butter the sides and bottom of a 9-by-5-by-3-inch loaf pan and line the pan with split ladyfingers. Pour in a third of the cream mixture, add a layer of ladyfingers, and repeat twice, ending with ladyfingers on top. Chill the dessert several hours or overnight. Unmold and serve with additional whipped cream and chopped hazelnuts. Serves 8.

Hazelnut-Chocolate Ice Cream

½ cup ground hazelnuts, toasted	4 eggs or 8 egg yolks
8 ounces sweet cooking chocolate	2 tablespoons gelatin
1 quart light cream	¼ cup cold water
1½ cups sugar	3 cups heavy cream, whipped
½ teaspoon salt	2 tablespoons vanilla extract

Toast the ground hazelnuts on a shallow pan in a moderate oven (350° F), stirring frequently, until they are lightly browned (15 minutes or less). Cool.

Melt the sweet chocolate over hot water. Meanwhile, heat the light cream over hot water also, until a film puckers on top of the cream. Stir the sugar and salt into the cream. Beat the eggs or egg yolks in a bowl and slowly stir in a little of the hot cream mixture. Then stir the egg-yolk mixture into the rest of the hot cream, stir in the melted chocolate, and continue cooking over hot water, stirring constantly, until the mixture coats a clean metal spoon. This makes a thin custard; do not overcook. Remove the custard from the heat. Soften the gelatin in the cold water, and stir into custard. Cool in the refrigerator or by placing the pan in another pan containing ice water until the mixture begins to thicken. Then add the vanilla and fold in the cooled, toasted hazelnuts and the whipped cream.

Pour the mixture into a chilled 1-gallon canister of a churn type of ice cream freezer and fit the dasher into place. Fill the freezer tub around the canister with finely cracked ice and salt, using 1 part ice cream salt to 8 parts of ice, or about 1 quart of salt for a gallon-sized ice cream freezer. Fill the freezer half full of ice before adding the first layer of salt, then alternate layers of ice and salt until the tub is filled. Freeze until the ice cream stiffens (about 20 minutes with an electric ice cream freezer). Then repack the freezer tub with ice, or remove the ice cream and place it in an ice cream mold, and let the ice cream ripen for several hours before serving.

To repack the freezer, remove the dasher, plug up the hole in the lid of the ice cream canister, drain out the salt water through the hole in the side of the ice cream freezer, and add fresh ice and salt to fill the freezer tub. Put cracked ice, but no salt, over the top of the canister, too. Cover the whole freezer with blankets or newspapers and let it stand in a cool place for several hours.

HAZELNUT ROLL

6 egg yolks
¾ cup sugar
1½ cups ground hazelnuts
1 teaspoon baking powder
1 teaspoon vanilla extract

6 egg whites
Confectioners' sugar, as needed
2 cups heavy cream
2 tablespoons rum

Beat the egg yolks with the sugar until they are light and thick. Mix the nuts with the baking powder and add them with the vanilla to the yolk mixture. Beat the egg whites until they are stiff but not dry, and fold in. Line a buttered shallow pan (12-by-18 inches) with buttered waxed paper and spread the mixture evenly into it. Bake for 15 minutes in a moderate oven (350° F), until a toothpick comes out clean. Do not overbake. Remove the cake from the oven and cover it with a damp towel until it is completely cool. Loosen the cake from the pan and turn it out on a piece of waxed paper on top of a towel that has been sprinkled heavily with confectioners' sugar. Peel the waxed paper off the bottom of the cake (which is now the top). Roll up the cake lengthwise in the paper and the towel and leave it until shortly before serving. Whip the cream until it is stiff and sweeten it with 2 tablespoons of confectioners' sugar. Stir in the rum and spread the whipped cream on top of the unrolled cake. Reroll, wrap with a cloth, and chill until serving time. Serves 8.

Hazelnut Soufflé

3 egg yolks
3 tablespoons sugar
3 tablespoons flour
¼ teaspoon salt

1 cup milk
¾ cup hazelnuts, ground fine
3 tablespoons butter
4 egg whites, beaten stiff

Beat the egg yolks until thick, add the sugar, and stir well. Add the flour and the salt. Heat the milk and the nuts in the top of a double boiler, then gradually stir in the egg yolk mixture and cook over simmering-hot water until thick, stirring constantly. Add the butter and cool. Fold in the stiffly beaten egg whites, pour into a well-buttered, sugared soufflé dish and bake over water in a slow oven (325° F) until the soufflé is well puffed (about 1 hour). Serve at once with Coffee Sauce (recipe below). Serves 6.

Coffee Sauce

Dissolve 1 tablespoon of instant coffee in ½ cup of boiling hot water. Add ¼ cup sugar and ⅛ teaspoon salt. Pour gradually into 2 well-beaten eggs. Cook over hot water until the mixture coats the spoon, stirring constantly. Chill. At serving time, beat ½ cup of heavy cream until stiff, then fold in the coffee mixture and serve it over hot soufflé.

Pecan Nut Log

Nougat Cream Center

3 cups granulated sugar
1⅓ cups light corn syrup
1 cup water
2 egg whites, beaten stiff
¼ cup melted butter
1 teaspoon vanilla extract
⅛ teaspoon salt

Caramel Coating

2 cups granulated sugar
1¼ cups light corn syrup
1½ cups light cream
1 teaspoon vanilla extract
¼ teaspoon salt
2 cups pecan nutmeats

Nougat Cream Center:

Combine ¾ cup sugar, ⅔ cup corn syrup, and ¼ cup water in a 1½-quart saucepan. Stir over medium heat until the sugar dissolves, then boil to 238° F on the candy thermometer or until a soft ball forms when a small amount of syrup is dropped into cold water. Pour the syrup over the stiffly beaten egg whites in a thin stream while beating with an electric mixer. Beat constantly until slightly cool (about 5 minutes). Spoon the mixture into a well-buttered bowl and make a well in the center. Let stand while making the second syrup.

Combine the remaining 2¼ cups sugar, ⅔ cup corn syrup, and ¾ cup water. Cook in a large saucepan over medium heat to 258° F. Pour the syrup all at once into the center of the egg white mixture in the bowl. Beat vigorously until well mixed. Stir in the butter, vanilla extract, and salt. Beat well. Let stand, beating occasionally, until the mixture is stiff and holds its shape. Transfer to a square pan (8-by-8-by-2 inches) lined with waxed paper. Chill for at least 2 or 3 hours (can chill for several days) and cut into 4 equal "logs." Cover each log with the caramel coating.

Caramel Coating:

Combine the sugar, syrup, and ½ cup of the cream in a 2-quart pan. Stir and cook over medium heat to 236° F. Add another ½ cup of cream and cook again to 236° F. Add the last ½ cup of cream and cook to 242° F. Lower the heat and stir often as the caramel thickens. Add the vanilla extract and the salt.

Dip each nougat log into the caramel and roll on all sides in the nutmeats. Chill before cutting each log into slices. Makes 4 logs.

PART IV

Continuing the Wild Feast

CONTINUING THE WILD FEAST

Whenever I think of the banquets of the meadows and woods, a feeling of felicity comes to me. It is as much a matter of nourishing the senses and the emotions as it is of finding our supper—or more. The sweet wild strawberries and the tart sorrel leaves that I find are only one course of the country feast. The crisp nuts and sour chokecherries in my basket are only the tangible harvest.

The pursuit of the wild flavor is one of the joys of my life. Every excursion into sunny fields yields the familiar bounties for our cupboard and often new wild foods I have not harvested before. The recipes accompanying this chapter are ones that I have tested in past seasons using the wild foods discussed here. At the end of the next harvest season—and the next—I will have added still more recipes and more wild foods to my ever-growing repertory. The new discoveries in store make me look forward to continuing the wild feast, year after year.

MAYAPPLES

In springtime, when we hunt for morels in the woods, colonies of mayapple plants (*Podophyllum peltatum*) are just beginning to unfurl green leaves. At the end of the mushrooming season, their large single and double leaves droop atop short, sturdy stems and the plants look very much like a crowd of miniature green umbrellas left open to dry. Some of the plants—those bearing a pair of large, similar leaves—have a single unpleasant-smelling white blossom. On these plants, an oval yellow fruit ripens in late summer, often as the plants are dying down.

The mayapple fruit, sometimes called wild lemon, hog-apple, or "mandrake," is the only part of the mayapple plant that is edible. *All other parts of the plant have poisonous properties.*

In August, when my nephew, Scotty Marshall, took me to a place in the woods where he had discovered a patch of ghostly Indian pipes, we found a colony of mayapple plants growing there too. The fruits were the size of pullet eggs and were a golden color. We sampled them and found them rich and musky-flavored. So, while Scotty gathered a handful of waxy-white Indian pipes, I filled my bandanna with lush, ripe mayapples for jelly.

MAYAPPLE JELLY

Wash ripe mayapples, cut away the stem and blossom ends, and any waste parts. Cut the fruit into pieces and place in a large kettle with water to cover. Bring to a boil, then simmer until the mayapples are tender, mashing during cooking. Strain the juice through a cheesecloth or let it drip through a jelly bag.

To 1¾ cups strained mayapple juice, add ⅛ cup of lemon juice and 3½ cups of sugar. Bring the mixture to a boil, stirring constantly, then stir in 3 ounces of liquid fruit pectin. Again bring to a boil, stirring constantly, and boil hard until the jelly stage is reached (see jelly test on page 00). Remove the jelly from the heat, skim, and pour into hot, sterilized jelly glasses. Seal at once with hot paraffin.

Double the recipe if you have plenty of mayapple juice. The amount used in this recipe is the yield of about 2 cups of sliced mayapples simmered in 3 cups of water—as many mayapples as I have found on one long walk through the woods. This recipe makes four small glasses of pale amber jelly with a special, almost tropical, flavor of its own. Serve mayapple jelly on hot breads or for a dessert with cream cheese and soda crackers.

FIDDLEHEADS

Fiddleheads, the coiled tips of young fern fronds, are a springtime delicacy especially prized by New Englanders and wild foods enthusiasts. Their season lasts only two weeks or so in May. Three kinds of the curled crosiers are gathered: those of the ostrich fern, the cinnamon fern, and the common bracken fern.

The fiddlehead is ready to pick when it is pushing up swiftly through the ground with its tightly coiled tip, shaped like the head of a fiddle. Fiddleheads are picked in the morning when they are woodsy-smelling and fresh flavored and snap off crisply into the hand of the picker. By afternoon the glowing green-coiled crosiers can have outgrown the edible stage, becoming unfurled fern fronds.

"I never gather any kind except the cinnamon fern," Mary Azarian told me. "There are great clumps of them down by the stone wall."

The cinnamon fern (*Osmunda cinnamomea*) fiddlehead is gathered when it is about eight inches tall. The crosiers and one-half inch to two

Cinnamon fern (*Osmunda cinnamomea*)

inches of the stems are eaten. A grayish-yellow woolly covering on the stems and tips must be removed (sometimes with difficulty) before the fiddleheads are cooked. They are washed and then rubbed to remove the fuzz. Fiddleheads will keep for a couple of days in the refrigerator after picking, but wild flavors and freshness are transitory. Better to pick fiddleheads in the morning and eat them before night—or freeze them.

Adele Dawson gathers the ostrich fern (*Pteretis nodulosa*) from the banks of the Winooski River which runs through the village of Marshfield, where our Vermont vacation house is. This fern is the tall, graceful plant that grows on stream and river banks where the water comes up in the early spring. So abundant are the ostrich ferns in the lush natural ferneries of the Winooski valley near Waterbury, Vermont, that quantities of the fiddleheads are harvested, packed in snow, and transported to Maine where they are canned for sale in specialty food stores.

Here in Indiana, our nearby woods and stream banks are not so ferny as our property in Vermont where Adele has found twenty-three of the eighty-plus species of fern that are native to the state. Every spring when I hunt morels and wildflowers in our Indiana woods, when violets are blooming with spring beauties and bloodroot and dutchman's breeches, and spring peepers are trilling in the creek that runs through the woods, I cross a boggy place where a small bed of bracken (*Pteridium latiusculum*) sprout. But I will not allow myself to take these tempting fiddleheads for our table because there are so few. When I picked them one spring and returned to the woods later to find some white trillium, I saw that I had diminished the lovely, lacy, clump of fern greenery. So now I content myself with fiddleheads gathered in Vermont whenever I am there, and canned ones at other times.

Fresh, crisp fiddleheads are steamed or boiled in salted water for 20 to 30 minutes, until just tender. Their flavor hints of asparagus and mushrooms combined, and they are delectable served with either of these compatibly flavored foods. But the best dish of plump fiddleheads is simmered gently and served hot, enhanced only by the simplest adornment of melted butter, served within hours after the crosiers are gathered—by yourself—from streambanks and along stone fences.

Bracken (*Pteridium latiusculum*)

Ostrich fern (*Pteretis nodulosa*)

FERN TIPS VINAIGRETTE

2 tablespoons vinegar
  or lemon juice
6 tablespoons melted butter
  or salad oil
½ teaspoon prepared mustard
½ teaspoon paprika
½ teaspoon salt

Freshly ground black pepper
1 teaspoon chopped chives
  or grated onion
2 hard-boiled eggs, chopped
2 cups fiddleheads, cooked
  and chilled

Combine all ingredients except the last two and mix well. Arrange hard-boiled eggs over top of the chilled, cooked fiddleheads and pour vinaigrette sauce over all. Serves 4.

MARINATED FIDDLEHEADS SALAD

Prepare 1 package of Good Seasons Italian salad dressing mix according to the directions on the package. Pour the dressing over 2 cups of cooked, drained fiddleheads. Let the fiddleheads marinate in the dressing overnight in the refrigerator.

Use marinated fiddleheads generously in a salad made of crisp lettuce leaves, sliced ripe tomatoes, and chopped scallions. Toss the salad with additional Italian dressing and serve with seasoned croutons scattered on top of the salad. Serves 6.

FIDDLEHEAD AND HAM CASSEROLE

4 tablespoons butter
4 tablespoons flour
2 cups milk
½ teaspoon salt
1 tablespoon chopped parsley

1 teaspoon chopped chives
1½ cups diced cooked ham
3 cups cooked fiddleheads
Buttered crumbs

Make a white sauce of butter, flour, milk, and salt. Add parsley and chives to sauce. In a casserole, alternate layers of ham, cooked fiddleheads, and white sauce until dish is filled, ending with a layer of sauce. Cover top of casserole with buttered crumbs and bake in moderate oven (350° F) until sauce bubbles and crumbs are browned (about 30 minutes). Serves 6.

FIDDLEHEAD QUICHE

1 cup milk
½ cup cream or evaporated milk
3 eggs
½ teaspoon salt
¼ teaspoon pepper
½ teaspoon dried minced green onion
  or 2 tablespoons fresh minced
  scallions

1 cup grated Swiss cheese
18 fiddlehead crosiers (not stems),
  cooked
4 slices crisp-fried bacon
Grated nutmeg
8-inch pastry shell, unbaked
  (page 44)

In a small bowl, combine the milk, cream, and eggs and beat with a rotary egg beater. Add the salt, pepper, and onions. Sprinkle half of the grated cheese in the bottom of the pastry shell. Arrange the fiddlehead tips over the cheese, then add the bacon, breaking it into bite-sized pieces. Pour in the milk mixture, add the rest of the cheese, and grate fresh nutmeg over the top. Bake in a moderate oven (375° F) for 30 minutes, or until a knife inserted in the custard comes out clean. Serves 4 to 6.

FIDDLEHEADS ON TOAST I

Cook fiddleheads and drain. Arrange on squares of toasted bread or on toasted English muffin halves. Pour rich white sauce with diced, hard-boiled eggs added over all. Serve sprinkled with paprika.

FIDDLEHEADS ON TOAST II

Cook fiddleheads and drain. Arrange on toast and top each serving with slices of crisp-fried bacon and a generous amount of white sauce, either plain or with cheese added.

FIDDLEHEADS ON TOAST III

Cook fiddleheads and drain. Roll fiddleheads in thin ham slices; broil and serve on toast or toasted English muffin halves with white sauce to pour over. Add cheese to the white sauce, if desired.

FIDDLEHEAD AND ONION SALAD

Cover chilled cooked fiddleheads and an equal amount of sliced, mild-flavored, raw onion rings with French dressing. Marinate for several hours, covered, in the refrigerator before serving.

VIOLETS

Every child knows that making sugared violets is as easy as mud pie and just as indispensable on the doll-house menu. But they also make great decorations for the elegant desserts or simple puddings on the grown-up's table, used like the expensive candied English violets that are sold in fancy-foods stores.

SUGARED VIOLETS

Wait until the morning dew has left the purple violets (*Viola*) before gathering them. Remove all of the stem portion and carefully dip each blossom into an egg white beaten until foamy with 1½ teaspoons water. Sprinkle each violet with granulated sugar, coating the petals evenly. Air-dry the violets on a cake rack in a warm dry place. When the violets are completely dry and brittle, store them in a covered tin with waxed paper between the layers until needed. Use soon.

NOTE: Mint leaves, rose petals, pansy blossoms, and borage flowers may be sugared in the same way.

VIOLET JELLY

½ cup fresh purple violet petals
1 cup sugar
3 cups water
1½ tablespoons plain gelatin

1 cup freshly-squeezed orange juice
Whipped cream
Fresh spring violets

Add fresh, fragrant purple violet petals, stemmed, to a boiling syrup made of the sugar and water. Simmer, covered, for 20 minutes. Strain and measure out 2 cups of syrup. Soften the gelatin in the orange juice and add. Pour into a mold and chill in the refrigerator until firm. Unmold and serve the dessert garnished with the whipped cream and fresh spring violets. Serves 4.

RED CLOVER

Red clover (*Trifolium pratense*) offers its delicately-sweet scented blossoms to wild-foods hunters and to bees from spring through fall. Its purplish rose flowers are easily discovered along roadsides and in sunny meadows. Its name, *pratense*, means "growing in meadows." In July, when clovers and many summer flowers are at the height of their blooming season, we make from the blossoms of red clover, white clover, and wild roses honey that could *almost* fool the bees. We make a clover blossom wine that has fooled a few of its imbibers, too. And we sometimes make a pleasant tea of the honeyed flowers.

In the middle of November, when my son Bobby and I walked along Grimm Road on a raw day, we found several red clover plants, still freshly blooming in spite of several frosts, and we picked enough of the pretty flowers for a bouquet and for a pot of hot clover tea.

Everyone knows white clover (*T. repens*), the creeping plant of lawns with a small, white, rounded bloom and its leaf with the three leaflets, among which we look for the lucky four-leaf clover. Its blossoms are also used in the honey and wine.

Clover Blossom Honey

5 pounds white sugar
1 teaspoon powdered alum
2¼ cups water
30 large red clover blossoms

40 white clover blossoms
Petals from 6 large roses
    or 2 cups wild rose petals

Combine the sugar and alum; add the water and stir until dissolved. Place in a large kettle over high heat and bring to a boil, stirring constantly. Boil hard for 1 minute. Remove the syrup from the fire and add the flower blossoms. Let them remain in the syrup for at least 15 minutes, then strain the mixture through a cheesecloth, pressing the

blossoms. Put the syrup in hot, sterilized jars (jelly glasses) and seal. This makes a light, golden honey-like syrup that will not granulate. Makes 8 jars.

Aunt Elsie's Clover Blossom Wine

1 gallon red clover blossoms	5 gallons boiling water
10 pounds sugar	5 cakes yeast or
1 dozen lemons, cut up	5 packages active dry yeast
1 box raisins	

Combine the clover blossoms, sugar, lemons, and raisins in a large stoneware jar. Pour in the boiling water and stir enough to dissolve the sugar. Cool to lukewarm. Mix the yeast with a small amount of the lukewarm liquid, and add to the jar. Mix well. Cover the jar with a cloth, tie it down around the top, and let stand for 5 days at room temperature, stirring occasionally. Strain through a double thickness of cheesecloth and pour into glass jugs. Cover the tops but do not seal tight until the wine stops bubbling and is still.

Aunt Elsie and Uncle Ollie always made this wine. The flavor is delicious. Aunt Elsie said, "The older it gets, the better it is."

NOTE: White clover blossoms may be picked for this wine, too.

Red Clover Tea

Put a handful of fresh red clover blossoms with a few of their leaves into an earthenware teapot, 2-cup size. Fill the teapot with boiling water, cover, and infuse for 5 to 10 minutes over very low heat. Set the pot on a trivet over the burner, if necessary, to protect it from breaking. Strain into a hot cup, add a twist of lemon and sweeten with honey.

Some fresh or dried mint leaves may be used with the clover blossoms, or several dandelion leaves, or both.

NOTE: Red clover blossoms may be dried to use for tea. Spread the blossoms out in a single layer on a tray and dry them in the sun. Use less of the dried flowers, 1 to 1½ teaspoons to 1 cup of water, to make the tea.

DAY LILIES

For years the lower end of Grimm Road was still a charming country lane, unpaved and overhung with an arch of tree branches and thickly rimmed with common day lilies (*Hemerocallis fulva*) that had nat-

uralized on the high roadbanks and proliferated, undisturbed, for years. We enjoyed walking and driving down the road when the tawny-orange day lilies were blooming in late June against a background of frothy white elderberry blossoms. There was such an abundance that we often picked the unopened flower buds for our table or huge bouquets for the house, although the blooms last only one day. How cheated we felt if the county-owned mowing machines came along before the day lilies, Queen-Anne's lace, and bright blue chicory finished blooming! But, fortunately, ours was a little-traveled road for many years and it was not until the summer before last that the road-graders finally uprooted and scraped away the lovely field of flowers.

"I don't like to come this way anymore," one of my sons remarked the next summer when we passed the place where the day lilies had always been.

But last summer, to our delight, we saw that the day lilies are beginning to grow back. With the increasing interest in preserving the natural beauty of our country roads, I am hopeful that these vivid flowers of the roadsides will again have their day of blooming.

DAY-LILY BUDS AMANDINE

2 cups green day-lily flower buds	½ cup slivered almonds
2 tablespoons butter	1 teaspoon soy sauce
1 cup sliced canned mushrooms	

Pick 2 cups of green, unopened flower buds of day lilies that seem ready to bloom in about two days.

Parboil the cleaned day-lily buds in salted water to cover for 1 minute. Pour off the water and drain. Heat the butter in a skillet and sauté the day-lily buds quickly with the canned mushrooms. Add the almonds and soy sauce and toss lightly. Serve at once. Serves 4.

BATTER-FRIED DAY-LILY BUDS

Dip opening day-lily flowers in batter and fry according to the directions given for Batter-fried Dandelion Blossoms on page 81.

WILD PLUMS

There were once two large wild plum trees shading a chicken house on the farm. I spent many mornings in the branches picking the shiny, sour, red-skinned fruits for Mother's jellies. The plums had to be harvested from the tree branches because the moment they fell, juicy with ripeness, the fat hens ran after them and pecked into their sweet skins, even before the plums had stopped rolling. Plum jelly was a bit tart to Mother's taste, so she sometimes combined the juice with that of greening apples or blackberries.

The old "wild goose" plum trees are gone now, but last April my sister-in-law and I found a new thicket while we were out looking for morels. The road bank in front of "Aunt" Bige's old homeplace, which we often walk by, was covered with a tangle of small wild plum trees (*Prunus americana*). So nondescript was the growth of the thicket before it was transformed by the mass of frothy white redolent blossoms that we had not noticed it in previous seasons.

Spring is often the best time to locate wild fruits with showy blooms. The flowering trees stand out against a green hillside or flag one's attention from a passing car. Sometimes we forget to return to the place of our discovery at the proper time. But "Aunt" Bige's plums were on the route of Pat's daily walk. When the small oval fruits were reddening, Pat reminded me of them. We picked enough to make a batch of tart, sparkling red-plum jelly.

WILD PLUM JELLY

Wash about 2 quarts of wild plums. Well-ripened plums may be used because this recipe uses a commercial fruit pectin. Place the plums in a kettle with about 3 cups of water. Bring to a boil and simmer, covered for 30 minutes. Let the juice drip through a jelly bag, squeezing to remove all of the juice, or strain through double layers of cheesecloth.

In a large kettle, combine 3½ cups of wild plum juice and 6 cups of sugar. Mix well and place over high heat, stirring carefully while the mixture comes to a boil. Add ½ bottle of liquid fruit pectin, stir, and bring to a full rolling boil. Cook and stir until the mixture reaches the jelly stage (see jelly test on page 129). Remove from the heat, skim off the foam, and pour into hot sterilized jelly glasses. Seal at once with hot paraffin. Makes 6 glasses.

Use this recipe to make Beach Plum Jelly, too.

Wild Plum Jelly Pie

¼ cup butter
¼ cup sugar
2 egg yolks
½ cup Wild Plum Jelly (recipe
   above)
⅛ teaspoon salt

¼ cup cream
2 egg whites, beaten stiff
8-inch unbaked pie shell
   (page 44)
1 cup heavy cream, whipped

Cream the butter and the sugar until light and fluffy, using an electric mixer. Add the egg yolks and beat well. Add the wild plum jelly, salt, and cream. Last, fold in the stiffly beaten egg whites, using a spoon. Pour the mixture into an unbaked pie shell and bake in a moderate oven (375° F) for 20 to 25 minutes, or until a knife inserted in the center comes out clean. Cool and spread the top with the whipped cream before serving.

RED RASPBERRIES

Red raspberries (*Rubus strigosus*) grow wild on our land in Vermont. They border the woods and the path along the waterfall. We harvest them at random. On a walk to the top of the meadow, we stop along the way by a clump of prickly canes and pick a sun-warmed handful of berries. At suppertime, someone goes out to the banks by the waterfall to gather a bowlful for the table. Our early-morning riser brings back a cupful, still wet with dew, to top his bowl of cereal. Last summer I hoarded a pint to add to the tutti-frutti.

But we never *really* have enough of the sweet wild berries from a summer's foraging to extend beyond the luscious raspberries and cream, raspberries and ice cream, and raspberries and cereal, and an occasional batch of jelly. Maybe next year . . .

Red Raspberry Jelly

Crush red raspberries, using about 2 pints. Add water to almost cover and simmer for 15 minutes, mashing and stirring as necessary. Strain the juice through a jelly bag. Squeeze the bag to extract all of the juice.

Combine 3 cups of the raspberry juice and 1 box of powdered fruit pectin. Stir and bring to a lively boil. Add 4 cups of sugar, stir, and

bring to a rolling boil. Boil hard, stirring constantly, until the jelly stage is reached (see jelly test on page 129). Remove from the heat, skim off the foam, and pour into hot, sterilized jelly glasses. Seal with hot paraffin. Makes 6 glasses.

WILD GRAPES

When I stayed in the cabin by my brother's lake during the beautiful days of early October, my eight-year-old nephew, Scotty, ran over from the farmhouse every morning to ask me, "When are we going hunting today?"

We would make our plans and later Scotty would take me from one place to another on the farm where he had made discoveries for me.

One day we walked on Havill Hill where he wanted to show me the orange-studded bittersweet vines twining over a cherry tree. When we looked up into the leaves, we saw another tree, just beyond, that was festooned with vines of wild fox grapes (*Virtus labrusca*). The leafy garlands were hung with dark clusters of grapes and, for once, not all of the vines were out of reach in the topmost branches of a tree.

"I can get those!" Scotty exclaimed, scrambling up the bank. The grapevines cascaded over a low tree branch that hung conveniently over the small bank where Scotty stood. He picked the long slender bunches of purplish black grapes as easily as if he were picking grapes from an arbor. He worked industriously, gathering the ebony, bloom-frosted grapes until the basket was overflowing.

The grapes were tart and juicy. Their flavor was foxy and wild. Picking them was much easier than removing them from the stems to make jelly. But when I finally used up all of our harvest, there were dozens of jars of jelly on my shelves.

At Christmas time, I intend to surprise Scotty with a back-pack basket that he can wear when we go out hunting together again next spring. In it I have packed wildflower, tree, bird, rock, and mushroom identification books, a red pocketknife, and six jars of grape jelly made from the wild grapes he discovered and picked for me.

WILD FOX-GRAPE JELLY

3 cups Wild Grape Juice
(recipe below)
2 teaspoons lemon juice

2 tablespoons powdered fruit pectin
3½ cups sugar

In a large kettle, combine the grape juice, lemon juice, and the pectin. Stir and bring to a boil, then stir in the sugar. Bring the mixture to a rolling boil, stirring constantly, and boil until the jelly stage is reached (see jelly test on page 129). Remove from the heat, skim, and pour into 4 small, hot, sterilized jelly glasses. Seal at once with hot paraffin.

TO EXTRACT JUICE FROM WILD GRAPES

Pick the wild fox grapes (*Vitis labrusca*) just before frost, if possible, or after the first light frost. The more frost touches the grapes, the harder they are to jell.

Stem and wash the wild grapes, including some underripe ones. In a large pan, combine the wild grapes with an equal amount of water. For every quart of wild grapes, 1 tart apple, unpeeled and quartered, may be added. Bring the fruit to a boil, then simmer about 20 minutes until the grape skins pop. Stir and mash the grapes slightly as they cook.

Let the juices drip overnight through a jelly bag. In the morning, pour the juice from the bowl carefully so as not to disturb the sediment in the bottom of the bowl or the tartrate crystals that collect on the sides of the bowl.

The pulp in the jelly bag may be used to make a puree for Grape Butter (see recipe on page 261), or it may be squeezed to extract more juice for a separate batch of jelly.

SPICED WILD GRAPE JELLY

Cook and extract the juice (see page 260) from 4 cups of stemmed wild grapes combined with ½ cup vinegar, 3½ cups water, 1 stick of cinnamon, and 1 tablespoon whole cloves. Then make the jelly using the recipe above for Wild Fox Grape Jelly. Serve the jelly with venison or wild duck.

WILD GRAPE–WILD CRABAPPLE JELLY WITH THYME

In a large pan, combine 2 cups of stemmed wild grapes and 2 cups of wild crabapples, which have been quartered but not peeled, with 4 cups of water. Bring to a boil. Tie a bunch of fresh thyme sprigs with a string and suspend it in the fruits. Simmer the fruits until they are tender, for about 20 minutes, crushing the fruits and stirring as necessary. Strain the juice through a jelly bag or through a double layer of cheesecloth.

In a jelly-making kettle, combine 3 cups of crabapple-grape juice and 2 tablespoons of powdered fruit pectin. Stir and bring the juices to a boil, then stir in 3½ cups of sugar. Bring to a rolling boil, stirring constantly, and cook until the jelly stage is reached (see jelly test on page 129). Remove from the heat, skim, and pour into 4 jelly glasses. Seal at once with hot paraffin.

GRAPE BUTTER

After extracting grape juice for jelly (see page 260), put the cooked wild grapes left in the jelly bag through a food mill to make a puree.

Measure the grape puree and add an equal amount of sugar to it. Bake in a slow oven (325° F) in a bean pot, stirring often, for 3½ hours. Seal at once in sterilized jars.

If desired, applesauce and grape puree may be combined, in equal parts, to make the grape butter.

CHOKECHERRIES

Chokecherry shrubs (*Prunus virginiana*) abound on the rocky hill directly in front of our red farmhouse in Vermont, and one August I made jelly from the small, astringent, red berries that hang in pretty clusters from the bending branches. The jelly was bittersweet and delicious with wild duck.

CHOKECHERRY JELLY

Stem about 4 pounds of fully ripened chokecherries. Place them in a kettle with enough water to barely cover the chokecherries. Cover and cook for 15 or 20 minutes. Strain the juice through a jelly bag or a double thickness of cheesecloth.

In a large kettle, combine 3 cups of the chokecherry juice with 6½ cups of sugar and stir to mix. Bring to a boil over high heat, stirring constantly. Stir in 1 bottle of liquid fruit pectin and bring to a full rolling boil, stirring constantly. Boil hard, while stirring, until the jelly stage is reached (see jelly test on page 129). Remove the jelly from the heat. Stir, and skim off the foam. Add ¼ teaspoon of almond extract. Seal the jelly in hot, sterilized jars. Makes 9 half-pints.

CHOKECHERRY-APPLE BUTTER

Make a puree of cored, unpeeled apples and ripe chokecherries by cooking the fruits separately until tender in small amounts of water. Put the cooked fruits through a food mill. Measure out 4 cups of apple puree and 2 cups of chokecherry puree. Stir and heat combined fruits

to a boil, then add 5 cups of sugar, lower the heat, and continue cooking and stirring until the butter is thickened. Add ½ teaspoon almond extract to make the cherry flavor stronger, or spice lightly with cinnamon and nutmeg, to taste. Pour the butter into hot, sterilized jars and seal. Makes 8 half-pints. Serve with meats or game or on hot bread.

PUFFBALLS

My son Jim rides his trail horse through the grassy fields near our home every day. In the late summer, after rains, he hunts puffballs (*Calvatia*) on horseback, often finding enough for our supper. The most common kind he finds in the meadows he rides in are the small, white puffballs that are shaped like pale muffins that have risen above

the muffin wells and are puffing over the edges. Once in a while we find a giant puffball, and afterwards we watch the place where we found it, for another mushroom will appear in due course. Every September a large, bucket-sized puffball rises under our Golden Delicious apple tree in the orchard. In Vermont, a giant puffball resides under the sugar maple by our front door and makes its yearly appearance in August. It was first discovered by Adele Dawson, who comes up the hill regularly to look for it when we are not there. These large puff-balls, round as melons, provide several delicious meals.

Puffballs are good eating when they have just fully emerged. Before eating, each puffball must be sliced cleanly through the center with a knife and examined. The inside flesh of a fresh puffball is as firm and white as divinity fudge and of the same texture. If there is a tinge of yellow coloring inside the puffball, it is already too far gone to eat, although not poisonous. If there is a definite silhouette of a mushroom inside the cross section, with the outline of a stem and cap running from top to bottom of the mushroom, *it is not a puffball* but possibly an immature amanita. *Do not eat it!* Do not eat any puffball whose interior is not pure white and free of the mushroom silhouette.

Puffballs stored in the refrigerator right after picking will stay fresh for several days, but they are best eaten soon after picking, as all foods are.

COUNTRY-FRIED PUFFBALL STEAKS

Clean the puffballs and cut away the thin outer skin, if necessary. Slice into ¼-inch-thick pieces, or slightly thicker. Dip each puffball slice in a mixture of 2 eggs beaten with ¼ cup of milk, then in fine cracker crumbs. Sauté the slices in a heavy skillet in several tablespoons of sizzling butter over medium to low heat, until the crust is browned and crisp. Season with salt and pepper and serve at once.

Adjust the measurements of the ingredients used according to the quantity of puffball slices being sautéed. As with most wild foods, the amount cooked depends upon how many are found.

SHAGGYMANES

When my husband and I were in Vermont in October, Adele opened the freezing compartment of her refrigerator and showed me the cartons, labeled Shaggymanes, in which she had frozen a surplus of the delicious mushrooms that she finds in abundance there in the autumn. Shaggymanes have never been so plentiful here in Indiana that we have enough to freeze, and the daydream that I might someday come upon quantities of them to fill my freezer, as Adele does, is my favorite reverie while hunting for them.

Shaggymanes are easily recognizable. They have nearly cylindrical caps that are white and softly shaggy, with large brownish tufts. They are usually about six inches high. The young specimens have a narrow, loose ring around the stem that soon disappears. Shaggymanes (*Coprinus comatus*) belong to the inky-cap group of mushrooms, and the lower edges of the pink-shaded white gills begin to turn dark

almost before the mushroom has fully emerged. They dissolve into a black liquid within a few hours or a day, cheating the wild-foods hunter of a luscious meal if he fails to keep close watch on the places where they grow, year after year, in grassy places and lawns.

Sauté the meaty shaggymanes in butter until they are tender and serve them with the sauce they make as they cook. Salt and pepper them before serving.

CRAB APPLES

This was a good year for wild crab apples. Often the only harvest we gather from the small, thorny trees is the spectacle of springtime, when thickets of wild crabs on my brother's farm are awash with ethereal pink blossoms that flood the air with waves of almond-scented perfume. But this autumn there were quantities of small, hard, sour, yellow-green crab apples (*Malus coronaria*) clinging to the black, twiggy branches, and when we were out nutting and gathering persimmons, we brought them home to make spiced crab-apple jelly.

Spiced Wild Crab-Apple Jelly

8 cups crab apples, cut
½ cup cider vinegar
2 sticks cinnamon
12 whole cloves

2 cardamom seeds
5½ cups sugar
½ bottle liquid fruit pectin

Prepare 4 cups of crab apple juice according to the directions given for red haws (page 219).

In a large kettle, combine the crab apple juice, vinegar, and cinnamon. Tie the cloves and cardamom seeds in a small square of cheesecloth and add to the juice. Bring to a boil, then simmer for about 5 minutes to extract the flavor of the spices. Remove the spices.

To the crab apple juice, add the sugar and stir. Bring to a boil, stirring constantly. Add the liquid pectin while stirring, then bring to a full rolling boil and boil until the jelly stage is reached (see jelly test on page 129). Remove the kettle from the heat, stir, and skim off the foam. Pour into hot, sterilized jelly glasses and seal at once with hot paraffin. Fills seven 8-ounce jelly glasses.

NOTE: To make unspiced crab-apple jelly, simply leave out the spices and vinegar and omit the directions that refer to the spices.

Serve the jelly with pork or game, or use it to glaze a ham.

IRISH MOSS

When my first seaweed pudding was a failure, my friend Ellen Wedeking brought me the Irish moss her husband, Don, had picked up on the sandy beach along the rocky shore of the Gulf of St.

Lawrence on Prince Edward Island. The Wedeking family was driving along the coast road of the island in August on a rainy day following a storm when they saw groups of men, dressed in hip boots, sou'westers, and slickers, working in the shallows and on the shore. The men were loading horse-drawn carts with a pink-colored material that they were taking from the water with rakes and pitchforks. Don stopped along the road and went down to the water's edge, curious, to investigate the activity. The men were harvesting seaweed to sell.

"We brought back quite a lot of seaweed," Ellen said, presenting me with a jar containing bits and pieces of lacy, brittle, ivory-colored seaweed. "I never thought we would use any of it, but this is the last bit."

I remembered the large clump of Irish moss (*Chondrus crispus*) that Ellen laid out on a rock in the sun to dry on the day the family arrived in Vermont to visit us after touring the Maritime Provinces. It was wet and colorful then, a pinkish, gelatinous mass, but the sun bleached it to a pale ivory color.

We made a pudding from the last of the small, coral-shaped fronds. We might have called it sea moss pudding or Irish moss *blancmange* or pearl moss pudding or carrageen pudding, after Carragheen, Ireland where this seaweed abounds. But to us, it was simply "Don's seaweed pudding."

DON'S SEAWEED PUDDING

1 cup Irish moss fronds
3 cups milk
⅛ teaspoon salt
3 tablespoons sugar

1 teaspoon vanilla extract
1 egg yolk, beaten (optional)
1 egg white, beaten stiff
 (optional)

Cover the dry Irish moss with lukewarm water. Soak for 10 or 15 minutes. Remove the moss from the water, picking out the discolored parts, and measure out ½ cup of the wet seaweed.

In the top of a double boiler, combine the seaweed and milk. Cook over boiling water, stirring often, for 25 minutes. Strain the mixture through a sieve, rubbing most of the softened seaweed through the sieve. Stir in the salt, sugar, and vanilla extract. If the addition of the egg is desired, the yolk should be stirred in at this time, while the pudding is still hot. Then fold in the egg white. Pour into molds and chill.

The pudding without the egg added is the traditional *blancmange*. Adding the egg gives the pudding a bit more flavor and makes it less solid. Both puddings are firm enough to unmold. Serve with fresh sweetened fruit or with chocolate sauce. Serves 4.

CATTAILS

As our wild feast continues in the seasons to come, we will return again to the thicket of cattails that rims the edge of my father's small, shallow pond. The boys have always liked to gather cattails because it makes sloshing around in the mud and water legitimate. They remember the cold Easter Sunday when they were permitted to wade into the chilly water, wearing their clothes, to pull up the tender inner shoots of cattail because we wanted "Cossack asparagus" to go with the leftover ham for our supper. They still talk about the time I was, literally, stuck in the mud when I ventured out to gather cattail pollen for pancakes and had to be rescued by Jimmy.

The family has enjoyed the flavor of cattail-pollen pancakes and breads and the tender "Cossack asparagus." But we have not eaten the

roots of the cattail. Nor have we tried eating the cattail spikes *before* they become covered with pollen, when they are said to resemble "roasting ears" in flavor, preparation, and manner of eating. Every summer we have intended to take some of the green spikes but suddenly they are covered with pollen and we have missed their season again.

And so it goes. There is always an untried wild-food plant or a recipe to sample, and another feast to anticipate.

COSSACK ASPARAGUS

In the spring, when cattail plants (either broad-leafed *Typha latifolia* or narrow-leafed *T. angustifolia*) are beginning to sprout, pull out the center of the plant by grasping the inner leaves and pulling upward. Then remove the outer portion and cut off the top of the leaves, saving the tender, innermost white stem which is very tasty, raw or cooked. The flavor of the cooked stems is better than asparagus. Wash the stems thoroughly before eating.

TO COOK: Boil the white stalks in salted water for a few minutes, until tender. Serve buttered or with hollandaise sauce.

TO SERVE RAW: Cut the solid white part of the inner stem into small pieces and add to a salad.

GATHERING CATTAIL POLLEN

In June, about the time dewberries are ripening, the stamens of the cattail flower buds in the bloom spike produce quantities of bright yellow pollen that is a nutritious, corn-flavored food. To gather the pollen from the pollen-filled cattail spikes, cover each spike with a paper bag, bend the plant so that the top of the bag can be grasped around the stem with one hand, and shake the golden powder into the closed bag. This is not always as simple as it sounds. Most cattails we find are quite tall and the spikes are often beyond my reach. When I go gathering cattail pollen, my teen-aged son who is 6-feet-2-inches in height, goes along. Not only can Jim easily reach the cattail spikes, he does not mind sloshing in the water and mud where the plants often grow.

Substitute the cattail pollen for part of the flour in any recipe for pancakes, biscuits, muffins, or bread, using pollen for up to half the amount of flour called for in the recipe. Sift the pollen through a fine-meshed tea strainer before combining it with the flour.

CATTAIL POLLEN FLAPJACKS

1 cup sieved cattail pollen
  (see above)
1 cup unbleached white flour
3 teaspoons baking powder
1 teaspoon salt

1 tablespoon sugar
2 eggs, lightly beaten
1½ cups milk
2 tablespoons butter, melted

Sift together into a mixing bowl the cattail pollen, flour, baking powder, salt, and sugar. Make a well in the center of the flour mixture and pour into it the eggs and milk. (Use more milk if thinner pancakes are preferred.) Mix only enough to blend, then stir in the melted butter.

Heat a pancake griddle over moderate heat until a drop of water flicked on its surface evaporates instantly. Grease the griddle lightly with a pastry brush dipped in vegetable oil and pour the pancake batter on the griddle to form pancakes 4 inches in diameter. Cook 2 to 3 minutes until small bubbles form on the surface of the pancakes, then turn with a spatula and cook on the other side until done. Serve the pancakes on a heated plate with melted butter and hot maple syrup. These bright yellow pancakes have a cornlike flavor. Serves 4.

When I think ahead of harvesting bounties of seasons yet to come, it reminds me of flipping through pages of a book of discoveries, catching glimpses of scenes and wishing to be transported to them instantly. I look forward to the sun-drenched June when I reach the ripe serviceberries before the birds strip the branches bare; to the greens hunt when Maude shows me her "cliff lettuce"; to summer in Maine when Irish moss washes onto a rocky shore for my seaweed pudding; to the first taste of wineberries and thimbleberries; to the coppery October when I find my father's tree where he filled his pockets with "red haws to eat in time of school." After years of gathering and preparing wild foods for our table, there are still unscanned fields and woods beckoning to me.

The pursuit of the wild flavor, like all quests, means discovery. Books about edible wild plants are as necessary to the wild foods hunter's discovery of his quarry as maps to a treasure hunter. *Edible Wild Plants* by Oliver Perry Medsger and *Edible Wild Plants of Eastern North America* by Merritt L. Fernald, Alfred Charles Kinsey and others are two general-identification books that anyone taking up the hunt should have in his library. Of the many useful books that are available, I find these particularly interesting:

The Edible Wild by Berndt Berglund and Clare E. Bolsby
Stalking the Wild Asparagus by Euell Gibbons
Using Wayside Plants by Nelson Coon
Free for the Eating and other books by Bradford Angier
The Savory Wild Mushroom by Margaret McKenny
Common Edible Mushrooms by Clyde M. Christensen
The Mushroom Hunter's Field Guide by Alexander H. Smith

Weeds of the Northern United States and Canada by F. H. Montgomery

The Golden Nature Guide Books: *Trees; Birds; Non-Flowering Plants;* and *Flowers, A Guide to Familiar American Wildflowers*

A Natural History of Trees, by Donald Culross Peattie

For city-bound residents who cannot search fields, woods, mountains, or seashores until vacation time, a sustaining taste of the wild flavor might be found via a different sort of wild foods hunt. A few—but only a few—wild foods may be searched out on the shelves and in frozen-foods departments of specialty food stores in large cities. Fiddleheads may be bought, frozen or canned; dandelion and mustard greens are available in cans; *pfifferlinge* mushrooms (chanterelles) can be bought in stores carrying German foods; game, both smoked and canned, is available and, of course, wild rice and maple syrup. Farmers' markets often offer fresh wild foods in season. Persimmons, morels, wild blackberries, mustard and dandelion greens, crab apples, wild grapes, sassafras roots, pawpaws, hickory nuts, black walnuts, and pecans are all available at times, in limited quantities, at the outdoor farmers' market near my home. At natural foods stores one can find seaweed and rose hip products and herbal teas such as elder flower, dandelion leaf, red clover blossom, and strawberry leaf. Wild-fruit jellies and syrups are usual in gourmet food stores, and there are mail-order firms that specialize in wild-fruit jellies and game.

The very scarcity of wild food products in city stores and the necessity of getting off the beaten path to find them provide two of the elements of an exciting hunt. Tracking down these suppliers in the city requires the same persistence and instinct to find that is needed in the field when searching for the elusive morel or the rare shellbark hickory tree. A trip to an Italian market in search of winter cress or stopping by a natural foods store for dried apples could prove as serendipitous an adventure as sauntering through a country meadow. An appetite for the wild flavor need not be starved if one cannot be continually in the country.

But, undeniably, the greater joys of nature's banquet await us in country places. The pleasures of continuing the wild feast are as unending as the flavorful bounties of the natural world, and they are ours for the finding.

When You Can't
Find Fiddleheads:
A List of
Substitutions

While some recipes in this book can be used successfully only with the ingredients given, many can be adapted by experimentally minded cooks for domestic or cultivated fruits and vegetables instead of wild ones. Here are some hints to help you in creating your own unique versions of my recipes and some warnings about certain substitutions.

1.   The fiddlehead recipes, in general, can be used with asparagus, wild or domestic, in place of fiddleheads.

2.   Domestic varieties of blackberries, elderberries, strawberries, blueberries, and apples may be substituted for wild fruits, but the amount of sweetening may need adjustment. Cultivated berries and fruits are often sweeter than wild varieties.

3.   The Japanese persimmon available in markets differs greatly from the native American persimmons used in my recipes. The flavor of the Japanese persimmon is more delicate and the fruit is juicier than the native American persimmon. The Japanese persimmon cannot be substituted for the native American persimmon in my recipes without risk of failure.

4.   Bananas can be used in the pawpaw recipes instead of the wild fruit, but the flavor will be banana, not pawpaw.

5.   Hickory nuts have their own flavor, which has no cultivated counterpart, but in general, nut recipes will work with nuts other than the ones suggested. English walnuts and pecans would be the best

choices to use instead of hickory nuts; pecans are a good substitute for butternuts.

6.   Use red raspberries instead of mulberries in all recipes except the jams and jellies.

7.   Try the Hoosier Poke Sprouts, page 79, using asparagus.

8.   Use broccoli instead of milkweed shoots in Milkweed Casserole, page 86.

9.   In place of maple syrup, dark corn syrup or honey could be substituted in most of the recipes, but the flavor will differ noticeably. In candy and jelly recipes, substitutions are tricky; do so only if you are willing to chance failure.

10.   Sorghum syrup or molasses will work in Vermont baked beans, glazed squash, barbecue spareribs, baked apples, and bread pudding as a substitute for maple syrup.

11.   There are no substitutions for morels or chanterelles which approximate their flavors, but the mushroom recipes can be made with the cultivated mushrooms available at groceries.

INDEX

All entries printed in roman type refer to text discussions; *entries printed ih italics refer to recipes.*